ALEC STEWART'S
ENGLAND DIARY

ALEC STEWART'S ENGLAND DIARY

CollinsWillow

An Imprint of HarperCollins*Publishers*

Brian Murgatroyd, who collaborated with Alec Stewart on the original hardback edition of this book, is the Media Relations Officer of the Australian Cricket Board, having previously worked in a similar position for the England and Wales Cricket Board. He has known Alec Stewart for over ten years.

Patrick Murphy, who has helped Alec update his book for this new paperback edition, is BBC Radio's Sports Correspondent in the Midlands, specialising in cricket and soccer. He has covered nine England cricket tours for the BBC and is a prolific author in his own right, having written in tandem with cricketers such as Allan Donald, Jack Russell, Dermot Reeve and David Gower.

First published as *Alec Stewart: A Captain's Diary* in 1999
by CollinsWillow
an imprint of HarperCollins*Publishers*
London

Revised and fully updated paperback edition published in 2000

1 3 5 7 9 8 6 4 2

A CIP catalogue record for this book is
available from the British Library

ISBN 0 00 218898 8

All photographs supplied by Graham Morris

Printed and bound in Great Britain by Clays Ltd, St Ives plc

Contents

Acknowledgments

First and foremost I'd like to thank my team-mates at Surrey and England, as well as all the support staff, for the work they have done and the way they have shared the highs and lows during my captaincy of the national side and after I stepped down in the summer of 1999.

Brian Murgatroyd ('Murgers') is also worth a mention for the way he's guided me through the perils and pitfalls of putting my time as captain down on paper. I think he deserves a medal for his patience as he's watched me try (and usually fail) to get to grips with a lap-top computer for the first time in my life!

For the updated paperback edition, the BBC's Pat Murphy stepped into the breach left by Murgers' departure to the ACB and proved to be a fine collaborator on the two new chapters covering the World Cup and the 1999/2000 South Africa tour. Thanks Pat, all those late nights were well worth it in the end!

It's certainly been an interesting experience re-living the events since my appointment as England captain, and it does make me realise how much has happened in what has been a very short space of time.

Thanks also to my parents, with dad's coaching, advice and experience a key factor behind where I am today, while I'm grateful to everyone at Midland-Guildford Cricket Club, and Kevin Gartrell in particular, for the welcome they gave me whenever we were in Perth during the 1998/99 winter tour.

To Tom Whiting and everyone at publishers HarperCollins, Jim Ruston, the staff at Diamond IT, the Gayleard family, Garry Rainford and the Catherine Hill Bay Bowling Club, thanks to you all for helping to make the idea of this book a reality.

Finally, to my family – Lynn, and children Andrew and Emily. Thanks for your understanding and patience in the face of my career which means I'm not with you as often as any of us would like. This book is dedicated to you.

Alec Stewart
Surrey County Cricket Club, London
March 2000

The England Captaincy

Introduction

Two years on from the day I got the nod to be England's Test captain, and I can still chuckle about it, despite the disappointments later on.

The reason is simple: at the time, I wasn't sure I'd been appointed! It was late April of 1998 and ECB Chairman Lord MacLaurin had invited Adam Hollioake and me for lunch at the House of Lords. Chairman of Selectors David Graveney joined us as well. The invitation was clear enough – but the reason wasn't. Neither of us knew if we were going along to be interviewed or appointed.

Ever since we'd got back from the West Indies two weeks earlier, there had been endless speculation among the media and the public about who the next England captain, or captains if the job was split between the Test and one-day roles, would be. According to the press, there were several candidates. Adam and myself were two of them, Nasser Hussain and Mark Ramprakash were two more, while some journalists, like former Hampshire captain Mark Nicholas, favoured going outside the current squad, with Matthew Maynard, who led Glamorgan to the County Championship in 1997, getting the odd mention in dispatches. And on top of that, there were also suggestions the captaincy would be split, with different men taking charge of the Test and one-day sides.

Adam had led the squad to our Champions Trophy win in Sharjah in December 1997 while Mike Atherton rested, and then, as vice-captain of the one-day side in the Caribbean, took over again when 'Ath' resigned. But England had never appointed separate Test and one-day captains before.

Ever since Ath had called it a day, there had been journalists knocking on my door to get my opinions on the subject. I was happy to talk about Ath the captain because I regard him as a good friend and have enormous respect for him and what he has done both for England and in the game. But I wouldn't talk about my chances of succeeding Ath as captain. That was a deliberate move on my part. For starters, I didn't want to be seen to be putting the selectors under any pressure by saying: 'I want the job.'

There were other reasons too. I didn't want to fuel the media debate so that it became a battle between me and Nass, or anyone else for that matter, as that could have got messy. And, if I had said publicly I wanted the job then didn't get it, I reckoned that could have been awkward for the man who did take over.

But I knew I was in the running for the job because David Graveney had spoken to me about it after Ath's resignation in Antigua, and I guessed 'Nass' was my main rival. That made sense as, to be honest, it would have been tough to appoint either Adam or 'Ramps' to lead the Test side when both of them were still battling to establish themselves in it. And if the selectors went outside the current squad they would be choosing someone whom they hadn't thought good enough to tour the Caribbean six months earlier.

I could see why I was in the frame. For one thing, I had experience. I'd been vice-captain for five years under first Graham Gooch then Ath, and had even led the side in Tests and one-day internationals when either man rested or was injured. On top of that, after a good tour of the West Indies, my place in the side was secure, and my image, something I knew the ECB thought was increasingly important, was of a clean-cut bloke.

But much of that also applied to Nass. He had scored runs in the Caribbean and had been Ath's vice-captain on the last two tours. And he was younger than I was, so he could have been a possible longer-term option.

The one thing I should say at this point is that I wanted the job, but unlike the last time I'd been in the frame, as a rival to Ath in 1993, this time I felt ready for it too.

Of course I was disappointed to miss out when Goochie packed it in, especially as I'd had a taste for the top job in New Zealand and the World Cup in 1992 and then in India and Sri Lanka the following winter. But although I would have accepted it if the then Chairman of Selectors Ted Dexter had called, I know now I wasn't ready for that level of responsibility then. I was only in my second year as Surrey captain and I had doubts I was experienced enough to handle all the pressures the job might throw at me.

This time was different. It's not for me to say whether I was a more mature person than in 1993, but I certainly felt more comfortable with the idea of being England captain. There was no longer the Surrey captaincy to worry about and I had five years more experience and five years more runs. And although I hadn't scored a hundred in the West Indies on the recent tour, I was as firmly established in the side as I had ever been.

With the real chance I could be offered the captaincy this time, I discussed it with my wife Lynn when I got home from the Caribbean. After all, it wouldn't have been much use if I'd accepted the job only for her to find some compelling family reason why I couldn't do it. We agreed I should take it if I got the call, but that was the easy part. After all, we both knew it would be very difficult to turn down the England captaincy if I was offered it. But we also thought about how we would handle it as a family. We knew there would be greater demands on my time, and that I would have a higher profile. Despite that, we were determined not to let it affect our family life.

People say I'm good at dividing my life up. I can be completely focused on cricket when I'm at the ground, but once I get home I switch off from work mode and give my wife and two children, Andrew and Emily, one hundred percent of my time.

We agreed that wouldn't change, and we also agreed we wouldn't seek publicity as a family. The reason people were interested in me was for what I did on the field, not at home, and that was the way we all wanted it to stay. Given the way parts of the media operate that may have been naïve, but we wanted the children to have as normal an upbringing as possible, and not spend their lives in a goldfish bowl. And looking back I think we have managed that pretty well over the year of my captaincy.

Despite all the speculation, I still didn't know the Test job was mine as Adam and I sat down to our lunch with David Graveney and Lord MacLaurin. The conversation began with a very general discussion about how we felt the West Indies tour went, for both the team and us. But then Lord MacLaurin started talking about what was expected of an England captain. He told us: 'Cricket is not a rich sport so we need to do the best job we can of selling ourselves. The England captain is our head of sales.

'The captain needs to be a role model for people. His conduct has to be exemplary and he has to project the right image, one that fans, and especially young people, want to copy and be associated with.'

As Lord MacLaurin continued to chat, Adam and I glanced at each other, and I knew we were thinking the same thing: 'Are we being told we've got the job?' But although we may have been thinking that, neither of us came out and asked the question. I think we both felt the same way, certainly in this situation: you are offered the captaincy, you don't ask for it.

The lunch ended, Adam and I shook hands with Lord MacLaurin and 'Grav', with both of them smiling broadly, and I think we both knew then that we'd cracked it. We got outside, looked at each other, and started laughing. Adam said: 'We must be England captains then!'

Grav confirmed it all when he called me on my mobile a little later to outline where and when the announcement would be made. We were to report to Lord's on Tuesday morning 5 May where he would tell the world that Adam would lead the one-day side for the Texaco series against South Africa, and I was in charge of all six Tests in the summer, five against South Africa and one against Sri Lanka.

To have someone call and let you know you are England's Test captain is an amazing feeling. My heart was racing, and as I drove home I stopped to ring Lynn and let her know. I don't think she'll mind me saying she was a bit emotional. She knew what it meant to me.

Once I was back home though, we tried to maintain an air of normality over the weekend before the announcement. After all, once Tuesday arrived I think we both knew that, try as we might, things were bound to be a little different.

Lynn was bursting with pride and so was I, but we were sworn to secrecy ahead of the press conference. We managed to keep it quiet, but we still had to side-step some pretty awkward questions when friends came to visit. Two people we did tell – the only two – were my parents. Dad was especially proud given his previous connection with the team, both as a player then manager.

It was the start of a very interesting year.

What Captaincy
is All About

If there is one thing that became clear to me during my year in charge, it is that captaining both your county and your country at the same time is now impossible.

How do I know? After all, I'm no longer Surrey captain, having resigned from that position at the end of the 1996 season.

Well, I did do the job for five seasons from 1992, and believe me it was hard enough when I was away every other week during the season as an England player, let alone the captain. But with the World Cup taking place every three to four years, and an increase in the scale of the international programme at home from the year 2000, I just don't think anyone can do the two jobs anymore.

Central contracting of England players, something I have been very much in favour of to ease the workload of internationals in the face of an ever-growing programme of matches, might help solve this problem. If a player was centrally contracted and likely only to play a handful of games, if that, for his county, it wouldn't make much sense to make him captain, so hopefully the danger of overload from someone doing two jobs would be removed. But what I am saying is if the candidate is a county captain I believe he would do himself and everyone else a lot of good by stepping down from his domestic role as soon as he took the England job.

I know how tired I feel after a Test or one-day international, and to ask a player to go straight from one of those matches to play for his county in a Championship match or even a domestic knock-out contest is tough. To ask him to go and captain that side is even tougher.

On top of that, an England player is away for so long during the summer he would miss at least half his county's Championship matches anyway, and that would do nothing for continuity. One week captained by the vice-captain, the next led by a player who might just be too tired to give it his best as the man in charge.

You just have to look at Ath before me. He's as mentally strong as they come and wasn't even captain of Lancashire, but after captaining an international match he struggled to produce his best consistently for his county. I'm not saying Ath or I just switch off and coast when we go back to play county cricket after a Test or one-dayer. But for me it is a relief to get back into the dressing room and not be the focus of attention and having to think about strategy and make decisions.

The media did enjoy making something out of what many of them felt was a change in direction and style when I took over from Ath as Test captain. I have to admit, on paper we are like chalk and cheese. He's Cambridge-educated, a northerner and fairly undemonstrative, while I am a southerner who has never been to university and someone who maybe wears his heart on his sleeve a bit more in public.

Those differences even extend to the dressing room. Ath can be a little untidy with his kit while I am quite the opposite, making sure everything has its place to the extent that my dressing room nicknames include 'Peter Perfect' and 'Squeaky' (as in squeaky clean).

But as captains I think we have plenty in common. Both of us will lead from the front and try to set an example to the other players. Opening the batting is a good place to do that from, and Ath was superb in the way he would set out to do it by blunting the new ball, as Goochie did before him.

Although maybe I am a bit more prone to clap or shout encouragement around the field than Ath, whichever one of us was in charge demanded the same level of commitment from the players as we showed ourselves, and that is total. It's just we had different ways of asking for it, Ath with a word, me with a clap or a pat on the back.

Despite these things, I will accept I ran the side a bit differently from Ath, and introduced a few things. But I think anyone would expect that because no two people are the same and everyone has different ideas. If we all thought the same way there would never be any point in changing the captain, except when he retired or lost form.

I introduced team meals for players and support staff and they usually took place two nights before a Test or one-day international. They were a chance to relax and get to know colleagues a bit better away from the cricket ground. Being an international side at home isn't always great for fostering team spirit, as you're not together all the time, so there is a danger new players can come in and feel like outsiders. The idea of the meals, which were relaxed affairs at local restaurants, was to try and break that down. This can also have the benefit of promoting a more open team environment when the time comes to talk tactics. In all walks of life people are generally more open and honest with others they know well, and the same applies in a team meeting. Experience of hundreds of these meetings has told me the new boys almost always say the least, even though they may have a valid point to make. So the quicker they don't feel like new boys the better.

In Australia, I was keen for players not involved in tour matches – not Tests or one-day games – to get away for a day or an afternoon. There's no point in resting a player if he then has to sit and watch four days of cricket. Better to keep him fresh by letting him take a car to get away from the ground, or even just having a lie-in if he wants one.

I've picked up these little things through experience, and I've got that experience not just from my time as a county captain, but also by watching all the people who have captained me. And I think experience, along with respect and luck, are the three most important factors that make a good captain. Without the respect of the side, which normally comes through achievements out in the middle, no captain can function properly as the team simply won't perform for him when the chips are down. And I defy anyone to name someone they regard as a good leader, who didn't also have a bit of luck here and there to help him along. The chance to have great players under your control, the odd lucky wicket here, the odd brilliant performance by a player there, and suddenly you are a winning captain. Easy really! And winning the toss is also a useful start to any game, as I found out in Australia when I lost five tosses in a row!

I've played under masses of people, from Ath, Goochie and Allan Lamb at international level to Roger Knight, Pat Pocock and Ian Greig at Surrey, and even former Australian leg-spinner Tony Mann, who was in charge of the club I played for in Western Australia. As for the best captain I've ever played against, that has to be Mark Taylor, who usually seemed to know what would make an opposition batsman most uncomfortable. He's had a great career, but it is always sad to see a great player leave the game. At least he's gone out at the top, which is a nice way to sign off.

Shane Warne is still learning the ropes as captain, and impressed us all during the Carlton and United Series out in Australia. He is a gambler as a captain, but maybe it is easier to gamble when you are not the first-choice captain of a team as you are under less pressure to keep the job. Who knows?

I studied every one of these captains and others in action, and slowly but surely my knowledge and understanding of the game increased until I got to the point where I was ready to take charge of a side myself.

It might not be the same for everyone, but that sort of apprenticeship was vital for me before I became a captain at international level. By the time I took over the reins in 1998 I was experienced and felt ready to do the job. And it was a job that involved more than just a role on the field and in the dressing room.

There's also the media to consider too, and even though we now have a team of media relations officers at the ECB to help out on this front, the increased exposure and the press still took a bit of getting used to.

The scope for slip-ups when facing a room of reporters every time you front up at an international with all the other on-field pressures to consider as well is daunting for a man who's played international cricket for as long as I have. It must have been much harder for Ath, who took charge less than four years after his debut. He enjoys his privacy, ended up hating that part of the job and it got him down a bit in the end. And while it might be too late for veterans like Ath and me, it's good to see the ECB has started to look at media training for the players. With so many sports competing for attention these days, we have to be up to speed on how to sell ourselves as players and our sport to the public.

I don't exactly love talking to the press, but I accept it is part of the job and has to be done to help us promote the game. But when I do speak to them, experience has taught me to do it on my terms. To start with, I speak to them before the match when I'm ready, which usually means after I've finished all my practice. They might not always like hanging around and waiting for me, especially if I'm last to leave the ground after nets, but if I mess up because I haven't got my preparations right, then I'm sure they'd be the first to let me know I failed.

I don't make any bold pronouncements as they can have a nasty habit of coming back to haunt you, but I do try to tell the truth.

Misleading the press is a sure-fire way of storing up trouble for later on. My manner with them is usually straight down the line, but I do try to inject a bit of humour into things. For example, at the start of the 1998 South African series, Brian Scovell of the *Daily Mail* asked me what I'd do if we won the toss at Edgbaston. The wicket was under cover and I wasn't sure, so I asked him what he'd do. Then I did the same throughout the summer and it always brought a smile and relaxed all the hacks.

I suppose my role as captain was unique, at least in recent England history, because I also filled the all-rounder's role, keeping wicket as well as playing as a top-order batsman, depending on the needs of the side. The 'keeping brings with it extra responsibility, but it does have its good side as I always have the perfect view of what each bowler is doing with the ball and how the batsman is countering it. When I was captain, it did mean I was restricted in where I could go and how many times I could run down to chat with the bowler, so my vice-captain also played a key role in relaying ideas and helping me shape tactics with the bowlers on the field. It also meant I couldn't really open the batting, at least in Test cricket, as I found that coming straight off the field and swapping one set of pads and gloves for another meant I didn't do either role proper justice.

It's been a source of frustration for me, as I've always made no secret of the fact I think I am at my best as an opener. But it's also an example of what captaincy is all about – putting team goals ahead of individual ones, and persuading the rest of the side to do the same.

England v South Africa Test Series 1998

A Promising Start to the Summer

From the moment I got the call from David Graveney to confirm I was captain, to the way we performed in the first Test of the 1998 summer series against South Africa, my first few weeks in charge went pretty well.

We might not have won the match at Edgbaston – the rain made sure of that – but we won plenty of fans for playing positive, attacking cricket. On top of that, there was a return to form for Mike Atherton, a successful return to the side for Dominic Cork, and we left Birmingham on something of a high.

Looking back, it was my honeymoon period as captain. That period had begun several days before the press conference at ECB headquarters with some serious talking to David Graveney because there were some key issues to be sorted out before we could front up to the media. Was I going to be a selector? Would I keep wicket? If I did, where would I bat? And would Ath still have a place in the side? It was no good facing the press for the first time as captain and saying: 'Well, we haven't thought about anything yet.' That would have been laughable.

The answer to the first question was pretty straightforward. The captain has the option of joining the selection panel, which consisted of David Graveney, Graham Gooch and Mike Gatting and, unlike Ath in his last year in the job, I took that option. As captain, you have to take a fair amount of responsibility for the results of the side, so I wanted a fairly big input into its selection.

The next two questions were a bit tougher. After I had kept for the

1996/97 tour of Zimbabwe and New Zealand and the home Ashes series in 1997, the selectors went back to Jack Russell for the Caribbean series.

It was a tough tour to keep wicket. The pitches were full of variable bounce, the outfields were uneven and although I thought Jack did as well as he could, he still struggled for form on both sides of the stumps, leading to calls for me to take the gloves again.

The selectors accepted that, but they weren't going to offer me the captaincy if I felt keeping wicket, batting and leadership would be too much responsibility. Grav sounded me out on the subject while I was still in the West Indies and I said I was up to it. Now I chatted with Grav again and confirmed as much.

I've never made any secret of the fact that, given the choice, I want to play simply as an opening batsman. The selectors went with that option in the West Indies, and I rewarded them with 452 runs in the series. But playing me as a keeper will always give us the option of picking an extra batsman or bowler in the place Jack had, depending on conditions, so I knew it made sense.

But if I was going to keep wicket, I had to decide where I would bat, and one thing I knew was I couldn't open the innings. I'd tried that in the Trent Bridge Test of 1997 against Australia. It was hot, we lost the toss and fielded for four sessions, and by the time I came to bat in the second innings I was knackered. And that was without the extra responsibility of captaincy.

On the other side of the coin, I wanted to stay in the top-order and not drop too far down to five or six, as I felt I do my best work dictating things nearer the beginning of the innings. I had batted at three on the 1996/97 tour, but I wasn't captain then, so we settled on number four, but no lower. That meant breaking up my opening partnership with Ath and that was the toughest part of it all. The selectors had restored me to open the innings with him in the Caribbean because our pairing was reckoned to be a real asset to the side. And even though Ath had a poor tour by his standards, we still produced two hundred partnerships.

I was determined Ath would be in the side for the first Test, and thankfully my fellow selectors agreed, despite his poor run of form in the Caribbean and a moderate summer against Australia in 1997. Some critics were suggesting his time had gone, while one newspaper report even claimed he wouldn't be welcome in the dressing room any more.

As far as I am concerned, that was rubbish. I've spent a fair amount of my career at the other end from Ath, with six hundred-plus opening stands to show for it, so I know what he can do. True, he was having a poor trot, but I still had faith in Ath and wanted him in my side.

It was good to clear up those issues, and it was also good to get a call from Nasser Hussain the day before the press conference, wishing me all the best. It mirrored what I did in 1993 when Ath was appointed and I'm glad he called me. I knew he would be disappointed to miss out so it would have been wrong for me to ring him just in case he still hadn't come to terms with not getting the job.

I know the ECB is keen on media training for the players, but no amount of it could possibly have prepared me for that press conference as Grav, Adam and I fronted up on Tuesday morning, 5 May.

There were eight camera crews, around fifty reporters and I think the announcement was live on BBC Radio Five and Sky News. Then, after the formal part of proceedings, there were other radio and television interviews to do, plus photographs, and the whole thing took two hours. Not that I minded too much. After all, it's not every day you're announced as the England Test captain so I just did my best to enjoy it.

I knew the next week or so would be busy in terms of media interest, so I had all press enquiries directed to the ECB. There, Brian Murgatroyd – 'Murgers' – the England team's media relations officer, would sift through them and decide what I would and wouldn't do, depending on whether time allowed.

We tried to fit in as many people as we could, but I had to ease up when Surrey coach Keith Medlycott got sick of me disappearing to speak to one television crew too many after I was out at Southampton. That was fair enough. I was trying to be helpful, but just for a while I forgot the game is my bread and butter.

At international level, Adam's appointment for the Texaco series gave me a real breathing space. Rather than go straight from the press conference to a Test, the one-dayers gave me time to come to terms with my new job and get most media commitments that came from my appointment out of the way by the time the Test came around. That allowed me to concentrate on the job in hand, the match at Edgbaston.

I had no problem with his selection either. After all, we were captain and vice-captain at Surrey, having swapped roles in 1997, so there was no awkwardness between us, and he had shown what a good captain he was by leading England to victory in the Champions Trophy.

If the selectors eventually decided they wanted to name one captain for both forms of the game then I was happy to fill both roles if asked, but until then I was delighted to play under Adam.

We may have lost the Texaco series 2–1, but I was still optimistic about our chances against the South Africans come the first Test at Edgbaston. After all, we had Darren Gough back after missing the winter with a hamstring injury, Dominic Cork was fit and firing having missed most of 1997 through a groin problem, and Graham Thorpe returned after missing the one-dayers with a bad back.

I have to be honest and say that while I always have a buzz of anticipation before every match I play, and a special one before every Test or one-dayer, the feeling I had before this Test, my first at home as captain, was extra-special. I didn't sleep much the night before the game, and by the time it came to toss up with Hansie Cronje the butterflies were really fluttering around in my stomach. I was still on edge as Mark Butcher and Ath went out to bat, but by the time they'd put on 179 for the first wicket I was much calmer!

It was a situation tailor-made for someone with Ath's temperament, and he didn't let us down. If Pollock or Donald beat him, he just put it behind him and got on with the job of playing the next ball on its merits, and I think Butch fed off that.

Nass was due to bat at three, but after four hours with his pads on I gave him a break just as Butch was out. I was happy to get into the action, but it also meant I was in the middle to congratulate Ath when he reached three figures.

After the way he had been written off in some quarters, I couldn't have been happier as he edged Pollock to third man for four to take him to his hundred. As we shook hands in mid-pitch, I said to him, 'You could have played a better shot to get there!' He smiled at that. Not bad for a bloke the press used to call Captain Grumpy!

Having the ex-captain in the side could have made my life awkward, but I never had any doubts that would be a problem with Ath. He just kept himself to himself, enjoyed being back in the ranks I think, and while he was happy to volunteer the odd thought on the field, he only did it if I asked him.

I'm happy to say Corky was another player I pushed for and I think that at his best he is a dynamic cricketer. He is aggressive and offers something with bat, ball and in the field and he looked fully refreshed here after his winter off. He took five wickets, but also took on added responsibility with the ball after Goughie was unable to bowl a ball when a Donald lifter broke his right index finger in poor light late on the second evening.

We got some criticism for having Goughie out there in the firing line to have his hand hit, but I would still defend the decision. There was no point in declaring as the light was too bad for South Africa to have batted that evening, and at least by staying out there we were taking the game forward by adding to our total. I would make the same decision again and so would Goughie, I'm sure.

I reckon we could have enforced the follow-on if he had been fit, but we still gained a first innings lead of 119, and that advantage had grown to 289 by the close thanks to some bold, attacking batting.

With heavy rain forecast for the last day it was possible to argue our approach was just an empty gesture, as we were never going to lose the match. But forecasts have been wrong before and I like to think we would have come close to a win on the last day but for the weather.

I was all set to declare at 10.49 on that last morning in the hope of making their openers have a bit of a rush to get their pads on, but just then rain began to fall, and never let up for the rest of the day.

All the same, I was delighted with the way we had bossed the game against a top side who had already shown they had adapted to English conditions by winning the Texaco Trophy. The critics seemed quite pleased too. 'STEWART BREATHES LIFE INTO ENGLAND' was one of the rave reviews we got in the press in the wake of the match.

I drove away from Edgbaston on that wet Monday afternoon really looking forward to the rest of the summer. That optimism was to be tested to the full over the next month.

'Sorry guys, the honeymoon's over'

I think it's fair to say that after the fun and games of Edgbaston, my honeymoon period as captain ended with a bang.

The following day Surrey lost a Benson & Hedges Cup semi-final to Leicestershire, with one of our old boys Chris Lewis helping to send us packing. During the Championship match that followed, against Essex at Chelmsford, Butch damaged his left thumb and my back went into spasm, throwing our plans for the second Test at Lord's into confusion.

Then, the Test itself, after a promising start, spiralled into disaster with two batting collapses, condemning us to a humiliating defeat with more than a day in hand. On top of that, Ramps was fined for showing dissent after being given out, and some critics laid into me for the way I left the crease after my second innings dismissal.

While all this was going on, I was immensely proud to be awarded the MBE in the Queen's Birthday Honours List. But that was about the only thing I had to celebrate. Welcome to the England captaincy, buddy!

My back spasm was obviously a cause of concern, coming as it did on the last day of the match at Chelmsford, just three days before the Test. At first, I didn't think it was huge problem. I get these spasms once or maybe twice a year, have come to recognise the symptoms, and if I catch it early enough a few hot baths and a day of rest are usually enough to ease the problem.

I even missed a day of Test cricket with a spasm, at Lord's in 1997, but was able to resume my keeping duties the following day after John Crawley stood in for me. But by Wednesday morning, I could still feel the problem and if the Test had started that day I wouldn't have been able to play, so we had to send an SOS for Graeme Hick and Jack Russell.

On the face of it, two players to replace one isn't ideal, but as I fill two roles in the side, top-order batsman and keeper, it had to be done.

But if I wasn't fit, it meant a change to the balance of the side, with four bowlers instead of five, as well as Nass taking over the captaincy. That meant Butch's bowling became more important, but he was struggling as well. He'd missed a stinging catch at slip towards the end of the Essex match, and had a badly bruised left thumb. It didn't stop him bowling, but with his hand coming off the bat in pain almost every time he hit the ball in the nets, we had to send for cover for him too.

Steve James arrived hotfoot from Cardiff, and after Butch had another net on the morning of the match, the Glamorgan opener came in for a well-deserved debut after years of prolific scoring at county level.

We were criticised for the way we handled the Butcher business as later x-rays revealed a crack. Those critics said the x-ray should have taken place on the Tuesday, so James could have been called up much sooner, rather than rushing down the M4 on the day before the game.

But with injuries like that, the issue is not whether there is a crack or not. In fact, most top players will tell you they have played with cracked fingers at some stage during their careers. I know I have.

The key is the level of discomfort the player is in, and whether it is bearable. We wanted Butch in the side, so were prepared to wait for him until Thursday morning. But when it was clear he wasn't fit, we went for James instead.

At least I was fit to play, and I knew it as soon as I woke up on Thursday morning. The rain that washed out the first three hours of play at least gave me the chance for another hot bath or two, but even if we had started on time, I would have been okay.

I felt even better when I won the toss so we could bowl first on a humid day after the pitch had been under cover for 24 hours. And a magnificent opening spell by Corky improved my mood still further if that was possible, as he reduced South Africa to 46 for four.

But from there, the wheels fell off rapidly. Corky got Rhodes caught by Ath at slip only to be pulled up for over-stepping, then Rhodes got another let-off when Ath failed to hold a rocket in the slips off Dean Headley.

Rhodes and Cronje chose to attack, and we obliged by bowling too short at both men. Rhodes, in particular, was savage on anything the least bit short, and they were away never to be caught.

The end result, a ten-wicket loss in four days, begs the question of whether we should have bowled first, but given my time again I would make exactly the same decision. First day conditions were helpful. But, apart from Corky, who bowled a full length in his opening spell and swung and seamed the ball, we just didn't use them well enough, and on top of that we missed our chances. The South African score of 360 was the sort of first innings total which meant you could usually boss the game.

They did just that, but that was still no excuse for the way we batted. True, Pollock and Donald bowled really quickly, but you expect that at Test level. We played some poor shots, the luck ran against us, and 110 all out was just not good enough. We knew it.

To add insult to injury, Ramps ended up in front of match referee Javed Burki after remarks he made to umpire Darrell Hair when he was given out caught behind off Donald.

Donald had ripped a ball between Ramps' bat and body, and it just flicked his back elbow on the way through to keeper Mark Boucher.

The appeal went up, and so did Hair's finger. Ramps delayed his departure for a few seconds, then as he walked past Hair he said: 'Don't you know you are messing with people's careers?'

I could totally sympathise with Ramps' frustration, especially as he was in the process of trying to fashion some form of miracle from our tail to get past the follow-on target. And to get a decision you know is wrong is never a pleasant feeling. But it doesn't alter the fact you must accept that decision, whether you think it's right or not. There's no way the umpire has deliberately tried to stuff you, and telling him about it for good measure doesn't win you any points either.

In all fairness, Ramps knew that as soon as he got back to the dressing room, and quite rightly accepted the punishment handed down to him by Burki, an £850 fine and a one-match ban suspended for six months, without complaint.

Burki agreed to delay announcing the punishment until after Ramps had batted a second time, and I thought that was quite right too, despite some howls of protest from the press who demanded to know what had happened. Ramps knew about it, of course, but I didn't want that to be an issue while we were still trying to save the game. There was plenty of time to chew the fat over that one after he was out.

One thing Ramps' behaviour did do was to get the media keen on finding other examples of dissent, and some of them homed in on me after I was out in our second innings.

Nass and I had fashioned a century partnership to take us to within touching distance of South Africa's score. We'd seen off Pollock and Donald, it was a hot day, and we had a real chance of getting a lead and then putting them under pressure with Thorpey and Ramps still to come.

At that point, I drove at Jacques Kallis, the ball went through to Boucher prompting South African appeals, and George Sharp put his finger up to send me on my way.

I must say I was really disappointed because I wasn't sure I'd got a touch, but I had to go. I set off for the Pavilion, but as I headed there I kept glancing around to see the replay of my dismissal on the giant video screen at the Nursery End of the ground. Some people – but thankfully not match referee Burki – took that gesture to be me showing dissent at my dismissal, but it couldn't have been further from the truth.

Of course I was disappointed at getting out. Who wouldn't be after the hard work Nass and I had put in to try and get us back in the game, especially as I wasn't sure I'd got a touch on the ball?

But it ignores the fact I usually look up at the replay screen as I walk off after a dismissal whether I've got nought or 100. In that situation it was only natural for me to try and catch a glimpse of my dismissal to clarify things in my own mind, and to do that I had to turn around as the screen was at the opposite end of the ground. On top of that, it would probably be the only chance I'd get to see the dismissal for some time, as the dressing room is at least a two-minute walk from the pitch. Often, by the time a batsman gets back there, the replays have run their course.

To make things worse, my fall sparked a dramatic collapse in which we lost six for 11 in 71 balls to end our interest in the match.

The biggest cheer of the day came when our last pair of Crofty and Gus scored the runs that made South Africa bat again, but things were wrapped up pretty soon afterwards, and a visitor's victory was a formality.

The crowd's ironic reaction when we avoided the innings defeat told us all we needed to know about how hacked off they were at the way we had folded. But we were just as gutted. And I really felt for Steve James too, as our effort robbed him of a proper chance to savour being presented with his England cap.

Ever since David Graveney took over as Chairman of Selectors in 1997, we have made a point of presenting a debutant with his England cap after the toss. It is something we have unashamedly pinched from the Aussies, but it is a great thing to do because as a professional cricketer getting your first cap is a career highlight, what you play the game for.

But although he had his cap to play in, with the toss and then play getting under way pretty quickly after the covers came off on Thursday afternoon there was no chance to have the ceremony, and on each of the following mornings the opportunity didn't present itself either.

We were going to do it on the fifth morning, but when we collapsed so spectacularly I ended up handing it over as we went onto the field for the last time on the fourth evening. It wasn't ideal, and that was a shame, but then neither was our performance.

Yet again we'd gone down at Lord's, my favourite ground in world cricket, but also one on which I have to admit our record is really poor.

Why that is I don't know. I certainly feel inspired when I play there, walking out to bat through the Long Room, past the paintings and memorabilia of more than 200 years of cricket history. And as I made my maiden Test hundred there, against Sri Lanka in 1991, the place is extra-special to me.

Unfortunately, the opposition often seems to feel equally inspired by Lord's, and after the drubbing we got there, it was us who needed some fresh inspiration.

The Turning Point of the Summer

As speeches go, my effort before we warmed up ahead of the fourth day of the third Test was no classic.

It was short and sweet, but there was no point in beating about the bush with flowery language. After all, we were 1–0 down in the series and had been completely outplayed for the first three days of the match. On top of that we were near-certainties to follow-on, and had been booed off the field after play by the Lancashire public on successive nights.

'The crowd was right to boo us,' I said. 'We've been second best all through this game so far. But the pitch is still good and I think we can get a draw.

'Whatever happens, whether we draw or even lose this match, let's at least show some pride in what we're doing. Just remember, we're playing for England.'

Words can only do so much though and it's actions on the field that count. And for a while the pattern of the match remained depressingly familiar. We did follow on, 390 runs behind, and quickly slid to 11 for two nine overs before lunch. At that stage, with the best will in the world, we looked unlikely to last the day.

But more than five sessions later I was racing from the dressing room and out onto the field to congratulate Crofty and Gus Fraser as they completed one of cricket's great escape acts. We had got the draw I asked for, and it was the result that kick-started our summer.

The match had begun in a haze of national sporting depression, with England's soccer team going out of the World Cup on penalties to Argentina the night before. The squad had all watched the match on a giant video screen at Manchester's Copthorne Hotel, and I think it's fair to say everyone was gutted when David Batty's spot-kick was saved. What was needed from us was a pick-me-up for the nation, a stirring performance to help everyone try and forget about France '98 as soon as possible.

But unfortunately we struggled to produce that, and with the ground little more than half-full on the first day, South Africa ground out the runs on an easy-paced pitch that offered our bowlers nothing.

All that prompted was more depression from everyone, including the press, who took one look around Old Trafford and said the game was in crisis, or even dying. To be honest, I could understand their frustrations. After all, we hadn't won a major five- or six-match series in twelve years, and with more and more sport now taking place in summer, cricket is facing competition for the punter's interest.

When I grew up I used to watch uninterrupted John Player League cricket on television on a Sunday. Now, the National League shares airtime with Grand Prix motor racing, golf, tennis and even soccer and horse racing.

With England's loss in France the previous evening and some pretty slow cricket on offer, there wasn't a lot of atmosphere in the ground, but I still think the way some writers painted us as a sport in crisis was a bit stiff.

The bottom line everyone measures the game's health by is how well the national side is doing. If we win, the game is in good shape; if we do badly, it must be dying. That ignores every other part of the game, and that is wrong.

Most of our Surrey squad, for example, came up through the Nescafé Coaching Scheme at the club, and that is still going strong.

I just think the combination of France '98, an average crowd and a poor day for us may have pushed some people too far. And I think my argument is borne out by the way, just over a month later, the grounds were full and cricket was the flavour of the month again when we won the series.

The ban on fancy dress inside the ground was a shame, even though I could understand why it was done. A small minority of fans who dress up just go to the cricket to get drunk and make fools of themselves and there's no place for them if they stop others enjoying the game. But a lot of other people dress up just for a bit of fun and to give everyone else a bit of a laugh. I know of a university lecturer in

Leeds who likes to go to the Test dressed as a carrot and I don't think you would have him down as your average troublemaker!

As long as any costume doesn't interfere with anybody else's enjoyment, I say let them in as the more fun we have at the ground, the better the atmosphere, and I love playing in a ground with a bit of atmosphere. The Aussies even encourage fans to bring banners, with the best one winning a prize. Maybe we should look at something similar.

Big crowd or not, we struggled to lift our level of performance on the first three days. Even with Goughie back after his finger injury we just couldn't make things happen, although we never let them get away completely as spinners Crofty and Ashley Giles, who had a tough Test baptism, toiled away.

'Ash's' selection meant there was no place for Ben Hollioake who was called up despite a mixed start to the season. Some people criticised us for that as they reckoned an injection of youth, in the wake of Michael Owen's success in France, was just what cricket needed. We had been hopeful of playing Ben, especially as we thought the pitch might suit his bowling after recent rain. But once we saw it was dry, two spinners made more sense. And in any case, Ben's presence gave him the chance to do some work with Bob Cottam, who spent the summer coaching our bowlers.

The good work of Crofty in particular meant South Africa delayed their declaration until the third morning, but once we batted we lost our way in pretty horrific fashion.

There were some poor shots – or in my case non-shots as I shouldered arms to Jacques Kallis only to lose my off-stump – but the luck also seemed to be running against us. Thorpey woke up on Saturday morning with a stiff back and spent most of the day flat out on the treatment table. Then, when he hobbled into bat late in the day, he appeared to nick the ball onto his pads only to fall lbw. And after the events of Lord's, Ramps had to keep his temper in check after being given out caught at the wicket after the ball seemed to hit his forearm.

But it was still pretty desperate stuff, and prompted coach David Lloyd, Grav and myself to go into thirty minutes of chat after play. We often do that during a game, and all three of us agreed we hadn't had the rub of the green with Thorpey's injury putting a tin lid on things, and we also agreed that these were basically the best players we could have picked. But all the same, we players had got us into this mess, so it was up to us to turn things around, and I told my team-mates as much on Sunday morning.

When we followed on I was at the crease much quicker than I'd hoped I would be, but I tried to view that as a positive. It allowed me to do what I enjoy best, to take the attack to the opposition early on in the piece. And with my old partner Ath at the other end it was just like old times really.

When you're batting to save a match, especially one where you are so far behind and there is so much time to go, it's important not to get distracted too much by the scoreboard. If you keep looking up at the score it's all too easy to think you are simply too far behind and the situation is hopeless. Or you might try and think too far ahead to the prospect of making the opposition bat again, making their task to win the match that bit harder, and to try and play too aggressively. It's vital to keep the board ticking over as that rotates the strike and poses the bowlers different problems with different players on strike. But the key is just to play each ball on its merits. If it's there to hit, hit it; if not, then just leave it or defend.

Ath and I have had the misfortune to play plenty of these rearguard actions down the years. It's a really comforting sight to have him at the other end in the form he showed here as he just never looks like getting out.

And if you can form a partnership it's amazing how the frustration among the opposition can grow. We managed it here, and suddenly the all-conquering South Africa became mortal again.

Donald had a sore ankle, although that didn't stop him running in and leading the attack superbly all through the match. Pollock was missing with a thigh strain, Klusener had a foot injury, Ntini was making his debut and spinner Adams couldn't get much turn out of the surface.

By the time I lashed the ball to the cover boundary to bring up my first Test hundred as captain and my first at this level since January 1997 we had won the day, but there were still six hours to go on day five.

We managed to get through the first session losing just one wicket, but after the break I fell hooking, as Ath had before lunch, and that seemed to send us into an apparently terminal nose-dive.

Donald had resorted to going around the wicket to me, banged it in short and I took up the challenge. But as I had to fetch the ball from outside off-stump I didn't get over it and gave deep square-leg a fairly straightforward catch.

Ath had perished hooking Kallis but I would defend both of us against a charge of recklessness. It's a shot that's brought us plenty of runs down the years so it has to be worth the risk. And by the time we'd got out we were in sight of making them bat again, something that would make saving the game easier, but we had to get to that total first.

Thorpey hobbled out but hobbled back pretty quickly after Donald dispatched him for the first pair of his Test career, and when Ramps and Giles fell soon after tea we had just two wickets in hand and almost two hours left to play.

In the face of those odds, Crofty, Goughie and Gus were heroic. We have been desperate for our lower order to hang around for longer as opposition players seem to do against us, and here they obliged, big time.

Crofty and Goughie batted for over an hour together to take us into the final fifteen overs, and by this stage the crowd of only a couple of thousand had begun cheering every ball they survived.

I'd spent most of the time after I was out pacing around, but settled on the dressing room balcony on the first floor of the pavilion alongside David Lloyd as the pair began their stand. I have to admit I can be superstitious in things like this, and as they kept batting I stayed rooted to the same place for fear of bringing bad luck.

It was a great effort by both men. Crofty had all sorts of problems against the short ball and Glenn McGrath in 1997, while Goughie was just back after having his finger broken. But both of them got right behind the ball and it took a searing bouncer by Donald to part them when Goughie was taken at short leg.

Enter Gus Fraser. I once saw him bat at eight for England as recently as 1993 and he got runs too, but these days his expectations as a batsman are fairly modest. But here he was going in with just a handful of overs to go and a Test to save.

He hasn't even got a bat sponsor these days and relies on a bloke in Kent to send him a piece of willow with an image of Gus carved into the back of it. But he braved it out here superbly.

In one final throw of the dice, Cronje took the third new ball and Crofty forced Ntini through the covers for two to level the scores. It meant South Africa had to bat again. There were four overs to go, but with the two overs taken off for a change of innings, plus any fraction of an over in progress, South Africa had to take the final wicket in the next over to stand a chance of winning the game.

Donald was the bowler, Gus the batsman. As I've said before, I have faith in Gus's batting, but it was still a miracle how he survived those six balls. They were lightning quick, he was penned in with men around the bat, but he just refused to back down.

Gus's method was simple. He played forward, or as far forward as he dared given Donald's pace, so that if he was hit on the pad he would probably get the benefit of the doubt in any lbw shout.

That still left him exposed to the short ball but he decided he just had to wear it on the body. He took some fearful blows, but when he survived the appeal for lbw from the last ball of the over I leapt up, punched the air and yelled 'Yeeessss!'

Everyone out in the middle seemed unclear on the regulations, including the umpires, so they played on for one more over from Adams, but I knew we were safe, and as soon as that over finished I was down the steps to welcome the two players in.

Crofty was exhausted but elated after 170 of the toughest minutes of cricket he'll ever play. Our dressing room was full of players high-fiving and slapping backs and it was just like we'd won the Test, not saved it by the skin of our teeth.

I thought we were going a bit over the top, even though we could now still win the series, but it was all put into perspective for me when I went down to say well played to the South Africans. They were silent, exhausted after almost three days in the field, and pretty dejected after failing to win a game they had in their pockets for most of its course. I had a special word for Donald. With Pollock absent, Klusener on the treatment table as well, and a damaged ankle into the bargain, he was magnificent. He just bowled and bowled for Cronje, always at top pace and I almost felt sorry he hadn't come away with a win after that sort of effort.

Almost, but not quite. Frankly, our need was greater than theirs but now we had to turn that type of fighting effort into a winning one.

Fighting Fire with Fire

The expression 'top class' can be overused, but not in this case. The duel between Allan Donald and Michael Atherton on the fourth evening of the fourth Test was one of the high points of the sporting summer.

On the one hand there was a brilliant fast bowler, straining every muscle in an attempt to generate top pace and achieve the breakthrough his side needed. And on the other was one of the world's best opening batsman, in a rich vein of form, and trying everything he knew to keep his opponent at bay.

It was a pivotal moment in the match, and, as it turned out, a pivotal moment in the summer. Because when Ath and Nasser Hussain survived that onslaught, they gave us the chance to press on for a win that not only gave us the Test, it also gave us a tilt at the main prize, the Cornhill series, by levelling things at 1–1.

But while all that was going on, spare a thought for the bloke in next – me.

I always back my own ability, and after my 164 at Old Trafford, I was full of confidence. But I also knew it would be an awesome test of that ability and confidence if I had to go in and face Donald that evening. He was flying in, and in that sort of mood, once he gets one wicket he can quite easily get two or three and that could have turned the match in their favour.

Nass and Ath bought us some valuable breathing space with their stand, showing the type of guts and determination you would expect from two players who sell their wickets so dearly. But whether Ath should have been there to play such a momentous innings was a massive talking point, and it still is among some people I would guess.

On 27, during the height of Donald's furious spell against him, he deflected a ball from round the wicket, which Boucher caught, diving low to his right. Donald was certain Ath had got a touch, Ath stood his ground, and umpire Steve Dunne shook his head and mouthed 'not out'. That provoked fury from Donald which grew even more intense after the next ball when Ath inside edged him past leg-stump for four. And when Boucher dropped a simple edge from Nass off his bowling soon afterwards, well, that just about put a tin lid on things for Donald.

Ath's let-off, together with Jonty Rhodes' dismissal in South Africa's second innings, when I caught him down the leg-side off Corky only for replays to suggest the ball clipped the pad, were just two incidents that provoked fierce debate and questions both in the media and among the public.

Those questions were usually: 'Why don't batsmen walk any more?' and 'Isn't there too much appealing in the modern game that puts the umpire under increased pressure?'

To me, the idea of walking, in other words leaving the crease when you know you've nicked a catch to, for example the keeper or short leg, is something that belongs in an ideal world. And unfortunately we don't live in that world any more, if we ever did. The world we do live in is governed by results, with big rewards for people who achieve them and very little for those who don't. In that situation, it might be asking too much to expect someone to slit their own throat by walking off of their own accord when by doing so they could be sacrificing their whole career. And that is especially true when there is someone there to make that decision for you.

The bottom line has to be that the umpire is in charge, and he should be left to make the decision. But that decision, whether it's right or wrong, has to be accepted without question or else the game falls into anarchy. To me, moaning at a bad decision is just not on, because on another day, that player might get the benefit of a lucky decision that goes for him.

I learnt to accept the umpire's decision pretty quickly when I went to Australia to play grade cricket for the Midland-Guildford club in Perth. In my first game for the club I took a slip catch off the man who went on to become the ECB's Chief Executive, Tim Lamb.

I gathered the ball cleanly at knee-height – that's no joke – and was just on my way to congratulate Tim when I saw the batsman still standing there. When I appealed for the catch, the umpire said 'not out'. Apparently, he thought the ball hadn't carried!

And whether I liked it or not, whatever I thought of the decision, I had to get on with the game. And so did Tim!

It cuts both ways and in an era when walking seems largely a thing of the past, players have to accept that, and if they do it will make the umpire's job much easier.

As for the amount of appealing that goes on, I do accept that cricket is a more pressurised game than it was even in 1990 when I started playing at international level. The all-seeing eye of television, the media, and increasing financial rewards have seen to that. But that doesn't alter the fact that if you don't bowl very well you are not going to be in a position to make many appeals.

I think it's fair to say that as the series against South Africa went on we bowled better and better. With Cork, Fraser and Gough in harness we got the ball to move around and created chances as a result. Those chances led to appeals, and we made those appeals. It was then up to the umpires to decide if they were out or not out. That is their job. They are paid to make those decisions and we have to accept them. If we don't, we are fined or banned.

My job, as England captain, is also to make decisions, and I made two of my best ones at Nottingham before a ball was bowled. I decided to go with Gus Fraser for the match and I put South Africa in.

And despite the odd moment when at least one of those decisions looked questionable – putting South Africa in if you were wondering – both came good with a vengeance in the end. We won, and Gus got ten wickets.

Gus admitted to me afterwards that he thought he was in real danger of being left out. He'd not set the heather alight with his figures in the first three Tests, but on a Trent Bridge pitch that was dry and well-grassed, I reckoned he was just the man for the job.

I was glad of him on the first day too, as he claimed four for 42 despite South Africa rattling up 302–7 with a Cronje century. Apart from flashes by Goughie and Andy Flintoff on debut, we didn't really bowl all that well except for Gus, and he kept us in the match.

Corky was especially poor on day one, but stories I tore him off a strip in the dressing room are absolute rubbish. Yes, I was disappointed at how things had gone, and yes he and I had a chat. But he is professional enough to know he'd bowled poorly, and he was at the ground before everyone else the following morning to work on his technique with Bob Cottam, with four second-innings wickets his reward.

Corky and Gus bowled superbly on the fourth day to give us a chance of the win after Ramps, Butch and Ath had all made fifties in our first innings and I was especially pleased when Gus got the man of the match award. There may have been some grass on the surface, but the pitch was basically good for batting, as it had been the year before when we played Australia, and he bowled with real discipline to wear the batsmen down. I know how much every England game means to Gus now after the long battle he has had with injury. And I was a really proud captain when I patted him on the back and said 'Well done mate' as he led us off the field at the end of South Africa's second innings.

Then, thanks to Ath and Nass we were able to ram home that advantage. Both put the side before themselves, especially Ath, who passed up the chance of a Test hundred in favour of a quick victory when he urged me to keep playing my shots as we neared the 247 runs we needed in the fourth innings.

I came in when Nass was dismissed with 55 runs still needed. At that stage Ath was on 88 and seemed certain to reach three figures if he stayed at the crease, but I felt in great nick right from the word go and started laying into Donald, who had every right to feel tired after his efforts through the match.

All of a sudden I was racing along, Ath had ground to a halt and there was a chance he would miss out on a hundred. I was keen for him to get it, as it was the least he deserved after the effort he'd put in, but his response was typical. 'Don't worry about me,' he said. 'Let's just get the win quickly.'

So I kept blazing away, to an unbeaten 45 in 34 balls while he missed out on the century he deserved, although he did have the satisfaction of hitting the winning runs through mid-on to take him to 98.

As we completed the final run, we shook hands, gathered up the souvenir stumps and then hugged each other out in the middle. It was a special time to be at the crease for both of us and we were pretty emotional. Then, as the near full-house of 12,000 fans raced onto the ground, we raced off for the sanctuary of the dressing room. Up the stairs on the right-hand side just inside the pavilion door, up to the top floor, where we were greeted by the rest of the team and support staff, everyone shaking hands, patting backs and punching the air.

All except Ath. He simply sat in his seat, just inside the door on the left-hand side with his pads on and took it all in. He's been through so much, seen so many defeats in his time as captain, I just think he wanted to savour what this really meant. I'm also pretty sure he was exhausted. His effort in the middle, spanning four minutes short of six hours was a monumental one, and by the end of the match he'd batted for more than 30 hours in the series.

Credit to the South Africans. They were hot on our heels up those stairs from their dressing room one floor below and they took the defeat graciously and had a drink with us afterwards too.

Once Ath had recovered, best of all was to see him and Donald having a drink in our dressing room long after most of the media had gone home. Whatever people say about how hard the game is these days, off the field, in the dressing rooms, the spirit between most international sides is as good as the old-timers say it was years ago.

My spirit was pretty good too. I'd just won my first Test as captain at the sixth attempt, and the win had come in front of one of the biggest last day crowds I've ever seen.

The buzz I got from their cheers as we moved to victory, and then the cheers after the match as we waved to them, was magic. Already the press was talking about the series-decider at Headingley. Not quite a sport in crisis I thought.

High Drama at Headingley

When the time came for the presentations, I knew what I wanted first.

As master of ceremonies David Gower reached down for the cheque that we'd earned for winning the Test series, I gave him a little shake of the head. It's not that we didn't want the £200,000 donated by Cornhill, Vodafone and the ECB. After all, we are all professional players, and cricket is our living. But long after we've all spent the money, the Cornhill Trophy commemorating our first win in a five- or six-Test series in twelve years will still be around.

That was what I wanted ahead of anything else. David duly handed over the trophy and I had my first prize as England captain in my first series after being appointed. The feeling I got as I held it aloft in front of all those thousands of smiling facing at Headingley that day was more than any money could buy.

It was Monday 10 August, and we'd come from 1–0 down in the series to beat South Africa 2–1. That was the ecstasy. But beforehand there was plenty of agony, even on that final, overcast morning.

I arrived at the ground not knowing if fate, or more specifically fitness worries to two of our leading bowlers would rob us of our victory chance.

Goughie, who'd spearheaded our victory charge late the previous evening, had been up for most of the night with an upset stomach. And Gus, who'd claimed his third five-wicket haul in a row in the first innings, had gone in the back.

Without those two I'd have still backed us to win, but I have to be honest, the 30 odd that South Africa needed looked a lot more realistic, even though they only had two wickets in hand.

It was down to the magic hands and tablets of our physiotherapist Wayne Morton to do the trick, and I have never been so relieved as I was when 'Fizz' gave me the thumbs up at around 10.30am.

All the same, it was still sad that we had to complete the win without a man who deserved to savour it more than most – Ath. He'd had an upset stomach for several days, and set off for the doctor just before play. Thankfully it was nothing serious, but he still didn't get back until just after we'd taken the final wicket, although that did give Yorkshire's Matthew Wood the chance of glory instead.

The workload that Goughie and Gus shouldered the previous evening was fabulous, so maybe it was no surprise when their bodies did cry out for mercy.

With South Africa chasing just 219 for victory while we needed 10 wickets, it was all or nothing stuff from both sides, and we went at it hard. Gus and Goughie roared in, urged on by a healthy Yorkshire crowd and in no time we had them reeling at 27 for five. Surely there was no way back for them now.

But that thorn in our side throughout the summer, Jonty Rhodes, and his experienced sidekick Brian McMillan, got them back in the game from nowhere. First they got a foothold, then as the ball went soft and our support bowlers struggled to maintain the pressure, they started to grow in confidence. Goughie came back late in the day as he made Rhodes his 100th Test scalp and then trapped Boucher lbw with some wicked reverse swing, but by then he was knackered, running on just adrenaline in front of his home crowd.

By this stage Gus had already pulled up lame, but although he wasn't fit to bowl, we kept him on the field as long as possible, just in case we could patch him up for Monday morning.

If he was off the ground for any longer than 15 minutes, he would have to be back on for the same length of time before he could bowl again. And if the game went to the wire we might need him sooner rather than later, even if he was only half-fit.

It was against that background that I was keen to come off when I had the chance to claim the extra half-hour that the regulations allowed. My bowlers were tired and we needed to regroup.

Now I know some people have criticised our approach at that point. They would argue we are in the entertainment business, there was a near-capacity crowd that had built up and the audience on BBC TV was growing by the minute.

Everything was set up for a finish that night.

But to those people I say this: what would you have said if we had stayed on and lost? We would certainly have been criticised then for running the bowlers into the ground and the English cricket bubble that had grown at Nottingham the previous week would have burst in a big way.

As it was, the public got another helping of the drama the following morning, and despite the fact there might only have been two balls of cricket, we still got another near-capacity crowd.

Then again, as we joked to Goughie afterwards, maybe it shouldn't have been a surprise that the Yorkshire public turned up in such numbers, as it was free entry!

And in any case, South Africa could have claimed the extra time if they had wanted, but by the time Cronje realised how tired we really were and sent a message out to the batsmen to stay on, umpires Javed Akhtar and Peter Willey had already picked up the bails.

We had no idea what to expect on that final day in terms of the crowd. When we finished practice at around 10.15 there still weren't that many people in the ground, a couple of thousand maybe. It was only when the bowlers came back in at around 10.50 and said the atmosphere was electric that we started to get a feel for what was waiting for us.

I had ordered Gus, Goughie and Corky, the three men I was going to rely on, to go out and have a warm-up as I wanted them to be totally loose for the first ball. With runs at a premium we couldn't afford an over costing 10 while any one of them just got the stiffness out of their limbs.

When they came back into the dressing room they said the crowd was massive, and Gus added: 'They were cheering every ball we bowled!'

There was time for one last pep talk: 'This is what we've waited for, boys. The ball is our court, let's go out and seize the day, nail down the coffin.'

Off we went. I opened up with Gus from the Kirkstall Lane End and Goughie from the Football Stand. Even half-fit, I knew they wouldn't give too much away, and with the match on a knife-edge I also reckoned Donald and Pollock, the not out batsmen, wouldn't be looking for too many big shots.

At first, it was frustrating stuff as they dripped the score along in ones and twos, and even a leg-glanced four by Pollock off Goughie as he strove for some late in-swing. The crowd cheered every time there was no run, but the ball was getting old and soft and the new ball, if it was needed, might come too late to help us.

Finally, after 20 minutes, Gus got the breakthrough. He had bowled an immaculate line and drew Donald into a forward push around off-stump. It was the thinnest of edges, Willey's finger went up, and we were one wicket away from winning.

But Pollock was still in. He is a good enough player to have scored first-class hundreds, and he has a Test ninety as well, but to get the winning runs here he needed the strike. And in the next over, from Goughie, we got him away from it just long enough to count.

There aren't many better bowlers than Goughie against a tail-ender because he is so expert at bowling the ball they seem to have most trouble with, the late, in-swinging yorker. This wasn't quite a yorker, but it was full, hit Ntini's front pad and straight away I knew it was out.

Javed Ahktar, the Pakistani umpire who was the National Grid Panel official for the Test, slowly raised his finger, and all hell broke loose. Stumps were harvested, players hugged each other and then it was a mad dash for the dressing room as the crowd came on from all directions.

Bumble was there to meet me at the gate and we hugged. He's a passionate man who'll always speak his mind, but he only wants what's best for English cricket, and although he said afterwards 'This is a day for the players', it was a great day for him as well.

Into the dressing room we raced, and we had a couple of minutes alone, players only, with Ath back to savour the scene. During that time alone, we rang Crofty and Thorpey, two men not around for varying reasons, and let them know what we thought of their absence on such a great day!

In came Lord MacLaurin to dish out the champagne, which tasted as good as any I've had, and then it was off to the presentation and some photos on the field. The ceremony itself seemed to go on for ages, but no one really minded, with Butch getting the man of the match award for his century on the first day, the only hundred on a good old-fashioned bowler-friendly Leeds pitch. It was a brilliant innings by Butch, and as far as I am concerned his partnership with Ath, especially as it is a left- and right-hand combination, was the find of the summer. They played well together, and although both of them lost form in Australia, they can still be good for England, I'm convinced of that.

I know a lot has been made of the standard of umpiring in this Test and the series as a whole, and there were those who feel we were lucky to get the success we had. Maybe we did get the rub of the green in the last two Tests, but there were still plenty of decisions that went against us. Poor Andy Flintoff bagged a pair, and his dismissal in the first innings, when he was caught at short leg off what appeared to be the thigh pad was a really tough one to take.

But I'd like to think both sets of players took the rough with the smooth, and it was nice to see match referee Ahmed Ebrahim, who took over from Javed Burki from the fourth Test, say well done to 'Fred' after the game for the way he'd behaved when he was given out.

He just walked off without a flicker, although I only found out why afterwards, when he confessed: 'I thought I'd been given out lbw!'

Overall, I think the standard of umpiring in my year as a Test captain was pretty good, although there is room for improvement, as there is with our play.

All we as players can ask for is that the officials are consistent in their decisions. And please, bring in fixed cameras for run-outs and stumpings!

The media circus seemed to go on for hours. After a while I went up to speak to 'Test Match Special', and then photographers came into the dressing room to snap me with the Trophy, which I wasn't letting out of my sight.

But eventually it all died down, the lads stated to pack up their gear, and that was the real sadness of the whole thing for me.

On the day of our greatest triumph in twelve years, Ath and Fred had to jump on a plane to get to Southampton for a NatWest Trophy semi-final the next day, Corky had a semi-final at Leicester the day after, and all in all only Nass, Butch, Ian Salisbury and me stayed in Leeds for a night out.

Gus had to be driven south because of his bad back, but before he went he made us all laugh. He could barely bend down to put his socks on, but all of a sudden he held up his glass of champagne and shouted 'Thanks for helping to pay for the new extension lads!'

Just a couple of days past his 33rd birthday, the old boy deserved the success we'd had more than most. But there was still plenty of the summer to go.

And although the South Africans were generous in defeat again, I knew they couldn't wait for us to go there in 1999/2000 for revenge.

England v Sri Lanka, Oval Test, 1998

'Kennington Oval, Colombo'

If English cricket was on a high after the success of the South Africa series, no one had bothered to tell Arjuna Ranatunga.

Just like Wimbledon Football Club in the Premiership, Ranatunga's Sri Lanka have specialised in ripping up the well-written scripts of opposing sides for quite a while now. They did it when they won the World Cup in 1996, and they did it again here at the end of the summer.

That script was pretty clear, at least in the eyes of the public. After beating Hansie Cronje's men in the Tests, we were expected to see off both them and Sri Lanka to claim the Emirates Triangular One-day Tournament before ending the summer on a high by winning the Cornhill Test against Ranatunga's men at The Foster's Oval. We weren't complacent and we knew it wouldn't be straightforward. But we still expected to do just that before heading off to Australia for the winter with success under our belts.

So it was a bit of a blow to say the least when Sri Lanka managed not only to beat us in the final of the Emirates, but also in the Cornhill Test at The Foster's Oval for good measure. On top of that, coach David Lloyd ended up in hot water with the ECB for publicly labelling the action of Sri Lanka's spinner Muttiah Muralitharan, previously no-balled for throwing at international level, as 'unorthodox'.

And while none of that could take away our earlier achievement against South Africa, it did have the effect of throwing a bucket of cold water over us at the end of a momentous summer for English cricket.

The Sri Lankans may be portrayed as amiable, smiling, happy-go-lucky, fun-loving cricketers by certain sections of the media, but that image couldn't be further from the truth. They are an uncompromising bunch, battle-hardened and tough, and they are skilled at playing to the very edge of the laws of the game. After all, they won the World Cup in 1996, beating Australia in the final, so they know what success is all about, and how to achieve it.

That success came about in part through wonderful, blitzkrieg batting from the likes of Jayasuriya, Kaluwitharana and de Silva, but it was no fluke. They developed a strategy for success, exploiting the fielding restrictions in the first fifteen overs of an innings, and followed it through clinically.

But that strategy has another aspect, namely playing the game at the pace they want. For example, next time you watch them bat, just count the number of times the twelfth man appears with drinks, fresh gloves or even new bats for the men at the crease. As a fielding side, you are under enough pressure in the face of their explosive starts without having to worry about over-rate fines as well. In that situation, it's all too easy to lose your cool, either as a captain or a bowler. You shouldn't get worried about it, shouldn't get dragged in, allowing yourself to get annoyed at the regular interruptions. But sometimes it's hard not to. If you do get dragged in, thinking about the delays, you risk losing concentration. And you can also be guilty of trying to make things happen either as a bowler or a captain, when often the best strategy is just to keep it tight and let the batsmen make the mistake.

The Sri Lankans are such good players that any error in length or line will usually be punished, so keeping your cool and focusing on what you are doing rather than looking at them is a key when you play them. We managed that pretty well when we came up against them first in the Emirates, winning easily in front of a full house at Lord's thanks to runs from Hicky and myself, and a sound bowling performance. The match marked the first time we wore coloured clothing in a domestic one-day international, something all the lads enjoyed, and the crowd seemed to respond, making for a great atmosphere in our first outing after the win at Headingley.

But if the atmosphere was great, so was the pitch, ideal for a one-day game. The ball came onto the bat to encourage strokeplay, but there was also pace and bounce to help the quicker bowlers and Goughie, Alan Mullally and Peter Martin exploited it to the full. The final however, four days later, was a different story. It was played on the same surface and four days on the track was worn, with the footmarks of the previous contest all over it. The ball was bound to turn, and there was little prospect of the pace and bounce we had seen in the earlier game. In short, it was made for Sri Lanka, who had really struggled against the new ball in our previous meeting.

I'm not for doctoring wickets to suit the home side completely, but I *do* believe there should be a slight advantage to the side playing at home. After all, we wouldn't expect to find a green, seaming pitch when we front up in Colombo, so why we provided a slow, low turner for this match is a mystery to me. It certainly wasn't what I would call a true English one-day pitch, but credit to Murali, he exploited the conditions superbly, and after a bright start we lost our way.

The combination of a slow pitch, a five-wicket haul for Murali and the ball losing it's hardness as the innings went on made it really difficult to force the pace, and we had to be content with 256–8 after being 191–2 at one stage. Then, once they saw off the new ball with just the loss of Jayasuriya to show for it, we were always struggling. And with Atapattu and Kaluwitharana making runs they got home easily.

It was a frustrating time to be on the field. They were easing to victory, we lost Nasser with a groin injury and I lost my cool with Tillekeratne.

Just before the end, Atapattu pushed the ball wide of the bowler Crofty, who tried to dive to prevent the run. At the very least Tillekeratne held his ground at the non-striker's end but in doing so, he blocked Crofty from getting the ball. Then, having done that, he ran the single.

In my book that was not on and I fully expected Tillekeratne to acknowledge his error by walking back to the non-striker's end to cancel out the run, in the same way that batsmen don't take overthrows when the ball strikes them. I couldn't believe it when he didn't, and before the next ball I shouted to the lads around the bat: 'Let's get this arsehole out then'. Unfortunately, that was picked up on the Sky Sports stump microphones and a couple of the tabloid newspapers started jumping up and down about it.

For my part, I couldn't see what all the fuss was about. It wasn't as if my remarks were aimed directly at Tillekeratne, they were more a gee-up for the lads after another frustrating incident in an increasingly frustrating day. And while I'm all for the enhanced coverage Sky

Sports has brought to the game by showing many more matches than we used to see, I was very disappointed that they broadcast my remarks.

As far as I'm aware the agreement between the ECB and the broadcasters is that the stump microphones are only for use between the time the bowler reaches his delivery stride and the ball is struck. Other than that they should be switched off. If the agreement does say this, then it seems to me that Sky did not comply with this aspect of it.

Let's be clear about this. It's a tough game out in the middle and things are bound to be said, but as long as it doesn't go over the top – and in this instance, neither the umpires nor the match referee thought I did – then that's fine. I've always worked on the basis that what happens on the field stays on the field, and all highlighting every little thing that is said in the middle will do is sterilise the game and take the passion from it. If that is what sections of the media want, then fine. But I am sure the game would lose something as a spectacle if that happened.

Defeat at Lord's was hard enough to take, but the Test loss that followed was even worse, especially given the pitch prepared for that match. During my time in the game, The Foster's Oval has usually been renowned for serving up pitches with pace and bounce that in turn have produced great Test matches. My first Test there, against the West Indies in 1991, was on a really quick surface, there were hundreds for Robin Smith and Richie Richardson, six wickets for Phil Tufnell and a win for England at tea on the final day.

But when we arrived two days before the Sri Lanka Test, we knew pace and bounce was definitely not going to be the order of the day this time. The surface was dry and fairly bare, and the little grass on it was cut very low. In short, it would be slow, with little pace, and was bound to turn as the match went on – just the sort of pitch you would expect to find in Colombo.

I know the Sri Lankans were worried about what they would find. They rushed left-arm quickie Chaminda Vaas back from injury expecting to play him, only to find a pitch that could have been designed for Murali. They must have been rubbing their hands at that one.

As at Lord's for the Emirates final, why such a pitch was served up is a mystery to me. Maybe Surrey were keen to avoid another three-day Test like the one they had against Australia in 1997, when the early finish must have cost them a fair amount of money in lost hospitality and catering revenue. But if that was the case, it was short-sighted because surely there is nothing more likely to generate extra interest in the game – and therefore more income – than a winning England side. We saw that with the public's response to our success against South Africa.

I'm not suggesting we doctor pitches to suit us and I know the ECB make a big play about not influencing Test grounds over the surfaces they produce. All very praiseworthy, but I still think that home advantage should count for something, however small.

We immediately called up Crofty alongside Ian Salisbury to give us some added spin potential. In the end though we decided to go with just Salisbury, alongside Gus Fraser, Ben Hollioake, Dominic Cork and Darren Gough as the attack we felt most likely to get us 20 wickets in the match.

The pitch wasn't the only problem we had going into the match. Nasser reported for duty but was quickly ruled out with the groin injury he picked up in the Emirates final, while Athers' bad back flared up again, forcing us to send for Steve James.

So, on a pitch likely to spin, we lost two of our best players of the turning ball, and two men who had formed the backbone of our batting all summer. A huge loss and one we eventually failed to get over.

Ben gave us another headache on the eve of the match when he turned up for practice 45 minutes late. He is a wonderful talent, but also very laid-back and loves to sleep. This was one doze he won't forget though, as it cost him a £1000 fine.

We got one bonus when Ranatunga put us in as we didn't want to be batting last on that pitch, and then we thought we had secured our position with top-class hundreds from John Crawley and Hicky, that took us past 400. Both played really well, and it was a hard decision to leave one of them – Hicky – out of the original Ashes touring party. As Grav said, that really was the toughest of all calls and there was nothing between them really.

But from then on it was largely one-way traffic. With the pitch offering no pace, bounce or seam movement, the Sri Lanka batsmen just clobbered us. Maybe our bowlers were tired after a long summer, but I wouldn't use that as an excuse for the way Sri Lanka motored along at almost four runs per over. There was absolutely nothing in the pitch for our attack and the batsmen must have felt quite at home on a surface which a few of us called 'Kennington Oval, Colombo'.

That wasn't being defeatist, and on the field we gave it everything we had, but it just didn't happen for us, and against the onslaught of Jayasuriya and de Silva, we were pretty powerless. By scoring 591, and getting those runs so quickly, they ensured we were still in danger of losing the Test on a pitch that was offering more and more help to Murali. That was frustrating in itself, as you don't often get over 400 in the first innings of a Test as we did, and then be in danger of losing. And maybe that frustration was behind Bumble's remarks about Murali after the fourth day's play, when he referred to the off-spinner having an 'unorthodox action'.

It's not for me to get involved in the rights and wrongs of that affair or to act as judge and jury on anyone's action, least of all someone like Murali, who has over 200 Test wickets. That's up to the umpires and the International Cricket Council, which has an advisory panel to do that.

But what I will say is that the row that blew up around Bumble didn't create any sort of distraction to the dressing room as we battled to save the game on the final day. In the end we were undone by a unique talent who produced an amazing performance of stamina as much as anything else to finish with figures of 16–220, the like of which I hope I never see again while I'm still playing for England.

Briefly, we threatened to save the match when Ramps and Goughie battled away for over two hours together, but in the end we were soundly beaten.

That was bad enough, but to make matters worse, by the time I'd finished my media commitments with BBC TV, Sky Sports, the written media and BBC Radio after the match, I got back to find the dressing room almost empty. Most of the players had already left for county matches the next day, which, at the end of a long and largely rewarding summer of international cricket, was all wrong as far as I was concerned.

It would have been nice to say a proper thanks to the lads for all their efforts, in this match and throughout the summer. But instead of a meal or get-together to celebrate our achievements against South Africa and look forward to the Ashes series, I had a drive to Leeds for a Championship match against Yorkshire starting at 10.30 am the following morning to look forward to.

I'll always play, and on this occasion I knew I had to as Surrey were in the running for the title, but to be honest, after five days of hard Test cricket, it was the last thing I needed. I arrived at the team's city centre hotel at 1 am I think, so I wasn't quite at my freshest for the game.

The Yorkshire match was played on a real green-top, which made the failure to prepare a pitch more suitable to our attack at The Foster's Oval even more laughable. And with Butch and Ben, like myself 'fresh' from the Test, also in the Surrey side for the match, maybe it was no surprise we lost.

We rallied and beat Durham in our penultimate game to set up a Championship decider against Leicestershire at home. But we were soundly beaten in that one too, and so memorable summer that it was, there was no fairy-tale ending to cap it all off.

1998/99 Ashes Tour

Prelude to the Tests

My First Tour as Captain

Tuesday 20 October

My first full tour as England captain – and an Ashes tour. For any English professional cricketer, it doesn't get any better than this.

I'd like to say it's a lifetime's ambition fulfilled, but for me it's slightly different. I'm honoured beyond words at the chance to captain my country, and it's something I cherish and respect. But I never went out of my way to publicly demand the job or throw my hat in the ring. If it came my way, fine; if not, then hopefully I'd still have had a good career.

The sense of anticipation I got when I woke this morning was tinged with another feeling, however. No matter how old you are or how many tours you go on, it never gets any easier to leave home, and that's especially true now I have a young family.

The life of a professional cricketer has many advantages, but the lack of family life is not one of them. Putting the finishing touches to my packing makes me realise just how much you miss seeing your children grow up.

My wife Lynn and two children – Andrew, who's five, and Emily, whose second birthday was last month – will be coming out with most of the other lads' wives/girlfriends/families during the Christmas and New Year period but it is hardly ideal in so many ways.

That period coincides with the last two Tests, which could be crucial in deciding the fate of The Ashes. If a player fails to perform because he has been up half the night looking after his child, then that can't be right. But, on the other side of the coin, what other sport asks its players to leave their wives and families for such long periods of time at a stretch?

In 1995/96, the arrival of the families was cited as a major reason why we lost the Test series against South Africa, as it was said to have disrupted our focus. A year later, we went to the other extreme and banned all families from a four-month trip to Zimbabwe and New Zealand, which also didn't work out too well with the players. The one thing that's certain is there is no easy answer.

An additional problem for everyone is the cost of flights for families. One of the ECB's World Cup partners, Emirates Airlines, have given us a deal for the girls to fly out for just over £800 each, with children getting a reduced rate again. But that is a cost each player has to bear. For someone like physiotherapist Wayne Morton, with a wife and three children, it adds up to an expensive Christmas, although the ECB does cover accommodation costs for the families.

Wednesday 21 October and Thursday 22 October

Just before lunch we headed for the flight, which turned out to be a real round the houses job. Emirates gave us a decent deal, but it involved us stopping at Dubai for two hours and Singapore for six more. If we'd gone with BA we'd have been there on Thursday afternoon local time; instead we arrived at gone midnight first thing on Friday with all the players washed out.

The trip itself wasn't without the odd tale to tell. I sat with Ath and Nasser and slept well(!) with Ath keen to show me how his computer worked. He said he's got an e-mail address and will be logging on throughout the trip, all a bit too advanced for me.

Our lengthy stop in Singapore allowed the lads to go duty-free shopping with Ben buying two Gucci watches. He also bought an alarm clock, about time too after he was late for practice before The Foster's Oval Test last summer after oversleeping.

The stop also allowed our version of The Shadows – Fizz, Butch and Creepy – to pluck their guitar strings and Big Al got his stereo out. It's huge, and he says he got it off Aftab Habib's dad, but it should keep the dressing room rocking throughout the tour.

The stop was so long there was time for a shower, and Nass, Goochie and I had a meeting to discuss the lads' dress code and behaviour for the trip. We came up with a four-tiered set-up to be policed by the team management. A verbal warning, or 'VW', is followed by a $100 fine. Then comes a $400 fine and finally you're sent home. It won't come to that, but the lads have got to know how important it is to be a team in every way, not just on the field.

I noticed first-time tourist Alex Tudor was a bit quiet, and wondered what he was thinking. He's been picked very much on potential rather than performance and hasn't yet proved his fitness after missing the second half of the season with a stress fracture of his left foot. But I know him from Surrey, he's got a great attitude and he can go far, if he takes advantage of the chance we've given him.

As we prepared to arrive just before midnight Perth time, I filled in my immigration card. Under 'Purpose of Visit' I wrote 'To win The Ashes'.

Friday 23 October

Things didn't start too well on our arrival. Rather than whisk us through customs and immigration, we were held up and made to clean all our boots to remove soil. Apparently it was to keep certain diseases out of Australia, but as it was already past 1 am in the morning it seemed a bit petty to us. Maybe the mind-games have started already, but as our sports pyschologist Steve Bull, with us for this leg of the trip would say, it's an uncontrollable so don't let it bother you. Corky was the only one to get away with this chore as he's bought new boots out with him.

Eventually we emerged into the glare of TV cameras and a few hardy souls waiting to greet us at a very late hour. I saw a familiar face straight away when Kevin Gartrell appeared. Kevin is a senior figure at the Midland-Guildford club in Perth, where I spent eight winters from 1981 to 1989. Together with former Australian Test players Tony Mann and Keith Slater, Kevin helped mould me as a cricketer, and it was great to see him again.

We finally got to the Hyatt Hotel, one of my favourite places to stay in the world, at around 2 am, and after picking up a stack of good luck messages and faxes, it's off to my room. Straight away I discovered one of the perks of being a captain on tour as I got a suite. I rang home to let Lynn and the children know I'd arrived, and finally got to sleep at 4 am.

I slept pretty well and my alarm woke me at midday. Goochie and I attended a press conference in the hotel at 1 o'clock that was pretty straightforward, as well as being our first view of the Aussie media. As usual at this stage of the tour, with little to write about before the cricket begins, things focused on the opinions of former players and what we thought of those opinions. This time it was Dennis Lillee, who claimed we're 'running scared' of Australia. I played that one with a straight bat, but admitted we are underdogs for the series. I don't see that as defeatism, just being honest, something I've vowed to be with the press.

Saturday 24 October

I slept well – much better than most in fact – and was really up for our first net session this morning. Thankfully, despite the effects of jet-lag, everyone else seemed to be raring to go too, and we had a great session.

The nets at the WACA, home to Western Australia and just across the road from the Hyatt, are a dream with pace and bounce, a real wake-up call for the lads after four weeks off, but just what was needed.

These net facilities were a real eye-opener for some of the younger players in the squad who aren't used to the quality or number of pitches available here. We used four nets, all offering full runs for the bowlers, and there are enough pitches in the net complex to make sure no one area ever becomes too worn.

I batted against Tudes and I can vouch for the fact he showed no ill effects from his foot injury as he almost knocked my head off. In fact, everyone was keen to impress and the session went really well.

After lunch with Deano and Ramps, we had a fielding session, again at the WACA, with Bob Cottam hitting some very tricky catches. 'PB' came into the set-up last summer to help the pace bowlers and impressed everyone enough to take over from John Emburey as Assistant Coach after 'Ernie' had done the previous two years. Allan

Donald and Shaun Pollock swear by Bob's coaching and I think that's a pretty good recommendation. If he can help turn Tudes into one of those two, he'll have done a good job!

Sunday 25 October

An early start today for 9 am nets, including fielding practice. For me, practice always takes a bit longer because I want to be happy with both areas of my game, batting and keeping, and to do that you have to devote the right amount of time to them. It means I often leave the nets after most of the squad, but that doesn't bother me if I'm happy with the work I put in.

PB helped with my keeping practice, throwing the ball at varying heights on both sides to get me moving and diving. That went well, as did the entire session. John Crawley and Graham Thorpe were especially impressive in the nets, which shouldn't be any surprise as these types of pitches, with pace and even bounce, are right up their street.

The one disappointment was the lack of net bowlers. It's all very well for us batsmen to face our best bowlers, but who bowls to them when it's their turn for an innings? We rely on the locals to provide good quality bowlers, and usually faxes are sent to make sure that happens. Today there weren't enough and it might count against us if the lower order isn't properly prepared. Every run could be vital.

At 4 pm we had a session with Steve Bull. He's just here for this part of the trip and then returns home when we move onto Adelaide, but he has a programme laid out with the first session called 'Do we think we can win The Ashes?' Steve usually starts with a short talk, using props and examples to get his points across, and then we break into small groups to discuss issues raised, before a member of each group reports back to the whole squad. The sessions usually don't take more than 40 minutes and I think they're really useful, helping us focus on what we want to achieve.

I had dinner with Steve after the meeting. He's been involved with us for just over a year and I think he's had a really positive effect on the team. Before he linked up with us, he worked with British Olympians and the England women's cricket team. They had a five-year plan with the aim of winning the World Cup in 1993, and they managed to do it, so he has a good track record.

Before Steve came on board, most of the players, when asked what might improve us as a side, said a sports psychologist was important. Many people might think that once you reach Test level you are at the top of your game and shouldn't need mental help. But that forgets the opposition who are firing in at you. If you can be encouraged to focus on your positives and dismiss trivial or negative things, it must be a boost. And even if it only benefits us one percent, that is good enough for me.

Monday 26 October

The day started on a disappointing note thanks to Ath's computer. He was up with the lark surfing the internet and found out that our one-day side lost to South Africa in the ICC knock-out tournament in Dhaka. Our boys got to 281 thanks to fifties from Adam Hollioake and Neil Fairbrother, but with Cullinan, Cronje and Rhodes in top form on a good pitch, they cruised home against us. It means David Lloyd and Brian Murgatroyd, both of whom were with the team in Bangladesh, will be joining us soon.

Before the winter touring parties were selected, there was a possibility that me and maybe Darren Gough would go to Dhaka, especially as the International Cricket Council was keen for every side to send their strongest squads. But it would have been impossible for us as an Ashes party to prepare properly if the captain and some of the squad weren't in Australia from the start of the trip. And if we'd made progress in Dhaka, we wouldn't have joined the tour until Adelaide. That would have meant coming to Perth for the second Test on a pacey pitch without having had any match practice there beforehand, which would have been all wrong.

As it is, our opening practice sessions here have confirmed to me the right decision was made, and we had more high-quality nets today, helped by the appearance of Kent's Ben Phillips, Andy Oram of Nottinghamshire and Somerset's Marcus Trescothick, all out in Perth playing and coaching this winter.

I did some extra batting work with Goochie, who is always happy to stay behind and bowl if asked, something last winter's tour manager Bob Bennett wasn't quite able to do.

What Injury Crisis?

Tuesday 27 October

Off to the WACA this morning for a session with former Australian Test bowler Peter Philpott on the art of leg-spin bowling.

Peter's been brought into the coaching set-up by Bumble on a part-time basis this winter to talk to us on how leg-spinners bowl and the options we have playing certain types of deliveries. He'll pop up every couple of weeks and stay for a few days, discussing things with us both individually and collectively.

I've known Peter for a few years and he even came and coached spin at Surrey for a season in 1995. Bumble has known him far longer, having played League cricket with him in Lancashire in the 1960s. He swears by Peter's skills on the subject, and that's good enough for me.

Judging by the number of reporters and television crews outside the WACA's indoor school this morning, it's prompted plenty of interest. The 'will-he won't-he' debate about whether the world's best leg-spinner Shane Warne will play this winter following his shoulder operation continues to rage both here and back home. And Peter's Aussie background, plus the fact he's also mentor to Stuart MacGill, the man currently deputising for Warne in the Australian side, also mean it's a big topic with the press.

It was a private session with Peter demonstrating every delivery in the leg-spinner's armoury and then inviting us to have a go. After a few tries, I could see why I've never been much of a bowler! The lads found it really useful, although the lower order all seemed to want to be told how to play each type of delivery. My philosophy is that each player should decide on a game plan and then stick to it.

In the evening we had the first team dinner of the tour, one more than we managed on the whole of the West Indies trip. We had a few of them last summer and they worked well, getting lads together, chatting and relaxing, fostering a team spirit, which isn't always easy with players from separate counties. The numbers were boosted by the arrival of Bumble and Murgers from Bangladesh, and it was a good night at the end of a very good day.

Wednesday 28 October

Nets again, with the first game just 24 hours away. Goochie took charge, allowing Bumble the chance to find his feet. Before we batted, each of us got our gear on and ran the equivalent of what would be nine lots of three runs. It got the blood pumping before we batted, but it also meant when we did bat it was much more like a match situation: you're a bit puffed and breathing hard – just like in a match – so you have to concentrate that bit harder to keep your wicket intact. Good practice.

Dean Headley bowled with a knee brace on, with seemingly no problem, but Nass was laid low with a cold and Thorpey rested his 'DIY injury'. He strained his wrist before the tour knocking his bat in with a mallet, but he claimed he did it doing some odd job at home. That would certainly make his wife laugh! He's now wearing a splint – what an iron man!

Another hard session, and the lads deserved an afternoon off to relax before the first game. I dozed in my room, looking forward to the challenges ahead. I love to just relax like that before a game, rather than rush about, so it was perfect preparation.

At 5.30 we picked the teams for the first two matches, against the ACB Chairman's XI and Western Australia. Our selection committee for the tour is me, Goochie, Bumble and Nasser, as vice-captain. That differs from last winter when the tour manager Bob Bennett wasn't involved. But with Goochie here in that role it would be madness not to use him.

We made sure everyone gets at least one game. Then at 6 pm we had another Steve Bull session for all the team, which again went very well, looking forward to the challenge of the matches to come and how we could be mentally right to win them. I'm a big fan of this positive thinking strategy, especially in a team like ours that is capable of such highs and lows.

After that, I announced the teams to the squad and both Goochie and I rammed home the same message: we must hammer sides hard. There are no easy games in Australia, and no friendlies, even though that's how tomorrow's game is billed. They might have some old-timers like Dennis Lillee in their side, but they'll be all out to beat us and set us off on the wrong foot from day one. If we win this match, the Aussies will forget it; if we lose, they'll remind us about it throughout the tour.

Thursday 29 October

A day that started full of anticipation ended on a slightly sour note when I felt a twinge in my back. I hope it's not serious, but it kept me off the field when we just about defended a total of 297 against a scratch side.

The back just started to stiffen up as I got going with the bat and I had to take an anti-inflammatory tablet during drinks. I got through to the end of the innings and felt I was hitting the ball really well for 74, but although I could have gone on to field if it had been a Test, I thought it stupid to risk making things worse just for the sake of it.

It's not the first time I've had problems with the back. I missed a day of the Lord's Test in 1997 and John Crawley had to keep then, and last summer I was a doubt to play in the Lord's Test against South Africa before it came right on the morning of that match. I don't regard it as a serious problem, it's just that it goes into spasm once or twice a year and that can sideline me for a few days until it settles. I just hope I've caught it in time now and that I'll be fine for Saturday's first-class opener with WA.

Dennis Lillee and Bruce Reid, two old headaches for England, had a bowl but we looked very good with the bat, with Creepy – like me another Midland-Guildford old boy – and Ath both playing well for fifties. There was another downer to add to my injury though when 'Pelly' (Ben Hollioake) damaged a groin turning for a run, and he too wasn't able to field. I hope that's not too long term, for his sake as well as ours.

A total of 297 should have been easily defensible, but we looked rusty with the ball, hardly surprising really. Tudes bowled well on his first appearance in England colours, but it was Goughie who saved us.

He wasn't even playing, but made a super-sub appearance in place of Pelly. His last few overs were nerveless, and he finished the job by running out Joey Angel off the last ball off his own bowling when they wanted two to win. He ran off, arm aloft and with the ball still in his hand as if we'd won The Ashes. Let's hope it's a sign of things to come.

Friday 30 October

I got up with mixed feelings. My back was still a little stiff, but it wasn't too bad. All of which means I'm hopeful of playing against WA tomorrow, but I know I can't risk it if I'm not one hundred percent fit.

I did very little at nets in the afternoon, desperate to play, and desperate to let my back settle, although I knew it still wasn't right. It's so frustrating, but I know I have just got to put up with it.

Steve Bull's final session followed in the evening, and it was another one full of positive thinking. We broke up into groups and had to think of all the things that could work against us or get on our nerves this winter. There were umpiring decisions, the crowds, media, even slow service at restaurants (Big Al's suggestion). Steve made the point that all these things are uncontrollable. As such, we should just ignore them and get on with what we can do something about – namely winning back The Ashes. It all seems so obvious, but I find it a real help to make these things crystal clear.

And with that, Steve's role on the tour officially ended. He'll still be with us for the WA game, but when we fly to Adelaide, he flies home. Looking around at the lads, I can't help thinking he's had a positive effect and the boys all like him too. I just wonder why he can't be with us for the whole tour, in the same way a physio is part of the back-up team. I think I'll make that point in my tour report.

Saturday 31 October

At 2.30 am I woke up and immediately knew I was out of the WA game. My back was in spasm and I had to do some hurried stretches to ease the discomfort, although even after that it still didn't feel right when I went back to sleep an hour later.

I knew I wasn't fully fit when we arrived at the ground, and although I was desperate to play I ruled myself out just before the toss. It would be wrong to play just for the sake of it when I could do some real damage to my back and, in any case, there are still two other matches before the Test for me to play and find some form.

The same went for Athers, who missed out with a bruise to his hip. It isn't serious and he can bat without problems, but it just stops him sprinting in the field – not that he does much of that anyway! – and so it was decided to rest the problem and get it fully right for Adelaide.

The good thing is that with the practice facilities here, as soon as either of us is up to it, we can get top-class work-outs in the nets. No Pelly to bowl at us though. His groin is still sore and he's on the treatment table.

Nasser took over the side and promptly lost the toss, not a popular move in very hot conditions. Goughie and Mullally made early inroads, but then Langer and Katich gave us an object lesson in how to play on the WACA pitch.

It's got pace and bounce, but they left the ball brilliantly, even straight ones as they will bounce over the stumps if they're not really full. They limited themselves to horizontal bat shots if the ball was wide, and straight drives and nudges, and although I wanted him out, it was still a pleasure to see Katich, a former pupil of mine, get to three figures.

On a hot day, all the lads stuck to the task well, and Ramps came on and nicked a wicket too. His off-spin could be vital in that fill-in role through the trip.

One downer was a couple of dropped catches, but that can happen after a long lay-off, although we must take all our chances to be competitive.

I spoke to the press during the day and apologised if I'd misled them about my back. I genuinely thought I'd play when I spoke to them after Thursday's game, but it had other ideas. My motto with them is to be straightforward, as if you try to be economical with things or even lie, it'll come back to haunt you when the chips are down.

Sunday 1 November

A treatment day. The back was still stiff and sore, but I've always worked on the basis that the mind can be a great healer so I was pleased it felt a bit better than yesterday. Fizz gave me some massage and I had six hot baths to try and relax the muscles.

Out on the field, we looked a little off the pace in the morning and WA had the luxury of declaring. Then we made a shocking start when Butch ducked into his second ball, which was only just short of a length, and copped it straight above the right eyebrow.

I have more than a passing interest in his health as he is my brother-in-law, married to my sister Judy, as well as a team-mate. We're quite close and so I was pretty concerned as soon as it happened. Fizz and I rushed out to see him and very soon there was blood everywhere. He was able to walk off with a towel clutched to his head, but once we got inside he went a bit dizzy before he had ten stitches put into the cut. It was all a bit shocking, especially as the ball sneaked between his helmet grille and peak, and it emphasised the extra pace in this Perth pitch.

Thankfully we were able to recover from that, and the early loss of Creepy, who was opening with Butch, thanks to Thorpey, Nass and Ramps. It was Thorpe's first innings of the tour, but he showed no ill effects from his back injury or the 'DIY' problem with his forearm, and hit the ball really well before top-edging a hook.

Got back to the hotel and spoke to Grav about the one-day squad. We will pick a 23-man provisional squad so that those players not involved here can get stuck into a training programme, and then whittle it down to about 16 in early December. I'm keen to get the provisional squad named as soon as possible as the players are already talking about it here. To them it will mean the difference between going home in early January or mid-February so it is quite important, and the longer the debate goes on, the more disruptive it could be.

We ended the day with a team meeting, which will become a regular part of life in the middle of matches on tour. Both Bumble and I stressed the need to be busier in the field, always on the go. We were off the boil a bit at times here, but maybe that isn't too surprising after six weeks away.

Monday 2 November

I was fit enough to have a net today, and felt great about that. If the game had started today I'd have played so it was a relieved man who walked back to the dressing room after a spell against Headless and Suchy. Maybe the tour can start now!

On the field, Nass and Ramps both make good contributions, with Nass's effort on his first-class debut in Aussie and on a quick pitch top-class. His judgement of what to play and leave showed he was been watching the WA players, one of whom, Matt Nicholson, produced a top-class spell to claim seven for 77.

It's only his third first-class match, and he's back after chronic fatigue syndrome threatened to end his career before it had begun. He bowled with pace and control. I like the look of him and reckon we'll see him again on the trip, maybe for the Australian XI in Hobart. He rolled over our lower order fairly easily, although Al slapped a quick-fire 25 to justify his rise in the order to number ten!

Poor Gussy got a duck as last man, apparently his seventh scoreless innings in a row. Goughie nicknamed him 'Astro' as in 'Astronought', and it may stick.

We batted a man short as Butch was pretty groggy after his blow. He came to the ground with a thumping headache and dark glasses, but that achieved nothing, so he went back to the hotel to rest. The swelling has now come out and his eye looks a bit of a mess.

If the first part of the day went well though, the second part wasn't great watching. WA opener Ryan Campbell, a bit like Michael Slater only more aggressive(!) slapped us everywhere and raced to a hundred in no time. We look ragged, while he looked like a World Cup candidate to me, especially as he can keep wicket as well.

Tuesday 3 November

I had two lengthy net sessions that went well, batting against Goughie and Gussy after lunch. By then WA had declared and Gus had taken a fair bit of hammer. His response was typical; he headed straight for the practice area to get things right.

I've no worries about Gus. After all he's got over fifty Test wickets for us this year alone so he must have done something right. He simply needs to adjust to bowling a slightly fuller length from the one that helped him pick up all those wickets last summer. The pitches here are so good that anything even fractionally short is just savaged.

WA set us 282 to win at around 4.3 runs per over. It looked on with Creepy and Chalks playing well, but when Creepy was out straight after tea for 65, it was time to shut up shop. With Ath and me injured, we'd only played six batsmen anyway, and with one of those suffering from an almighty headache, time in the middle was much better for the lads than death-or-glory stuff. Chalks moved smoothly to a fifty and we finished 90 short with a satisfying draw.

Yes, there's plenty still to do, but Perth's extra pace and bounce is unique, and all things considered I thought we did okay for a first game. As I said to the press afterwards, there were plenty of plusses, like Al and Goughie's bowling and runs for Ramps, Nass, Chalky and Creepy. Corky was a worry as he picked up 0–109 and looked out of touch with the bat. But he has the character to come good, and with Ath and myself hopefully back for the next game, we can only get stronger.

Before we left the ground, Big Al had an injection in his left shoulder. Bowling isn't a problem, but he's had a sharp, stabbing pain in it when he throws, so hopefully the needle will hit the spot and clear the problem up. It'll probably stiffen up though, so I think he'll be rested for Adelaide, no bad thing really as he's shown here he's a real contender for the Test side.

I never lie to the press, but I didn't volunteer that news, as I know how these things can get out of hand. Ath, Pelly and me have already missed this match, Butch has a headache and a black eye and if I told them about Al too, that spells an obvious headline, even though most of us should be fit for the next match: 'ENGLAND IN INJURY CRISIS'. We don't need that at this stage.

Butch made it to the ground today, which is good news, but he just sat quietly watching the television, and there was no chance he'd bat. He's still got a headache, no surprise given the blow he took, but Fizz expects he'll be fit for Adelaide.

Welcome to Adelaide

Wednesday 4 November

The start of the internal flights merry-go-round this morning with the first of 17 internal flights in three and a bit months. Air travel might seem glamorous, but packing every week, and, during the one-dayers every three days, gets you down after a while as you just long to be in one place for a bit of time.

The television crews were buzzing today because of quotes from WA captain Langer in this morning's papers claiming we should have gone for their target, and that if we play with such a lack of ambition throughout the trip it will be a long, hard tour. I play those sort of comments down in public, merely stating everyone's entitled to their opinions, and I can't see the need for a war of words.

Privately I'd say that our philosophy against WA was like it always is – to win every game. But if you can't win you make sure you can't lose. I'm a big fan of keeping a '0' in the loss column for as long as possible as that can only breed confidence.

With the two-hour time change, we arrive at the Hyatt in Adelaide at around 4.30 pm and I wandered round town with PB and Al to stretch the legs after a long flight. Al is a big U2 fan and bought their new Greatest Hits CD. As he also carries around his huge ghetto blaster wherever we go I'm sure we'll be sick of that CD by February.

An evening meal at the Earl of Aberdeen pub with a few of the lads followed with English football on a big screen television there. It reminded me of home, and when I got back to the hotel I rang the family, something I do every two or three days as a rule.

I managed to interrupt breakfast, never an easy time for Lynn as a lone parent, and speak to Andrew. The hardship of touring came into sharp focus straight away when he told me about his swimming lessons and then asked: 'Dad, when are you coming home?' What can you say?

Thursday 5 November

Bonfire night back home, but no fireworks here as they're banned by the Aussie Government for being too dangerous. If they'd wanted to set them off this morning they'd have been a damp squib anyway, as one look out of my window when I woke up showed rain.

That was bad news for practice and nets had to be cancelled, but thankfully it wasn't too damp so we still went down to the Adelaide Oval for some exercise. Our departure on the team bus, set for 9 am, was delayed though because Tudes overslept and incurred the first verbal warning of the tour.

It wasn't that he'd been out partying the previous night – he's a teetotaller, and a quiet lad too – but he just slept through his alarm. Hardly surprising really as 9 am in Adelaide is 6.30 am in Perth with the time change. Pelly rang him at 8.55 when he showed no signs of surfacing, and he was still asleep. He eventually arrived at 9.10 looking very sheepish, with everyone deliberately staring at him for good measure.

Once we got there, Butch was soon in the wars again. We were playing 'Crows and Cranes' which is basically a game of tag to get the blood flowing at the start of a session. Two people stand next to each other, one is the crow and the other the crane. If Riddler calls 'crane', each crane has to sprint away from the crow next to them without being touched. Everyone's keen to be quick off the mark but it can lead to confusion as Butch and Suchy proved when they ran into each other. Butch got a cut above his left eye to go with the stitches over his right one, while Suchy got a graze on the bridge of his nose which needed a plaster and left him looking like Robbie Fowler. Thankfully neither problem is serious and both are still available for the South Australia game starting on Saturday.

Friday 6 November

I got dressed in whites to start the day as we headed off to the ground for the official tour photo before practice. One gets done for every tour, but this is extra special for me as it has me in the middle of the front row as captain on an Ashes tour. A dream really.

Adelaide is the perfect location as it is one of the most beautiful grounds in the world, with the Cathedral in view behind the old scoreboard, and we got a great day for it too with sunshine and a clear blue sky.

Nets were testing as the practice pitches were pretty juicy after yesterday's rain, but sometimes that can work in your favour as a batsman. If the ball darts around you tend to concentrate even harder than usual to keep an eye on any movement off the seam.

Tudes was really impressive and has come on heaps in a short space of time with Bob Cottam. PB has cured his tendency to no-ball using the same technique he employed with Dean Headley in the summer. Both Deano and Tudes were never sure where their feet were landing in their run-ups and it affected their rhythm. They ended up being more concerned where their feet were going rather than the ball, and that is a road to ruin for a bowler.

PB's answer is to measure their run-ups, watch a few deliveries and then draw a box on the turf about halfway to the crease, and the aim is for the bowler to get his foot in that box. As long as they do that, they know their approach is okay, so they can then concentrate on where they are bowling. Seems simple, but the best ideas often are, and it works for both men.

Tudes' effort was particularly good because he is having real problems with blisters on his feet. He's been using new boots, but they don't seem to be doing his feet much good, so I rang Kookaburra to get him some other shoes, although size 12 or 13 aren't always easy to come by. In the meantime, he is now using a spare pair of Al's.

After nets, PB gave me a good work-out at my keeping in the middle. It's an important session as I tried out some new gloves. As with most things in life, you do a better job if you are confident in your equipment and that certainly applies to my keeping gloves. I've had the other pair for five years, and although they are a bit tatty, they are also supple and comfortable. I always remember Steve Davis saying how much he struggled when he changed his cue, and the same applies to these gloves. The new ones will take some getting used to, and there's probably an element of superstition about keeping the old ones too, but I need to have a pair ready for match action just in case.

We picked the team at the ground and Tudor, Headley, Such, Atherton and me came in from the side that played in Perth. But I didn't tell the press what the team was when I saw them later as I wanted to tell the lads first. In my experience there's nothing worse that finding out a side through the media, especially if you're not playing, and I'm keen to make sure that doesn't happen while I'm captain. Instead I told the players at the evening team meeting with details to be released after that.

The meeting included some discussion and video analysis on leg-spin from Peter Philpott, useful as he discussed the techniques used by different bowlers. A lower arm usually means less flight but more spin, while a higher arm can mean more bounce but less turn. Things like this can be a real help, especially for the lower order.

Saturday 7 November

After the problems with my back in Perth, today marked the real start of my tour, but by the end of it I was wishing it was just a bad dream and that I could start again.

The weather forecast wasn't great, but by the time the toss came around it was fine, and although there was just a hint of damp in the surface, I had no hesitation in batting first when my call of 'heads' came down correctly. Most Test pitches have a bit in them for the first session, but if you can survive that period you are usually half way towards bossing the match which is what a good first innings total always allows you to do.

The only trouble was we hadn't read the script, and by lunch we were in tatters at 50 for four. Jason Gillespie, back for the first time since a back injury cut short his Ashes tour in 1997, looked sharp, and he got good support from left-armer Mark Harrity. But too many of us threw our wickets away as if it was the last ten overs of a one-day game instead of the start of a four-day match, and that was just not good enough.

I was the prime culprit too. Keen to get off the mark, I slashed at a wide ball angled across me and edged to third slip, an ugly shot, and not one to be playing on nought. After all the frustrations of the previous week, it wasn't the best of starts.

Ramps and Nass tried to rebuild things but both then fell to poor shots against the spinners, and although Corky and Tudes then played well down the order, by then the damage was done. 187 against a side that has a modest attack apart from the opening pairing was simply not good enough.

We couldn't redeem ourselves with the ball either. Their openers looked fairly solid in the 11 overs before the close, but even when we did create a chance it wasn't taken. Tudes got Martin Faull to drive at a wide ball which flew straight past Headless, who was making his debut at third slip. He didn't pick it up against the background in order to drop it, but it means he'll probably go back to his specialist position of fine leg from now on!

Down was how everyone seemed in the dressing room after easily our worst day of the tour so far, but we only had ourselves to blame. I was keen to look on the brighter side though. I said: 'I know there aren't too many plusses from today, but what's happened has gone. The key thing is to learn from this, and if we do then we'll be on the right road.' Let's hope we do.

Sunday 8 November

Today we got a glimpse of one of the reasons Australia are such a good side at the moment – strength in depth.

Greg Blewett scored a really classy hundred, and frankly, apart from a streaky edge to reach three figures off Gus, he never really looked like getting out. Here was a class batsman keen to take advantage of a flat pitch on a fine day, and he did just that.

After reaching three figures he opened out and made his last 43 runs in just 46 balls before Ramps spun one back sharply to bowl him as he cut. A top class innings by a man who always seems to get runs against us, and yet he is nowhere near their Test side if the local pundits are to be believed.

With Blewett playing superbly, SA were in real command at one point on 214 for two. But the lads stuck to the task well, especially Tudes and Suchy who both bowled without luck, and by the close, they were still in sight at 262 for five, a lead of 75. Tudes really impressed me with his pace, line and length, and I just wonder whether, if he keeps making the progress he has thanks to PB, he could repeat the success of Bob Willis in 1971. Bob came out to Aussie as a raw quickie, came on in leaps and bounds, and finished with over 300 Test wickets. We can only hope!

Monday 9 November

Not one of my better days!

I managed to miss a stumping off Suchy then padded up to an inswinger from Blewett to complete my first pair for England, and only the second of my career after one I picked up in Derby more years ago than I can remember.

The stumping was frustrating as it would have given Suchy his first wicket, and after the way he bowled it was the least he deserved, even though it was the number eleven, Harrity. He went down the pitch, missed a ball which turned between bat and pad, and I was a bit slow across to the ball which just missed leg stump. No excuses, just a mental note to maintain concentration, even with the last pair together.

As it was that last pair of Harrity and Gillespie added 23, which just took the gloss off a good effort in the morning by all the bowlers. Gus was much more like his old self and Corky seemed to have benefited from his knock on Saturday, bowling with much more confidence. The only downer to our efforts was that we just couldn't seem to make the Kookaburra ball swing. Back home we use Dukes and Reader balls and they will usually move in the air at some point, either with conventional or reverse swing. The Kookaburras just aren't going off the straight so far which is a worry, especially for Corky, who relies on swing so much.

Butch failed again, another worry as I wonder if the blow on the head has affected him more than he's letting on, but then Athers and Nass played well to set us up nicely. At that point though we had a crazy ten minutes at the end of which we had masses to do to save, let alone win, the match.

First of all Nass got a shooter from Harrity to fall lbw. He's had more than his fair share of shockers over the past twelve months, even managing to get out to the seventh ball of an over in the West Indies, and this continuation of ill fortune didn't leave him all that chuffed.

Next over, I committed suicide to Blewett, and even though replays weren't conclusive, I only had myself to blame by not playing a shot. Maybe I was a bit tentative after falling to an aggressive shot in the first innings, and maybe it might not have hit off stump. But with a bat in my hands, I controlled my destiny until I shouldered arms. Not too clever, but at least Steve Bull would be pleased with my thoughts: 'Things can only get better' I told myself as I slumped in the dressing room!

Our nightmare was complete when Ath, backing up too far was run out when the bowler deflected Thorpey's straight drive onto the stumps. Ath had already managed to get out in bizarre fashion in the first innings when he clipped Gillespie off his hip straight into short leg's midriff, so this completed a notable double. He knew he was out and walked without waiting for the television replay, a bit foolish as they almost didn't have a conclusive picture. We shouted at him to stop and he waited halfway to the pavilion, but eventually the red light came on, and we'd slipped to 80 for four.

At that point, we could have lost in three days, and by an innings too, but Chalky and Ramps played well in the last hour to take us into the lead. At 149 for four though, we were only 11 ahead at stumps and still with plenty to do.

Tuesday 10 November

A big day then, as we tried to keep a zero in the loss column, and the early news wasn't good. Thorpey had an upset stomach, didn't do any of the pre-match warm-ups, and only batted after first having a lengthy net to prove to himself he was up to the task.

Before play, we had an open team discussion about the importance of supporting each other. Nass was upset yesterday when, just before tea, Corky was walking around the ground to do a television interview at the interval. It's awkward, because the local television station covering the matches has been very helpful, providing us with tapes of the play. But Nass felt if players aren't practising they should be in the viewing area supporting their team-mates on the field, and in the dressing room at the start of an interval to offer encouragement. So, it was agreed we would still do the interviews, but any player who did them would have to be in the dressing room at the start and end of an interval. And during play, at a drinks break for example, only non-players or management could do the interviews.

Harmony restored in the dressing room, I spent most of the rest of the day practising. I had a good outdoor net before play against a lively

Goughie – he got me out once, but only after I'd got off the mark! Then, after lunch, I went indoors to face the bowling machine under the watchful eye of Goochie. By the end, I was pretty happy with my head and foot positions, and I reckon I was timing the ball well.

Meanwhile, out on the field, Chalky and Ramps were busy ripping up the record books. The pair started cautiously, as you'd expect given our position, and they also had the new ball to contend with in the first session. But once they were through that, they just got better and better and never really look like getting out.

By lunch, we were 91 ahead and already looking better, then after the break it was carnage. The pair cut loose and were particularly severe on the two young spinners making their debuts, Arnold and Crook. At one stage, they savaged the young leg-spinner Arnold for 50 in five overs and the home side began to look a bit ragged. In fact, the way the ball started to fly around, it resembled a benefit match.

The home side got frustrated and Gillespie and Harrity even resorted to clowning around, flapping their arms and pulling faces as they were running in to bowl to try and put the pair off. Maybe that clowning counted against Gillespie, because when Ramps offered him a hard caught and bowled chance just before the end he shelled it, which left us laughing and joking no end.

At tea, the lads had put on 343, with Thorpey easing past 200, a great comeback after all the back trouble he had last summer. To be competitive on this tour, we really need the little man to be at his best, and he and Ramps were certainly in that type of form this afternoon, adding 194 runs in just 33 overs between lunch and tea.

The rain still hadn't arrived, although the odd drop of drizzle was falling, and we had it in mind to bowl at them for an hour, just to give Tudor, Fraser and Cork another run-out. That closure had to wait though until Ramps and Thorpey broke a few records.

Two runs to Ramps in the first over after the break gave them the highest stand by an England pair against SA, previously 344 by Colin Cowdrey and Tom Graveney in 1962/63. Then two more to Thorpey just before the rain became too heavy to continue made sure they became the holders of the highest partnership by any touring side in Australia for any wicket, beating Wilfred Rhodes and CAG Russell, ironically against SA in Adelaide way back in 1920/21. It was a fabulous performance, and made sure we didn't just save the game, we ended it in credit.

By the end, the new record stood at 377 when they came off and everyone was really buzzing. To think, in all tour matches by all sides, dating back to the last century, this was the highest stand ever. Fabulous.

I fancied a day off from the media tomorrow, and so rather than speak then, I faced them after the match, along with the two stars. There was no point in getting carried away, because all we had done was bat to draw the game, but it was still a great achievement by the pair and I said so. There were plenty of questions about my form, but I played a straight bat to those. I feel in good nick in practice, but I do know good form in the nets counts for nothing if you're not scoring in the middle. I know I need runs in Cairns.

The press conference took place in the dressing room after the other players had left, and it gave the hacks something to hang their story on. On the dressing room notice board we'd pinned a copy of the local paper which rubbished us, claiming we were far too tentative against SA's rooky spinners, and that Warne and MacGill would be rubbing their hands together. By the end of the day, Thorpey and Ramps had written a suitable reply to that message.

Into the Heat of Cairns

Wednesday 11 November and Thursday 12 November

This is the side of touring that people don't realise. A 6.15 am alarm call for a 7 am leave, three separate flights – Adelaide-Melbourne, Melbourne-Brisbane and Brisbane-Cairns – nine hours travelling door-to-door, plus a change of time-zone. Amazingly, despite the team meal last night, everyone made it to the bus on time for the early start, so maybe the system of 'VWs' and fines is working.

We eventually arrived in Cairns at about 4 pm and straight away almost everyone was struck by the humidity here in Northern Queensland. Unpleasant it may have been, but the obvious thing to be aware of is that playing in these sorts of conditions can only do us good ahead of the Brisbane Test next week. On my two previous tours, we've played the game before the Brisbane Test in Hobart, which is about as similar to Queensland as Loch Ness. This, to me, is ideal ahead of the Test.

Goochie, Bumble and I headed off to the ground to check things out soon after we'd checked into the team hotel in town. The locals said there's been plenty of rain around recently, and true to form the pitch was covered when we got there. The outfield was also saturated, and it'll take a good drying day tomorrow to help us get away on time come Friday. Facilities are pretty basic, but everyone is bending over backwards to help and they are determined to make this game a success so good luck to them.

Facing a Queensland side including seven internationals, we decided to play a near-Test side ourselves to give everyone a run-out ahead of the Gabba. We named 12, resting Chalky, with the only decision to be made tomorrow being who to leave out. I favoured Gus, who's a banker for the Test, providing he's happy with the amount of bowling he's had.

Friday 13 November

I woke early, buzzing at the prospect of this match. They are really going to test us, but I'm confident we have the lads here to do us proud.

We left Gus out, the sensible move given that after this match, the first two Tests are back-to-back. It was sticky even at 8.30 in the morning, but all the lads wanted to bowl first as the pitch, which had been covered, seemed to have some damp in it, and the outfield was still slow after the recent heavy rain.

I called correctly – heads – and the suspicion that the pitch had some juice in it was confirmed straight away in a dramatic opening over. Second ball, Goughie got one to lift from just short of a length to smash Matty Hayden on the hand. He required lengthy treatment and we all reckoned it was broken. He batted on, but three balls later we all walked off when Goughie went flying as he slipped in delivery stride. Sawdust for the footholds was needed, but although the umpires had asked for it to be made ready the previous day, none could be found. So off we trooped while someone cut down a local tree.

We all came back 25 minutes later, all that is except for Matty, who was heading to the local hospital to confirm what we all guessed was the case – he was out for the match. Conditions weren't easy for either side. It was cloudy, and as humid as anything I've ever played in with the possible exception of Sri Lanka. Then, just when you thought it couldn't get any worse, the sun came out, prompting Crofty to shout: 'Would someone shut the oven door, please!'

The lads kept their spirits up well and gave as good a performance with the ball as they had done all tour. Crofty, in particular did well, and benefited from a long bowl which put him in contention for a Test spot. The fielding was sharp too, and by the time the close came with bad light followed by a torrential thunderstorm, we'd reduced them to 193 for eight, effectively nine wickets down with Hayden's injury.

The only blot on the day was a dropped catch that cost us dear, and I was the culprit. Ian Healy is a good friend, but he is also someone who has specialised in holding us up whenever we think we're through to the tail, so any chance he offers really needs to be taken. He slashed at Corky and I saw it all the way, but I just misjudged the pace of the edge as it flew at shoulder height to my right and all I ended up doing was parrying it, Peter Bonetti-like, round the post for a single to third man.

It was a disappointing miss as I would have expected to catch it most times, and as Heals and Geoff Foley added 90 for the fifth wicket, important runs in what could be a low-scoring match, I would be lying if I said I didn't occasionally think about it. But thankfully we nicked Heals out before the close, and we could still reflect on a good day in really tough conditions.

Cramp can cause real problems in that sort of heat, so it was back to the hotel swimming pool after play to stretch out the muscles. Allan Donald swears by the method and reckons just a few minutes stretching in a pool usually stops any stiffness. We'll soon see if that's right when we all pitch up tomorrow!

Saturday 14 November

We arrived at the ground by 8.15 am for an earlier start at 9.38 because of yesterday's storm, and the mood was good. Ath even joked: 'If we take the last wicket quickly, Butch and I could be out before the normal start of play!'

Unfortunately, that joke almost came true, as after Goughie cleaned up Foley, the pair were both back in our viewing tent just 12 minutes after the normal starting time of 10 o'clock, victims of seamer Adam Dale. Ath continued his run of bad luck, caught down the leg-side first ball, then Butch played all around a straight one. Hardly the best start for our Test openers, both of whom are struggling for form, but both are mentally strong and I reckon they'll come good.

It brought me in with the pressure on, and I managed to respond by getting my first runs in first-class cricket on the tour as Nass and I tried to rebuild the innings. It was hardly entertaining cricket – a desperately slow, low pitch and even slower outfield saw to that – but it was just what I needed. You can have as many nets as you want, but time in the middle is the key, especially in such humid conditions, which we expect to find in Brisbane too.

Nass and I batted for the rest of the first session and into the afternoon, on a pitch that was starting to keep lower and lower. If the ball was straight, the priority had to be survival, but even if it was off line, there was so little pace on it to allow you to steer it for ones and twos. The crowd must have been bored stiff, and it was a battle for every run, but it was just the type of tough cricket I relished.

One member of the crowd, a local barracker who seems to know the whole Queensland team, lightened the mood with his constant calls to 'Give Jimmy Maher a bowl!' He did bowl the last over before tea, sending down some flattish off-spin, but on that pitch, it was always going to be the quicker bowlers who would do the damage.

We reached 104 for two at one stage, a great effort, but after Nass was given out caught at slip hooking and I was trapped lbw by Dale pushing forward we lost our way. We felt we might have received the benefit of the doubt with a couple of the lbw shouts that went against us, and we finished the day at 182 for seven, still 27 behind.

I spoke to the press afterwards, relieved to get some runs under my belt, and stressing how much we wanted to win this match. That was the theme I took up again in the mid-match team meeting back at the hotel. Runs were getting harder and harder to come by with the last two sessions of the day producing just 57 and 65 runs respectively and I said that as we had to bat last any lead we could get on first innings would be crucial.

Bowling straight and to a good length is the key as Dale showed, and we also debated the way Queensland had used their bowlers during the day. Heals gave them one over spells at one stage just to make sure they stayed fresh, and while some of our lads like Goughie and Al were in favour of that, others like Deano preferred slightly longer to get some rhythm. 'I don't want to rush in thinking I have to make something happen this over or I'm off again,' he said. Fair enough and each to his own, but I'm all for learning off the opposition if we can.

One thing that pleased me at the meeting was that no one was drinking alcohol. Our team room at every hotel is well stocked with soft drinks and beer, but after two days in the sauna everyone has got the message that alcohol, sun and work don't mix.

Sunday 15 November

Hardly the ideal start to the day with the news that Ath was struggling again with his back. He spent the day in the viewing tent, occasionally stretching and taking drinks out, but he was very stiff, not what we needed with the Test less than a week away.

On the field, it was a mix of the good and the not so good as we battled to get the win we desperately wanted. The lead I'd hoped for just didn't arrive as Dale helped blow our last three wickets away for just 10 runs in only 5.2 overs. He gets in close to the stumps and bowls a very tight line, similar to Mark Ealham, if a bit quicker, and with the Aussies naming their team for the Test tomorrow he is bound to come into contention. But even though the Test is on home soil for him, I can't see the strip for that game looking too much like this one.

Goughie got us a couple of early wickets when we bowled again, but after that we were very flat and they cruised past 50 by lunch, looking far too comfortable. Thankfully, we clicked back into gear just in time, and with all the bowlers showing some discipline, we bowled them out just before tea to leave ourselves just under four sessions to get 142.

That was a tough ask, especially after Butch failed again. He might have been lbw to his first ball but for a nick onto his pads, and he was definitely lbw to his second, trapped on the back foot by a fast full-length ball from Andy Bichel. He now has more stitches – ten – than first-class runs on tour – nine. I'm still keen to play him in Brisbane, but we'll have to watch him in the nets beforehand to make sure he's happy with his game.

At that point it needed someone to be positive, and Corky, promoted to open in place of Ath, played just the innings we needed. He and Nass added 45 for the second wicket with a mix of watchful defence and desperate attack to any ball less than perfect. But just when they appeared to be cruising, we lost a cluster of wickets to leave us just second favourites.

It was that sort of pitch. You were always likely to get one that shot along the ground, but if you managed to get in first, you at least had a slightly better chance of keeping it out because you had your eye in. My shooter came first ball, so I was left with three ducks and a fifty to take into the first Test.

Ath's back had eased through the day, but because he had been off the field for so long, he couldn't bat until five wickets were down. Then, when Corky was out in the last but one over of the day, Deano went in as nightwatchman to protect him.

Just over halfway to our target but with only five wickets in hand, it would be a tense last day, but before that the tour selectors – Goochie, Bumble, myself and Nass – had to discuss what to do about Ath. He and Fizz were both confident he would be fit for the Test, but if he wasn't and another batsman went down on the morning of the match, we would be left with just five specialists. We couldn't risk that so would have to send for cover.

Goochie had anticipated this, and had spent most of the day tracking down likely players already in Australia and New Zealand. He'd settled on two names, neither of whom had Test experience, and was happy to go with either man, as I think were the other two selectors. I argued against them though, and said we should get Graeme Hick on a plane as soon as possible as cover. He had been to Bangladesh with the one-day boys and was also on standby for this tour, so he wouldn't be totally out of nick. And as far as I was concerned, if we did need someone at short notice in the Test, I would rather an under-prepared Hick than a Test novice walk out for me.

That swayed the room. Grav was contacted back in England and he put the wheels in motion, ringing Hicky. By ten o'clock, he was set to fly on Monday evening and would be in Brisbane as 'reinforcement' for the tour party by Wednesday morning. Murgers ran a statement round to the press hotels while I joined a few of our lads for a drink with the Queensland boys in a local bar before returning to the hotel to pack. We knew the match wouldn't go much beyond lunch on Monday whatever happened, so we brought our flight to Brisbane forward to teatime.

Monday 16 November

An amazing day began with what I expected would be a leisurely breakfast. But as I sat there, John Crawley came to join the rest of us looking like he'd gone fifteen rounds with Mike Tyson. He had a plaster above his right eye and a fat lip and although he tried to raise a smile, it did prove difficult.

It struck me straight away that Creeps had been at the same bar as me the night before, enjoying a drink with the Queensland boys. His part in the match was over so he had every right to relax, but I couldn't remember any trouble before I left. It was a mystery why he looked like that now.

There wasn't really time to establish what had happened before we left for the ground as, after all, we still had a game of cricket to play – and win. Goochie was away co-ordinating our afternoon departure for Brisbane, but everyone knew he would have to look into the matter as soon as possible. Until then, we all tried to remain focused on the day ahead, keen to keep a zero in the loss column, while Creeps stayed at the hotel to rest.

Goochie arrived at the ground soon after play started and immediately headed back to the team hotel with Murgers to get the facts from Creeps. It turned out he had left the bar after 11 pm and came across a man as he wandered through the town. The man started shouting at him 'Are you Irish?' and when Creeps said no, the bloke punched him to ground. Creeps managed to stumble back to the hotel and summoned Wayne Morton, who cleaned him up, but even so, he was a mess.

Goochie and Murgers got back to the ground and we discussed the matter with Fizz, Bumble and Nass. With Creeps' facial injuries it would be pointless trying to pretend nothing had happened, and Murgers and Goochie were in favour of just telling the truth. After all, there was no point in making something up, and we had nothing to hide. After all, Creeps was perfectly entitled to go out for a drink, especially as he had nothing more to do in the match.

We thought some of the press might read something more into the whole episode, so we just decided to have a further think about it on the flight to Brisbane and chew things over again once we got there. As it was, if we had said something at that stage, it would only have started a media frenzy, and we wanted to make sure we were doing the right thing first. On top of that, there was still a cricket match going on, and the last thing we needed was a distraction to the guys in the middle.

Those guys were getting less by the minute by that stage. We got to 89 for five before the wickets started to tumble, Ath among them, stumped for just one as he reasoned it was a hit-out or get-out pitch. We slumped to 106 for nine when Goughie was out, and it looked as if we were heading for certain defeat, but then along came Alan Mullally.

Al's catchphrase for the trip has been 'Bosh, bosh, job done', in other words, nothing is ever a problem. Most of us begged to differ at 106 for nine, but slowly and surely he and Crofty inched towards the target.

Amazingly they hardly looked like getting out, and by lunch they'd added 22 with just 14 more to get. The only real alarm came just after the break, when Al top-edged a pull for four, but that apart, they played superbly.

Ath took the reins as the dressing room bookie, quoting odds for both sides as the target came down, and that helped to ease the tension. But nothing eased it quite as much as Crofty's push-drive for a single off Kasprowicz which gave us the winning run.

You'd have thought we'd just won The Ashes given the cheer from our tent, but it was a great victory, full of fight, and it meant we went to Brisbane with a great win. All of a sudden, all the chat was of the success, not Creepy's injuries, although that was still a concern.

We had to get away quite quickly to get back to the hotel for our afternoon departure, but not before Goochie sat everyone down on the team bus and explained what had happened to Creepy. He said we'd make an announcement about it when we got to Brisbane, but that all media enquiries had to be passed to Murgers. The only thing everyone else should be bothered about was the Test to come.

With that settled and a win under our belts, the flight to Brisbane was a pretty relaxed affair, although I ended it with severe earache after sitting next to Al, who talked me through his innings ball by ball.

Prelude to the Big Show

Tuesday 17 November

I took the opportunity to go to the Gabba with Tudes and Ramps to have a look at the pitch and have some throw-downs in the impressive new indoor school. A first look at the pitch was reassuring as it looked flat with a fair covering of fine, live grass that should produce a good Test. There was some moisture there too, but I reckoned that would be gone given two days of fine weather before Friday.

The late afternoon fielding session saw us pick up an unwanted injury, but at least it wasn't to a player. Fizz fell on his right shoulder, dislocating it and ran back to the dressing room in agony. Goochie followed him to see if there was anything he could do, but then probably wished he hadn't, as Fizz got him to help put the shoulder back in place. Fizz went white as a sheet, but typically didn't make anything of it in front of the rest of the lads, all of whom seemed in great spirits during the session. His injury could be a real blow to me as he's my personal throw-down man before each day's play!

After practice, the four selectors sat down to pick the Test squad. We came up with 12 names, including all seven batsmen, and will release it to the media tomorrow after I've spoken to the players missing out. It looks an obvious 12, but both Deano and Suchy were unlucky, and I'll tell them so. It's nice to be able to leave players out rather than scratching around for 11 blokes, most of whom are out of form.

Wednesday 18 November

We had a long but very good practice session this morning, which showed me the lads are really up for this one. The quicks all came steaming in, and the batsmen all looked in good nick, even Butch, which pleased me, as we're backing him here despite his lack of runs in the warm-up matches. I talk to Butch a lot, and not only because he's my brother-in-law! He's got a great cricket brain and his advice is often spot-on, and by chatting to him I can also tell what sort of state of mind he's in. He seemed in great spirits, and as he said to me before he had a knock: 'How do I know if I'm out of form? I haven't been in long enough to find out so far on the trip.'

The only problem with Butch as far as I'm concerned is that he's not bowling at the moment because his groin feels a bit tender. He's had surgery there before and so it's fair enough he's not charging in, but if he could bowl on a regular basis it really would benefit the balance of the side. What we've lacked for too long is someone who can fill in for ten overs a day, like Basil D'Oliveira did twenty years ago. Someone who could do that role would be a real bonus now.

The session was long because it was held up for an hour by a passing thunderstorm that skirted the ground. It was very humid, but the lads were fine, thanks, I reckon, to the time we spent in Cairns.

Mum and dad arrived this morning and came straight to the ground to see me. It was great to catch up with them, and mum was very quickly wearing my trademark 'zinc lips' on her cheek to prove it. Dad meanwhile could have a look at my technique, and he felt my head was falling over too early, leaving me off balance at the crease. It's just a case of waiting a bit longer before moving and if I can do that I should be okay, especially as I reckon I'm hitting the ball fine.

Grav, Hicky, and Simon Pack, the ECB's international teams director who heads the Team England administration unit, were on mum and dad's flight, and Hicky appeared for practice with the rest of us – looking pretty pasty it must be said. But he hit the ball pretty well for a first net, and I was delighted to see him here as our reserve batsman. Also on their flight were masses of supporters, and the more the merrier as far as I'm concerned. I love all the noise and support we can get wherever we go – maybe that's why I've always done well in Barbados – and I was delighted to be told that the national anthems are going to be played before every Test. I've wanted that for years, as has Goochie, but when he asked for it as England captain, he was told it was too hard to do. How hard can it be to stick a tape recorder in front of the PA microphone? It's certainly something I'd like to happen next summer, especially with the World Cup in town.

The press quizzed me about our squad after practice, but in true Glenn Hoddle fashion I gave nothing away. We were keen to release a 12 to show the Aussies we were clear about our plans, but it still gives us the option of playing either six or seven batsmen. I'm fairly clear we should play six as it is an attacking move to help us bowl them out twice, but I didn't tell anyone that today!

There were plenty of questions about Ath too, but I played them with a straight bat. He's fed up with talking to the press about his back, but I expect him to play, although he will have to tell me he's fit for that to happen. We can't risk him breaking down in the middle of the match, like he did in Cairns.

Thursday 19 November

The last day of practice before the Test, and the chosen twelve got priority in the nets ahead of the rest of the squad, but I was delighted with the way everyone looked going into such a big game.

The bowlers all operated off full runs to test the batsmen, who all looked in good nick, including Butch once again. For a bloke who's only got nine runs on tour, he seemed to be hitting the ball like a shell! And despite building work around the Gabba, there was still a bit of an atmosphere there thanks to around a hundred fans and the masses of media that followed every move of every player.

I felt happy too, especially after my chat with dad yesterday, and by the end of the net I felt I was really timing the ball well on top net surfaces. Ramps took a ball on the back elbow, something he seems to do a fair bit, and it caused him some pain, but that apart, there were no problems at all for us.

PB put me through a long work-out with the keeping gloves on after I batted, then Crofty bowled into my gloves for 20 minutes. Keeping is like batting for me, both are about timing and rhythm, and I felt good by the time I took the gloves off after the session.

The one thing I insist upon at practice is getting what I consider to be the right amount of work on all aspects of my game. And if that means I have to stay longer than anyone else because I need to work on my dual roles of keeping and batting then so be it. I know that annoys the press because it means they are always hanging around for me to finish, but when I do finish I like to think I give them all the time they want. It's a two-way street too. I know they would be the first to let me know if they thought my game wasn't up to scratch in any area.

After I finished at the ground, I headed back to the hotel and spent an hour wandering around town on my own. This time alone has always been vital to me in the lead-up to a Test, as it allows me to focus on the job in hand, the problems I'm likely to face and how I might overcome them. And being captain, it's best to get away from the hotel on the day before a Test, as if I stayed there I'd only get bothered.

Back to the hotel for a 5 pm meeting with the bowlers, along with PB and Bumble, and we discussed how to bowl at the Aussies. We looked at Allan Donald's article in *Wisden Cricket Monthly* and it seemed spot-on. Key points for us are to keep their players tied down by bowling with discipline to a set line and length on or about the off-stump. Stopping the Waugh twins from getting off the mark is especially important as they can fret, while Slater likes width but can be loose outside his off-stump. Taylor, who's set to play his hundredth Test, is one who loves to cut, but if you bowl too straight at him he will work you through the on-side all day. Langer showed us in Perth how effective he was at leaving the ball so we must make him play and bowl fairly full at him, as he can leave the ball on length, while Ponting is another player we must tie down by bowling a tight line around off-stump. Healy, we know all about after so many annoying innings against us. He will cut and slash to his heart's content if we give him room, but he loves to pick the ball up over the on-side if we bowl too straight at him.

Bumble was especially good discussing strengths and weaknesses and the meeting was a really positive one, as was the team meeting that followed. Bumble, Goochie and I all said our pieces about how important the game was, but I got Gus to really ram things home to the lads with his views on the Test and the series. Gus made his debut just before me, when the Aussies won back The Ashes in 1989 and, like me – along with the rest of the squad – has never won a series against them. He made that point but added: 'This is our chance to win them back. We're capable of doing it. We know we are. There are masses of people who would love to be in our position now, ready to take part in an Ashes series, so enjoy it and make the most of every chance you get. This is what we all play the game for, so let's go out and make the country proud.'

I thought getting someone like Gus, who is universally liked and respected through the team to make that sort of rallying call was exactly what was needed. It went down well too, with just one addition from me: 'Make sure at the end of the Test and the end of the series you have no regrets.' Let's hope that rings true.

Australia v England
Test series 1998/99

Australia v England, First Test, Brisbane, 20–24 November 1998

Friday 20 November, First Test, Day 1
Australia 246–5 (S Waugh not out 69)

One of the proudest days of my life – and, at the end, also one of the most frustrating.

After all the planning, all the warm-up games, all the waiting, here we were at the start of an Ashes series we hoped would finally spin the wheel of fortune round in our favour after a decade of Aussie domination.

But even though we ended the day with five wickets under our belts, it could have been so much better. We gave lives to both Steve Waugh and Ian Healy, two players who've hung around like bad smells throughout my entire time as an England player, and with cricketers of that calibre it is something you just can't afford to do.

Al botched a throw of mine to run out Steve Waugh. Then when we took the new ball in the last 40 minutes of the day Goughie had Heals dropped by Gus at third man and Waugh missed low at slip by Nass in what turned out to be the last over of the day.

First things first though. I woke with a real buzz of excitement, even more so than normal. I felt fine, which was a relief after the back trouble I'd endured earlier on in the tour, and I couldn't wait to get to the ground.

We gathered in the lobby of our hotel for an 8 o'clock leave and already there were a few supporters milling around to wish us all the best. A few people shook my hand as captain, which was nice, but I didn't need reminding what I was about to undertake. Even though I never sought the captaincy, the chance to lead England in an Ashes series is a dream come true, and I wanted to take in every moment of it.

In that sort of mood, you tend to notice the little things, and this morning I noticed how quiet the team bus was on the five-minute journey to the ground. I expected players to be nervous – I know I was – but I felt everyone was still focused and ready for the job in hand.

Once at the ground, apart from warm-ups with Riddler and pre-match nets, we had to decide which player to leave out. We went out to have another look at the pitch to see if that offered any clues and I reckoned it looked a good surface. Given that fact, I thought we should bat first and play five bowlers as we would need some variety to bowl them out twice if the pitch played well. The other selectors agreed, so Creepy was the unlucky man in the twelve.

Telling players they are not in the side is not the sort of job that anyone wants, but as captain it's up to me to do that on these occasions. Creeps took it well and wished us luck, but I knew he was a bit down about it. It's been quite a week for him after all, and he was still covered in plasters and cuts on his face.

The first morning of a Test can be a busy time, and this was no exception. After nets, it was quickly into the whites and blazer for the toss. There was just a nagging feeling in my mind that we should bowl as I thought if the pitch was going to do anything it would do it early on. On balance I was still going to bat though, until the choice was taken out of my hands by my call of 'heads' turning out wrong.

Mark Taylor decided to bat, then we both had to do three separate interviews, one with Channel Nine, one with Sky Sports and one with ABC Radio. I'm all for selling the game and promoting it, but not when it interferes with a player's preparations for the game itself. Time doing those interviews was time I could have spent preparing to play, especially as they were then followed by both sides' national anthems and a presentation to Mark Taylor to mark his 100th Test cap.

We stood arm in arm for the National Anthem, with even the management joining in. I know that gesture caused some surprise, as did the decision to wear black armbands on the first day in memory of Goughie's grandfather Fred, who passed away on Wednesday night. The news really upset Goughie, who felt pretty helpless in Brisbane while a family tragedy was unfolding on the other side of the world.

He asked if he could wear one as a mark of respect, and I said we would all wear them. These things were labelled as silly bonding exercises, but I really thought they were important. It showed we were all in this together, even the non-players, especially when we joined together for the National Anthem. It's crucial that we are a 25-man squad, not just 11 blokes out on the field, each doing our own thing and with no support.

Time for one last word with the lads before we went out, and I stressed we had to hit the ground running in the first session. Everyone had been keen to remind us about the start of the series four years ago when Slater battered Daffy DeFreitas in the first over, and that set the tone. We couldn't afford a repeat.

Thankfully, we didn't get one. Goughie and Corky took the new ball, and they both bowled tidily. Goughie was really fired up, while Corky was steady, although he didn't really swing the ball as I hoped he might, the main reason for getting him on first.

In fact, it was Big Al who made the first breakthrough. He'd already got Slater to drive loosely just wide of third slip, so we moved Butch into the floating slip position. That move doesn't always work as it can leave too much of a gap either side of the fielder, but on this occasion it came off with the edge going straight to him at head height. He took the catch easily and they were 30 for one.

That was our only wicket before lunch, but as they'd only reached 58 in 29 overs in the session, that was fine. A quick pep talk at the break – 'Keep doing what we're doing lads and the wickets will come' – and things then got even better. First Goughie, who'd bowled brilliantly, trapped Langer on the crease, then we got two wickets in successive balls.

Al was the man who had looked to swing the ball most out of our attack, and he did just that, back into Mark Waugh as he attempted to force. The ball took a fine inside edge and I tumbled slightly forward and to my left to take the catch. Straight away I said to Mark Waugh 'That's out', but he waited for the umpire's decision. Darrell Hair (we jokingly call him 'Pubic' in the dressing room) asked KT Francis at square leg whether it carried and third umpire Peter Parker was called into action. But replays quickly removed the doubt and we had another victim.

Next ball, from Corky, Taylor got a ball that lifted and left him from nowhere and Nass did the rest at second slip. 106 for four and we were buzzing. Ponting and Steve Waugh consolidated, but they never got away. And we were definitely helped by the chance to keep our bowlers fresh by a break for bad light in mid-afternoon. That was a really sore point with the Aussie crowd and journalists too.

When we arrived in Perth, the Australian Cricket Board tried to get us to agree to play Tests under lights if it got too dark to play in normal conditions. That was all well and good, but we weren't going to agree to that without having the chance to practice in those conditions first, and that didn't seem on the agenda.

On top of that, we'd heard there had been problems in South Africa when Pakistan played under lights the previous year. The red ball proved tough to spot out of a dark background, and we weren't going to start experimenting in Tests. Even Mark Taylor admitted to concerns when the subject came up in last summer's ICC Captains' Meeting, but that wasn't mentioned by the media here.

Of course, we were labelled 'Whinging Poms' spoiling the enjoyment of the crowd when Goochie faced the press after play, but the playing conditions said both sides had to agree to the use of lights and we wouldn't, especially as we felt we were being steam-rolled into it. I'll fight for the rights of my side every time.

When play resumed after the break Ponting looked out of touch, and struggled for his timing. Our bowlers gave him nothing, especially Crofty, who bowled two successive maidens at him, and it was no surprise when he eventually ran out of patience and drove a good-length ball straight to Butch at cover, who took a good, low catch.

By that stage though, Waugh was already on his second innings. At 147 for four, in the first over back after a break for bad light, Ponting had clipped Gus to fine leg. He was always looking for two, as I could tell from his call, but Waugh, on 29 at this point, wasn't so sure. Ponting was determined to get back on strike though, and came screaming back for the second as Goughie's throw was arrowing back to me. By this stage, I sensed Steve Waugh was a little slow off the mark for that second run and so I whipped off my right glove just as the throw was on it's way. Without looking up, I gathered it, turned and threw straight at the stumps at the bowler's end, the end Waugh was now making for. It's the sort of thing keepers have to do, especially with the amount of one-day cricket played these days and I like to pride myself on the fact that I hit the stumps more often than not.

Today was no exception either. Or at least it wouldn't have been if Al's hands hadn't been in the way. Al had been at mid-on, and good team man that he is, he took up a position over the stumps at the bowler's end after the shot was played with Gus still at the end of his follow-through. Maybe I should have shouted for him to leave it, but I was certain he wouldn't try to stop the ball that was on course to hit the top of middle stump on the first bounce with Waugh straining for his ground. Unfortunately he did.

Al wasn't quite sure of the position of his hands and thought the ball was just going to bounce over the stumps, so he was trying to gather it quickly knowing how tight the run would be. The ball bounced off his hands, which broke the stumps as they recoiled from the blow.

He appealed to Hair, but I think he knew straight away he'd made a huge cock-up. The rest of us guessed as much too, Gus, standing just yards away, and myself at the other end of the pitch, in particular. That was confirmed pretty quickly when the big screen, square of the wicket in front of the building work showed as much. If Al had left it, Waugh would have been out by six inches.

The incident left us flat, but we all knew we had to knuckle down again. After all, up to then we had a good day. But even though we got Ponting, the worst was yet to come.

Goughie, who'd had no luck all day, charged in with the new ball trying to break the Waugh-Healy stand. Heals tried to whip a ball on his body over square-leg but only succeeded in getting a massive, spinning, leading edge. We all took a second to sight it, then realised it was heading for third man. Nass set off from second slip, but it was Gus's catch as he ran in. He was slow to spot it, but then picked it up and started to move in. He was late to move, but still got there with the ball at around knee height. He stooped, thrust out his hands – and spilled the catch.

The cheer from the home fans was deafening and Goughie was desperate. But he kept running in, only to suffer more torment just before the close.

By now, it was almost an hour after the scheduled close thanks to the bad light earlier in the day, so the shadows were lengthening. We knew the umpires would offer the batsmen the light at any time so Goughie was flying in to try and get that wicket. He bowled the perfect ball to Waugh, on about off-stump and bringing him forward. He edged fast and low to Nass at second slip, and for a second I think everyone reckoned he had it. But just as we were about to jump for joy, the ball squirmed out, and for Goughie, it was the final frustration.

He roared 'F***!!' at the top of his voice, and even the match referee would have sympathised with him for that one, especially as we came off at the end of the over.

The dressing room was a quiet place when we got there, with Goughie and Al leaving almost straight away, bitterly disappointed with the way things had gone. 'Well done boys, a good day and we're still in the game,' I said. But we all knew it could have been so much better.

Saturday 21 November, First Test, Day 2
Australia 485 (Healy 134, S Waugh 112, Fleming not out 71, Mullally 5–105); England 53–1

Another frustrating day, although we rallied well at the end with Butch and Nass hitting the ball well.

Before the start, we knew we had to get rid of the overnight pair quickly, especially as the new ball was already eight overs old. But although they had some early luck, both playing and missing at Goughie with Heals playing on to the same bowler without dislodging a bail, they got away from us early on and added 102 in the session.

Both men had hundreds by lunch and there was a real contrast between the noise from the crowd as we left the field at the interval and the quiet in the dressing room once we all got in there. But there was no point in moping about. Bumble and I both stressed before we went out again: 'We still only need one wicket to be into their tail. We can still be batting by tea.'

Unfortunately that didn't happen. We did pick up two quick wickets with Al giving me two regulation catches from Waugh and poor Kasprowicz, who'd sat for over two sessions with his pads on only to fall third ball to a cracking away-seamer. But then Fleming took the attack to us, swung the bat and had one of those days where everything came off for him.

With Healy nudging the ball around at the other end, it was easy to get frustrated, especially for Goughie, who had bowled brilliantly but had little to show for it. Fleming's charmed life included nicks wide of and through the slips but he played just the right innings for the occasion. He got on with things, put runs on the board and annoyed us no end.

As a captain, all you can do in those sorts of situations is keep changing the bowling and hope the luck turns in your favour. Bowlers are tired, the ball either seems to miss the edge or go for four, and it is all too easy to lose the plot. Hopefully we just about managed to hang in there, but it must have been frustrating to watch for all the fans out to support us. God knows, it was frustrating enough to be involved in.

Even MacGill chipped in with 20, and by the time their innings finished, we were faced with a formidable total of 485. At least on the plus side, Big Al picked up his first 'Michelle' (Pfeiffer – as in 'five-for') in Tests and the decision to go in with five bowlers had been justified. All five had to work their socks off and if four had to get through the same workload, there might have been real problems.

That said, even four might have been enough if we'd taken our chances. But the fact was we hadn't, and now we were batting a rearguard action.

I was down on the scorecard to bat at four, as I did for most of last summer against South Africa and Sri Lanka, but after five sessions in the field I needed a break, so Chalky spelled me for half an hour while I had a shower and relaxed. That was just as well too as if he hadn't I'd have been scrambling for my pads pretty quickly. Ath was snapped up at second slip by Mark Waugh off Glenn McGrath in just the fifth over, but thankfully Butch, playing really positively, and Nass ensured there were no further alarms before stumps.

Afterwards, some of their boys came in for a drink, something we're looking to start on the second and last nights of every Test. Some series may need match referees, but in my experience an Ashes contest isn't one of them. The two sides get on very well, maybe because so many of the Aussies have played county cricket and know our team anyway.

I spent most of the time chatting to Mark Taylor. It was small-talk, but I think both of us knew how important tomorrow could be for the rest of the series. We must make a good fist of things to let them know we mean business.

Sunday 22 November, First Test, Day 3
Australia 485; England 299–4 (Butcher 116, Thorpe not out 70, Hussain 59)

Sometimes as a selector, you take the flak for backing a hunch that goes badly wrong. Thankfully today was not one of those days as my old pal Butch scored a brilliant century, which, with support from most of the batsmen, helped keep us well and truly in the match.

I think his summer against South Africa really convinced him he is a Test match player, and here he showed it big style. He and Nass really took the fight to the Aussies first thing, playing positively, and they rattled them.

They took 22 from MacGill's first three overs of the day, and fifteen boundaries in the first 19 overs, forcing Taylor to use five bowlers in the first 70 minutes play. We were sailing along at 145 for one, when Nass pushed at one from Kasper and got the finest of edges and that brought me in, fresh after a night's sleep and keen to carry on the positive work.

I thought it might have been my day too. Off the mark first ball from Stephen Waugh, three more runs clipped away off Kasper, I was feeling good. The luck was with me too as I even clipped a low full toss from MacGill straight to short leg, only to see it fall to ground.

But that luck didn't last long. MacGill, who'd not bowled well all morning under the assault from Butch and Nass, served me up a waist-high full-toss. You don't get too many of those in Test cricket, so I was determined to put it away.

'Here's four more' I thought, and swatted it away without hesitation.

Unfortunately, I didn't swat it hard enough or high enough and it turned into catching practice for Kasper at deep backward square leg. The golden rule with those deliveries is either to roll your wrists and hit the ball down or hit it for six. I did neither, and paid the price.

Two wickets in quick succession and it could have been worse if Butch hadn't been bowled by a no-ball from Kasper on 92, the only real blemish of his innings. Thankfully Hair raised his arm, and we got through to lunch on 179 for three, still 107 away from the follow-on.

The rest of the day was all ours, as we lost just one more wicket before a spectacular electrical storm ended play 66 minutes early. Butch reached his hundred with a sweet four from MacGill, and the viewing room was full to applaud him for that one.

Even when he was out to a slightly tired drive and a brilliant caught and bowled from Mark Waugh, Ramps kept things going by giving Thorpey good support as the little man did what he does best – scoring runs against Australia. It was a gamble to bring him here with little form and fitness behind him after a back operation, but already he's on the way to paying us back for that show of faith.

We cruised past the follow-on, but with the storm looming, it was crucial the lads kept their concentration as it was obvious play would be called off early. Thankfully they did, as it meant we could enjoy the thunder and lightning safe in the knowledge that it was a good day at the office.

We said as much in our mid-match team meeting too, where the mood was pretty buoyant. There were cheers and applause all round for Al and Butch, but I stressed we were now in the match, competing. It was important for all the remaining batsmen to support each other and make sure we got as close to Australia's score as possible, if not past it. 'They'll come at us hard tomorrow, so we must be ready,' added Bumble.

A good day, made even better when we had dinner at a local restaurant, with several England fans coming up to tell us to keep up the good work. They were quite happy too.

Monday 23 November, First Test, Day 4
Australia 485 & 237–3 declared (Slater 113, Langer 74); England 375 (Thorpe 77, Ramprakash not out 69, McGrath 6–85) & 26–0

What a difference 24 hours can make. We ended yesterday buoyant, but now, although we can still win, it will take a huge effort on a wearing pitch after we got blown away.

No excuses, just the thought that we have still got a long way to go to be as hard as Australia. We had a good day on Sunday, and we lacked sparkle today. Maybe it's complacency, I don't know.

We had to be at the ground early to make up some of the time lost yesterday evening and as it was a batting day, the lads were allowed to do their own warm-ups, but that didn't work. It was all too leisurely, and maybe we just weren't focused enough going into the day, despite what was said.

Anyhow, we lost Thorpey in the first forty minutes a bit unluckily as he cracked a hook shot from McGrath straight to square leg. But after that, Crofty apart, we batted pretty unintelligently and left Ramps high and dry.

McGrath bowled fast and straight, but he just got to too many of our players, especially Corky and Al, who both seemed determined to hook him into next year rather than let the bouncer pass and support the batsman at the other end. It was daft cricket, and with Ramps unbeaten on 69, we were bowled out by lunch.

That gave them a lead of 110, and with five sessions left, licence to play their shots and set us a target to put us under pressure in the last innings. Even if we'd batted for another hour into the afternoon it wouldn't have come to that, but we played poorly and now got punished.

We'd been in this situation before and the bowlers responded. In Port Elizabeth in 1995, South Africa had a similar lead, but we then hit them hard to peg them back and could even have bowled them out but for a hundred by Gary Kirsten. We drew that game easily, but now they came at us and we couldn't respond.

Before we went out I said: 'Early wickets. If we can get them we're still in the game. It will put them under pressure, and that's the key.' But although Corky got Taylor for the second time in the match for his first Test duck in Australia, Slater just took the game away from us.

He attacked from the outset, it was a perfect situation for him, and he clobbered Goughie out of the attack. I think Goughie might have been feeling a bit sorry for himself after the first innings when he didn't really deserve figures of one for 135, but for once he couldn't lift himself in the face of Slater's onslaught.

Langer played the perfect supporting role, and Slater waltzed to as carefree a hundred as you'll see. I'm getting sick of seeing his wild celebrations when he gets a hundred against us, punching the air, kissing everything in sight and jumping all over the place, especially as he seems to have done it so often while I'm still waiting for my first in Ashes cricket. Can't blame him though. It must be a great feeling.

Although Al was tidy again, it soon became a holding operation. But at least I was able to take heart from the end of their innings. The Waugh twins came in and just patted it around, adding only 38 in 12 overs before the declaration. I couldn't understand that as another fifty runs at that stage would have taken the game away from us completely, even if they'd got out.

Being set 348 in 98 overs wasn't an easy ask, but I stressed the importance of taking each hour at a time. 'And make sure, whatever you do, you're positive, both in attack and defence,' I added. 'Even when you're defending, still looking for runs can keep the board ticking and them on the back foot.'

Thankfully Ath got off his pair with a four, third ball from Fleming, and we closed on 26 for no wicket. They played positively and that will be the key on the final day, whether we're looking to win or draw. If we go out just trying to hang around, that is a recipe for disaster.

Tuesday 24 November, First Test, Day 5
Australia 485 & 237–3 declared drew with England 375 & 179–6

It's cost us plenty of chances to win in my Test career – Trinidad 1990, Old Trafford 1994, Barbados and Edgbaston 1998 – but the rain had never saved an England side I've been involved in from defeat. Until today.

And what rain it was. The players left the field for bad light at 2.20 pm with storm clouds already encircling the Gabba, and within minutes the deluge had started. It was as black as night – not even floodlights would have been any use here – and the rain was so heavy, the water was flowing off the pitch and down the steps of the players' tunnel into the dressing rooms. Thankfully ours stayed dry, but the Aussies' rooms weren't so lucky, and they had to use mops and brushes to stem the flow of water.

Even so, the Gabba is an amazingly quick drying ground, so it wasn't until almost 4.30 that the umpires finally called play off. By then the rain had eased to a drizzle, but parts of the ground looked more like a boating lake than a cricket field.

Publicly I maintained I still thought we could have survived for a draw, but I have to accept we were lucky to get away with this one. By the time the players left the field in light which meant Taylor couldn't bowl McGrath or Fleming, we were six wickets down, all our top six batsmen were back in the hutch and we'd long since given up hope of winning. It was backs-to-the-wall stuff.

We started positively, even though Ath fell again to McGrath, this time hooking high to fine leg. By then though, he had played some shots and Butch and Nass looked equally positive as we approached lunch just one wicket down.

That all changed when Butch and I fell in quick succession to send us to the interval in a tail-spin. Butch was really struggling against MacGill, who was turning the ball sharply on a wearing pitch. He didn't really look as though he knew where he was going to score, and when he padded up to a leg-break, Hair sent him on his way.

I followed three overs later. I will admit I'm not the best starter against spin, and with Mark Waugh on at one end and MacGill at the other it was hard work. Waugh bowled cleverly to me, floating it up on about off-stump, and my tendency to go hard at the ball cost me dear. I lunged at a good-length delivery, got a pad-bat to silly point, and was off before the appeal finished. A soft dismissal and a poor end to a poor match with the bat.

The slide continued gradually after lunch, Chalky, Nass and Ramps all falling to the pepped-up Aussie spinners sensing blood on a wearing pitch with men around the bat. By this stage, I was up in the viewing area above the dressing room with one eye on the weather.

I have to admit, my heart rose when the umpires finally offered Corky and Crofty the light, and they couldn't get to the dressing room quick enough. Then it was just a case of waiting for the game to be called off.

I got asked the standard questions about why we hadn't agreed to play under lights and enjoyed a joust on that one with an Aussie journalist called Malcolm Conn, which went something like this:

'Why didn't you agree to play under lights?' he asked. 'The paying public were robbed on that first day because of it.'

'We've not played with a red ball under lights before, and a Test is hardly the place to start,' I replied.

'How will you ever get practice if you don't start?'

'But we are starting to install lights in England after experiments last summer, and the sooner we do the sooner we can practice.'

'So why didn't you practice in the lead-up games?'

'We were never offered the chance.'

Conn's a typical Aussie, very much behind his side and railing against all things Pommie. I think we'll have some fun on this tour.

After play, we found out they've left MacGill out of their side for Perth. I can understand why, as Perth never spins much, but it does bounce, and although he does bowl the odd bad ball, I thought he did well on the last day here. Still no sign of Shane Warne though. His comeback appears to be going more slowly than most Aussies hoped.

Discussing a match straight away isn't always the best thing to do as people can still be wound up and unable to look back at events objectively. But I decided just to say a few words to the lads after I got back from the press conference. I knew we'd got away with things, but I decided to emphasise the positive.

'Well done lads,' I said. 'It might have been tough if we'd stayed on, but I had full confidence in you remaining batsmen to see us through, as you did at Old Trafford last summer.

'We've not played anywhere near our best, but we still created chances, and managed to rattle them a few times. No matter what you might read or hear, it's still 0–0 and we've managed to keep that zero in the loss column again. If we can keep doing that we can only get stronger.

'I think you all know we've not played to our potential here, but it's up to us now to lift our game for the next Test. We've been to Perth already, we know what's it like, and we know we can do well there. We can beat this lot, we've shown that in this match, so relax this evening, and then let's get ready to do just that in the next Test.'

Back to the hotel to pack for an early departure back to Perth tomorrow morning. Thank goodness it's still 0–0. We'll need to improve to compete, that's for sure, but I've seen enough here to still leave me optimistic for the rest of the series.

Australia v England, Second Test, Perth, 28–30 November 1998

Wednesday 25 November

Any flight to Perth is a long one as I'm told it's the most isolated city in the world, and this one is no exception. It takes around six hours, with a two-hour time change, via Melbourne, and by the end of it there were some tired looking lads who trooped off the plane.

Some of that tiredness was no doubt caused by a late night but that's okay as far as I'm concerned. After a week of high intensity international cricket – the two build-up days plus the match itself – some players will always want to let off some steam by having a drink or two, safe in the knowledge that there's no practice the next day. Every one of them knows that no one will have a go at them for that, but they also know that if they're not in top form when we hit the nets, then there'll be hell to pay. Goochie said as much publicly at the start of the trip, but thankfully this is a dedicated bunch and I don't expect any problems in that department.

I stopped to have a look at some of the papers in the newsagents at Melbourne airport, and they all seem to think we were very lucky to survive. Maybe we were, but the fact remains, the score is still 0–0, and that's all that counts.

The flight passed uneventfully, but I did notice that Thorpey spent an increasing amount of time out of his seat. There aren't enough business class seats on internal flights in Australia to allow us all to travel in style, so we go economy, and that's rarely a hardship as most flights here are relatively short. I just hope he's okay.

I spent most of the flight dozing and reading Glenn Hoddle's *World Cup Diary*. It's a good read, and certainly strikes a cord with me given the fact that we have the World Cup next year. It's also quite amusing to remember where we were when each of the matches took place, especially the game with Argentina. That took place just before the Old Trafford Test against South Africa, and we all watched it in a meeting room at the Copthorne Hotel. I can still remember all of us leaping up when we thought Sol Campbell had scored the winner, only for it to be ruled out for an elbow on the keeper by Alan Shearer. Remind me not to elbow Adam Gilchrist in the Final at Lord's next June!

We've switched hotels from our last stay in Perth, moving from the Hyatt, which is next to the ground, out to the Burswood Resort, which includes a Casino and a golf course, about a five-minute drive out of town and just the other side of the Swan River. I would have preferred to stay at the Hyatt, even though the Aussies are there, but, to be honest, this is still top-class, although some of the lads might end up a little light in the pocket by the end of the stay thanks to that Casino.

I ended the day having dinner with Kevin Gartrell from M-G, including some superb garlic prawns. It was a relaxing evening, but even though I've got so many good friends here in Perth, there won't be too many nights out during this visit. As captain, I must throw myself into the business of this Test, and anything else has to come second. Sad but true.

Thursday 26 November

'Back to the nets, idiot!' That was the line Ian Healy used on Ben Hollioake after Pelly cracked 63 in 48 balls in the Texaco Trophy match at Lord's in 1997. It was meant as a serious sledge, but all of us have adopted it as a rallying cry for practice.

It was back to the nets today in the build-up to the Test, and although I'm certain they are the best facilities in world cricket, I felt sluggish today. My timing was off and I ended up having two nets to try and get things right. It's back to that problem of hitting a rhythm, and as I haven't spent too much time in the middle so far, I don't appear to have a great deal of it.

The Aussies practised at the opposite end of the net complex and that created problems of its own. Even though there was a length of netting between the two camps, it was only about ten feet tall, so hits back over the bowler brought plenty of calls of 'heads' and wild ducking. No one was hit, but I think they won 7–3 on shouts!

We did have a concern with Thorpe, who 'rocked up' (an Aussie expression for arriving somewhere which we are all picking up on) with a stiff back. He had a gentle net, but was clearly unhappy. Wayne Morton examined him and couldn't find any major damage and I'm confident he'll be okay for the Test.

We went out to look at the pitch after the session and it looked good: hard, flat and with the promise of pace and bounce from the groundsman. Having seen it, we decided we might as well pick the Test squad, so we sat down to do it in our viewing room while the press waited outside.

It was a tough job. Gus Fraser has been such a brilliant servant to us this year, but so far he has looked short of his best. I had no worries about him after the state game here, but he didn't look all that effective in the first Test, and also failed to keep it tight, what he normally does best of all, with just eight maidens in 43 overs.

That, coupled with the need for a bit of extra pace, made us look elsewhere, and we settled on Tudor and Headley. Normally we'd have liked to name just 12, but we couldn't decide between the two. I knew Tudes would welcome the extra bounce, but both men had looked sharp in the nets, so we decided to sleep on it.

With the doubts over Thorpe's back, we decided to include Graeme Hick in the squad. He's not played since arriving but looked in good touch in the nets, and as I said in Brisbane, there aren't many better players to have on stand-by than 'Arnie'. In fact, we named all eight batters in the squad to cover all our options. At least Ath appears to be fine now.

I've always enjoyed working with 'Smokey' (Adam Hollioake). Here we are after he took over from Ath as captain for the Caribbean one-day series.

Waiting for the presentation ceremony after we collapsed to lose the sixth Test of the 1997/98 West Indies tour in Antigua. None of us knew Ath was about to resign.

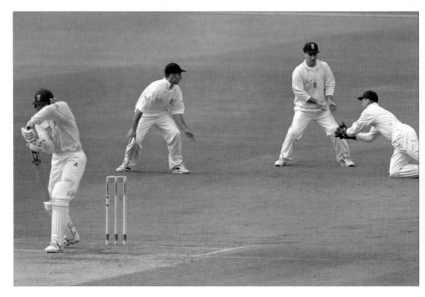

'Gotcha!' My first catch of the 1998 summer as captain removes Jacques Kallis off Corky, who returned to Test cricket with five wickets at Edgbaston.

'I thought you said captaincy was easy!' Chatting with Ath at Old Trafford, where our fight-back against South Africa began – eventually.

Contrasting emotions at Headingley. For Shaun Pollock, the bitter taste of defeat and for me, a series win as captain – and a souvenir stump.

Aravinda de Silva and
friends enjoyed the slow,
turning pitch served up at
the Foster's Oval that
helped end our summer
on a flat note.

A rare attacking stroke from me as we
battled to save the last Test of the summer
against the wiles of Muttiah Muralitharan.

Above: A career-first for me in Brisbane at the start of the 1998/99 Ashes tour as rain helped us save a Test, although even without it we might still have got a draw.

Left: 'Well done Tudes!' Congratulating our Perth debutant, whose five wickets gave us something to smile about despite our three-day defeat in the second Test.

Above: 'What have I done?' Reflecting on a poor shot as our second day revival goes up in smoke at the WACA, Perth.

Jason Gillespie, who wrecked our comeback hopes with a fiery third-morning spell in Perth, celebrates removing Hicky, who had hammered him the previous evening.

Goughie. Fit, fast, consistent and unquestionably our man of the tour. How many wickets would he have got if we held all our catches?

Gus celebrates his recall in Melbourne. His presence was reassuring after one of the most frantic build-ups to a Test I can remember.

Dominic Cork gets a wake-me-up from Damien Fleming at the WACA, where the pace and bounce of the pitch proved awesome at times.

Justin Langer's amazing concentration in Adelaide's heat helped him make an unbeaten 179 that set up Australia's victory and ended our interest in the Ashes.

Ramps, who along with Nass was our most consistent player in the Test series, pushes Colin Miller for more runs in Adelaide.

The Barmy Army, part of our magnificent travelling support, even managed a song in Adelaide after our chances of regaining the Ashes disappeared for another series.

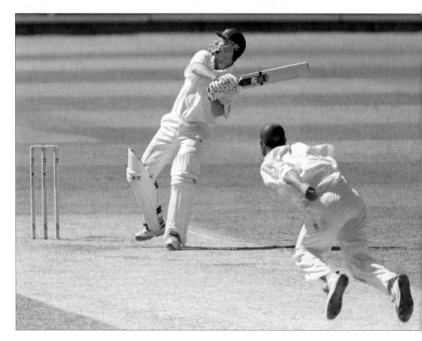

Stephen Waugh takes on Deano in Melbourne. Waugh's decision to expose his tail-end partners in the second innings gave us our victory chance.

After our very public discussion, it was time to face the press in my pre-Test conference. They all pushed me on whether we'd picked a side, but I wasn't about to tell them ahead of the players, who'll find out before training tomorrow morning. I said the chat had just been a 'preliminary discussion', which it was given our doubts over Thorpe and our bowling line-up.

Thorpey also came up in conversation, and I decided to come clean; lying to the press has a nasty habit of rebounding on you, and there was no point in covering things up.

'I won't lie to you,' I said. 'Thorpey's arrived a bit stiff after the flight from Brisbane, but that's hardly surprising as it's his first concerted period of cricket since the operation. I'm pretty sure he'll be okay to play.' And I believe that too.

By the time I'd finished with the press it was mid-afternoon, and time for a rest before we had to attend another pre-Test function. This one, put on by the Western Australian Cricket Association, was in many ways worse than the one in Brisbane which featured a choir singing 'Go Aussie Go'. There were a few of my old friends from M-G there, but it was just as jingoistic as before.

The evening began with the players of both sides being brought on, one by one, before we stood for the Australian National Anthem. Most of us then stayed standing for our Anthem – but they didn't play it!

Then we had to sit through 25 minutes of Aussies taking wickets and scoring runs in the past three Ashes series, with barely a stroke played in anger by our lads. You had to laugh. It went on and on, and even the locals around our table began to start squirming by the end.

The food followed but it was along the same lines as Brisbane with one course, followed by an interview or an auction, then another. In fact, by the time we left at 11.15, we still hadn't had dessert.

I was again invited on stage as I had been in Brisbane, along with Mark Taylor, to answer a few questions, before Taylor and Goochie were given photos to commemorate them both topping 400 runs in a Test. Goochie did it against India at Lord's in 1990 when he made 333 and 123, and when he was asked what he remembered about it, he said with a smile, 'Not much, it was a long time ago and I had less hair then.' That brought a laugh, as since then he's had a hair transplant, and he has been promoting it wherever we go.

The main speech was a disaster. Sam Loxton, one of Don Bradman's great 1948 side which went through a tour of England unbeaten, was the speaker, but he was, quite simply and very sadly, past it. It was the only speech I've ever listened to where the person talking actually forgot a story halfway through. It was one of those occasions when you just felt embarrassed, especially as he went on for over half an hour. At one stage he even admitted: 'I don't feel too flash', and I had visions of him passing out on stage, but thankfully for all of us he made it to the end.

The only redeeming features of the evening were a comedian who used latex face masks and got us all laughing with a brilliant impersonation of Rambo, and the announcer who introduced us to the crowd as we arrived. Gus was called on stage as a 'swing and seam bowler', which he loved as people have spent his whole career telling him he can't swing it. But the biggest laugh of the night came when Deano emerged as 'all-rounder Dean Headley'. Afterwards he refused to admit he'd written the guy's script.

Everyone accepts we are ambassadors for our country; but we shouldn't have to sit through Aussie flag-waving dinners like this just because we're English. The Aussies wouldn't put up with it when they tour our country, and neither should we.

Friday 27 November

Whoever said being a captain is easy can't have done the job. At least that's the way it appears to me after a tough day at the office.

It didn't exactly begin smoothly. Telling someone he's not going to play in a Test is a bloody difficult thing to do, but as captain I have to do it, so at 8.15 am I had the task of knocking on Gus's door to break the bad news to him. It wasn't a long meeting, there's not a lot you can say at a time like that, and trying to say too much can often make things worse. I just told him why we'd reached the decision, and urged him to keep going as there's still plenty of time left on the trip. He knows how things can turn for you better than anyone: four years ago he wasn't even on the Ashes tour, but joined late after a few injuries and helped us win in Adelaide.

Gus took it well, but I knew he was gutted. Being the pro he is though, he still knuckled down in the nets, bowled his heart out, and was even willing to speak to the press after practice where he maintained a diplomatic tone despite his disappointment.

Nets were better for me today, I felt my feet moved well and I played more positively, but I had 20 minutes on the bowling machine afterwards just for good measure. It was good to see Adam Hollioake too. His parents live in Perth, so he's been on holiday here while working on his fitness ahead of the one-dayers and he came down to practice today. A few of the press were wondering if he'd been added to the squad, but we had to disappoint them on that one.

Things weren't quite so good for Thorpey though. He arrived at the ground and announced he felt worse than yesterday and sat out the entire practice session in the dressing room. If he can't practice, I can't see how we can risk him in a Test, and his loss will be a huge hole for us to fill. He's been in great form on the trip so far and made a century in the Test here four years ago. Thank goodness we've got Hicky here as cover. He looked good in the nets today, especially in the face of some top quick bowling by Tudor, Headley and Gough. All three of them screamed in at him and it's going to be a tough call to decide which man to leave out tomorrow.

Nets over, I spent the afternoon with Peter Carlstein, a former Rhodesian cricketer who now lives in Perth. I know Peter from my time playing grade cricket here, and he's also a long-time friend and cricket advisor to Adam and Ben Hollioake. Peter took some weight off one of my bats and we just talked cricket, very relaxing and just what the doctor ordered ahead of the Test.

Back to the hotel, and it was team meeting time ahead of the match. Serious stuff too, with a fax from Peter Philpott. Although we've used Pete at various times through the trip, he's not been with us on a full-time basis due to other commitments, but he still let us know his views on the first Test.

He made some good points both on the way we played spin, and on our general approach. He was quite right when he said we needed to maintain our intensity in the field at all times, and be careful when we swept. We must get our front pad in the way to prevent being bowled around our legs, although that won't be an issue here with MacGill not playing. He also stressed we need to either hit the ball along the ground, or hit it for six, something I know all too well from my time in Brisbane.

The spin we'll face in this match will come from Colin Miller, a bit of a journeyman in Aussie cricket, who's with his third state – Tasmania – and has only just come to international cricket in his mid-

30s. He can also bowl seamers and has just got back from the tour of Pakistan.

We have some footage of him, but Bumble still gave everyone a laugh when I asked whether anyone knew anything about him. 'He lives in a pub,' said the coach, which at least let us know he might like a drink if nothing else.

A more serious part of the meeting was how to play on the Perth pitch. We'd already seen how it played in the state game and knew it would have pace and bounce. Bumble stressed their players would be looking to leave the ball on length as much as line, so we had to bowl a strict line on off-stump, making them play as much as possible. Given the bounce we could expect, it was better to be too full than too short as at least we could set fields for the ball to be driven.

As batsmen, I said we could learn a lot from the way Langer and Campbell had played against us in the state game. They got all their runs from either driving or horizontal bat shots, the cut and the pull. Goochie added to that when he said, 'In these conditions the danger ball is the one down the channel just outside off-stump. Whatever you do, don't try to force it with a straight bat as the bounce will catch you out and bring their keeper and slips into play'. Everyone nodded.

The meeting broke up in a confident mood, with the batsmen staying behind to watch footage of Miller and Gillespie, who also didn't play in Brisbane. We can win this game, I'm sure of that, as long as we do the basics right.

Saturday 28 November, Second Test, Day 1
England 112 (Fleming 5–46); Australia 150–3 (Taylor 61)

Perth is my second home, so I woke this morning with a special feeling of anticipation for this Test. Unfortunately, by the end of the day, that feeling had become an enormous let-down. Just about everything that could go wrong did go wrong, and after just three sessions we are staring down the barrel in a big way.

What made it worse was that most of the problems we suffered were self-inflicted. Yes, I lost the toss for the second Test in a row, and yes, we had to bat on a pitch that had some damp in it. But we still threw our wickets away for the most part, then dropped catches when it was our turn to bowl.

At least the day started with a pleasant duty, telling Tudes he was playing, which I did after we loosened up. I'd decided in my own mind that he should play the night before as with his extra height, he was bound to get a bit more bounce than most, but I just slept on it to be sure in my own mind.

I've known the big fella since he first came to Surrey as a 16-year-old and it was a real pleasure to let him know his ambition was about to be realised. I think he was quite chuffed too, judging by the appearance of his pearly white teeth in a huge grin when I told him he was in.

By the same token, I had to break the bad news to Croft and Headley. Crofty was unlucky and hadn't done much wrong in Brisbane, but the pitch had a history of giving the spinners next to nothing – even Shane Warne's never taken a five-for here, so after a final look at the pitch, he had to make way.

Deano was just as unlucky. Once we decided to leave Crofty out, we were never going to play five seamers; the tail would have been too long for one thing. It meant we would be going in with seven batters including Hicky at seven, but given the way the tail had played in Brisbane I reckoned that was no bad thing. We'd tried to play an all-rounder there for most of the summer against South Africa and Sri Lanka and the person batting there had averaged seven. It was time for a specialist in that spot. In any case, given the history of the WACA pitch, I reckoned four seamers plus Hick and Ramprakash would be enough, and I was convinced we got the selection spot-on.

Before the toss I chatted with Tom Moody and he said he'd bat first. I felt the same because even though I noticed a bit of moisture in the surface, I still thought it would play okay. That moisture wasn't there the day before, but I reckoned the groundsman was keen to make sure it didn't crack up like recent Perth Test pitches. You accept a bit of something in most Test pitches on the first morning knowing if you can get to lunch in good order, you can then dictate the match.

The decision was taken out of my hands though when I called wrong again – heads – and after the endless interviews I had the pleasure of presenting Tudes with his cap before heading back to the dressing room to get ready for a batting day. It was good to see that most of the squad came out for the ceremony, and that was an indication of how popular he is. Tudes is no socialite – he doesn't smoke or drink – but his sense of humour and willingness to learn has marked him out as a favourite with everyone.

There was no point in any words before we went out, everything had been said the night before, but very quickly it all went pear-shaped. Athers, Butch and Nass all fell caught behind, and within 45 minutes we were 19 for three.

Let's be clear about this. They bowled exceptionally well. McGrath, Fleming and Gillespie all bowled a great line on or around off-stump, but we did ourselves no favours by playing at balls we could have left alone.

The top three falling so cheaply was bad enough, but it could have been even worse. McGrath was really flying in and bowled a wicked short ball at Ramps that followed him as he attempted to sway out of the line. He ended up having to take it on the body, and it just grazed his chin before dropping to the ground.

Ramprakash is a hard man, and a very focused one too. He just stood there, refusing to be fazed by McGrath and remained completely concentrated on the job in hand. But pretty soon the blood began to flow and it was obvious he'd have to go off for treatment, a fact confirmed by Wayne Morton when he arrived in the centre.

I said as much to Ramps, but the reply I got made it crystal clear he was going nowhere in a hurry.

'I'm not going any f***ing where. I'm f***ing staying here to battle it out with you.'

Fizz and I didn't really know what to say to that one, but thankfully the umpires used the delay to call for drinks and they were happy for Ramps to go off, get taped up and come back without the need for a new player.

Back he came, and for a while we made some headway. I took four boundaries off McGrath, including 14 from one over, and he was in the tenth over of his spell when that little bit of luck you need went his way, not mine.

He bowled me a full ball just outside off-stump and I went for the drive. Late on, it nipped back in a fraction, took the inside edge, onto my pad and then back onto the stumps.

I was gutted. It was the best I'd felt since the first match of the trip at Lilac Hill, and if ever I'd needed to kick on it was now. And what made things worse was that my wicket was followed by Creepy and Hicky, both edging Gillespie, before lunch.

A score of 76 for six at lunch on the first day made for a pretty quiet dressing room, and there was nothing much to say except to urge the remaining players to sell their wickets dearly. Tudes did just that, and played with real composure on his debut, but 112 all out at 2.09 on day one left us with a mountain to climb.

After everything that had been said beforehand about making sure we didn't bring their close catchers into play, nine of our ten wickets had fallen to nicks to either the slips or keeper. A disaster.

But there was no point in dwelling on it, and I said so before we went out. 'What's done is done, we can't change anything. What we've now got to do is bowl with their discipline and we're still in this game.'

Hard though we tried though, it just didn't happen. There were bright spots, like Tudes' first over to Taylor, which gave the Aussie captain a little bit of a wake-up call when he copped the second ball in the ribs then edged through the slips for four, but by and large it was depressing stuff.

Catches went down again with Hicky missing a sitter at second slip from Taylor, while Slater got another life when Ben Hollioake, on for Ramps who was resting after having seven stitches in his chin, couldn't cling on to a lopping edge in the gully. Both chances came off Goughie, who was beginning to wonder if his luck would ever change.

It did when Butch eventually clung onto one from Slater at third slip, and Ramps managed to nick Langer out before the close, miscuing a sweep to short leg. Corky made it three when he got Taylor for the third time in as many innings in the series, the victim of late seam movement, and reward for a good spell. But there was still no getting away from the fact we had a huge task to get back into the match.

We'd kept our heads up in the field and that was pleasing, but as we walked off at the end of the day I reckoned that it was as bad a day for any England side I'd captained. The only rival to it was Old Trafford last summer when our batsmen had been booed off on Saturday evening, and I could at least take heart from the fact we came back to draw that match. But there were still four days left here.

There was no point in a mass enquiry there and then, it wouldn't do any good. Everyone knew what had gone wrong. Now was a time to go away, reflect, and come back ready to fight again tomorrow. I did just that, with some room service and no calls.

Sunday 29 November, Second Test, Day 2
England 112 & 126–5; Australia 240 (Tudor 4–89)

My message was short and sweet before play: we had to fight. I said: 'If we can bowl them out for 250 or less, we're still in this match. But if we just lie down and die, they'll walk all over us. Let's get into them.'

It was a hot day, Mark Waugh was in, Stephen Waugh, Ricky Ponting and Ian Healy were still in the hutch, and if we didn't get our skates on we were set for a real grilling. But there was a light breeze off the Swan River which Al used beautifully from the River End, and with Goughie firing in from the other, the Aussies never got any sort of momentum going.

We couldn't get any wickets either in the first, frustrating hour as nightwatchman 'Dizzy' Gillespie hung around, but it wasn't for want of trying. Al was just too good for both players, producing the best spell of left-arm swing bowling I've ever seen. Eventually he persuaded Dizzy to nick one, but that only let in Stephen Waugh, and he immediately tried to dominate.

Waugh slashed Al over the slips, but pleasingly we kept it tight, and by lunch they'd added just 44 runs in the session. If we couldn't get wickets, control was the next best thing, but I asked the lads for another big effort after lunch to try and break through.

Containment was one thing, but with only four sessions gone in the match they could still have afforded to bat like that for two days to put us out of the game completely. That was why I took the new ball as soon as it was due, one over into the afternoon session.

I gave it to Tudes alongside Goughie, partly because, unlike Al or Corky, he was fresh having bowled just one over before lunch, and partly because I wanted to see how the Waughs handled his extra bounce.

At first, things continued to go wrong. Al missed Steve Waugh above his head at mid-off as he drove at poor old Goughie, and then he took three fours in a row off Tudes. But even then, I guessed we had a chance of getting him.

Tudes immediately slipped into a great rhythm and Stephen didn't like the pace and bounce he was generating one bit. He played one classical on-drive, but expecting a short ball next up as a result, gave himself some room. Tudes read that and fired it in full and fast, and though Stephen managed to get it away for four more, the advantage was now with the bowler.

Goughie caught the mood, hitting Mark with a sharp lifter in the next over, before Tudes finally got his man with a beauty. He began the over with two short balls that forced Stephen back. Then, with the batsman stuck in the crease, he found a fuller length just outside off-stump and when the ball broke back it burst between bat and pad to knock the castle over. Tudes just didn't know what to do with himself and spread his arms as if to say: 'What happens now?' What happened was that we all mobbed him to celebrate a notable first Test scalp.

And he carried on the good work in his next over. A perfect length on off-stump brought Mark forward, and as he reached for the ball, it just moved away, caught the edge and Butch, who had been our safest slipper on the trip, pouched it easily.

All of a sudden we were buzzing again. Goughie got in on the act by removing Healy and Fleming in successive balls, and with the Brits in the crowd now in a frenzy, a hat-trick would have brought the house down. Goughie had been on one last summer against Sri Lanka and missed out then, and now was no different, Miller surviving a rapid ball on off-stump.

Still we missed catches, with Goughie flooring a Ponting hook at fine leg off Tudes, but the big fella wrapped things up soon after to make light of that one. He finished with four for 89 on debut including four for 24 after lunch as Australia lost their last six wickets for 31 in 39 balls. All out 240, and we were back in it.

There wasn't much time for a chat before the batsmen went out again, but the dressing room was buzzing after that comeback. All I said was: 'Right. Well done. We've done what we had to do and we're back, but this is where it counts. Runs here and we're in the game big time.'

It wasn't to be though. Fleming, who'd looked ordinary in Brisbane, had really found some rhythm, and he tormented us around off-stump with pace, bounce and movement, both in the air and off the seam.

Butch, an old mate of his from grade cricket in Melbourne, was the first to fall to a beauty. He avoided his pair, but then got one that swung in before seaming away and he did well to edge it to third slip. Century in one match, one run in the next. Poor Butch.

Nass went next, trapped half-forward, before Fleming made it three in three by suckering me big time. True, I walked to the wicket less than forty minutes after having kept for 90 overs, but I can't hold that up as an excuse for the shot I played. All our pre-match talk was of not playing forcing shots outside the off-stump with a straight bat, but I did just that to give Taylor a regulation catch. No excuse, poor shot, and we were in big trouble.

At least Ath looked good, pulling strongly whenever he got the chance and scoring 35 out of 40 either side of tea while Ramps hung on at the other end. But just as it seemed we'd weathered the storm and Ath was set for the big one he needed to kick-start his tour, Fleming found a good one for him around off-stump and Taylor snapped up the nick again. They were missing nothing, and we seemed to be heading for a two-day defeat.

That feeling grew when Creeps and Ramps were separated after a stubborn sixteen-over stand. Miller, who had, up to that point, done little, was thrown the ball, and he found some extra bounce, which caused Creeps to offer short leg a regulation catch.

Still 61 behind and with our last batsman striding to the crease, things looked hopeless, or at least pretty desperate, but I had a feeling Hicky might do something special. He had seemed very relaxed, and even dropped off to sleep in his chair in the dressing room during the early part of our innings.

He was, of course, on a pair, but I had faith in him. God knows, he's a good enough player to take most attacks apart, and he was my first choice to come out as cover when Ath struggled in Cairns.

My message to him was short and sweet: 'Go out and show us all what a good player you are.' And he did just that.

Right from the off, he looked in prime form, square-cutting his first ball from Miller for four. He did have one slice of luck, top-edging a hook from Gillespie over the keeper, but when they tested him with the short ball again, he mashed it.

Gillespie had switched to the River End to replace McGrath and banged in his first ball just outside off-stump. Hicky saw it early and dispatched it over midwicket for six, the ball just clearing the rope some fifteen yards inside the fence. Next ball was short again, this time outside off-stump and Hicky pounced once more, this time cutting it for four.

Gillespie wasn't used to this sort of treatment, and banged the next one in, much quicker and shorter. Hicky was back in a flash and hooked it high into the seats out at square leg. Six on any ground, and 16 runs in three balls. The crowd loved it.

Ramps caught the mood, and with Gillespie losing his rhythm completely, the over cost 23. Fun while it lasted, and the pair survived until the close to leave us at 126 for five. It had been a brilliant counter-attack by Hicky, who scored 42 in 33 balls, but the dressing room was still a flat place. Once the dust had settled, we were still two runs behind and no major batsmen to come. Somehow we needed to find another 150 runs from somewhere and that meant we needed to be batting at tea the next day. It was going to be a really tall order.

Once again, they showed why they are the best side in the world. They came at us hard, we needed to survive and couldn't. That is what we must learn to do.

Monday 30 November, Second Test, Day 3
England 112 & 191 (Hick 68, Ramprakash not out 47, Gillespie 5–88, Fleming 4–45) lost to Australia 240 & 64–3 by seven wickets

I took some time to speak to the batsmen still 'alive' before play. There was no point in lecturing them about how to go about things; that was up to them. All I could do was encourage them, and let them know they should sell their wicket dearly. It was the type of pitch where you were never really in on, so if we could get a lead then anything was possible.

Unfortunately, that didn't include miracles. Early on, Ramps and Hicky continued their good work of the previous night, but runs were much harder to come by against an Aussie side focused and knowing that just one wicket would expose our tail.

Hicky had some luck, top-edging a hook from McGrath fine for four, but the pair saw off the opening onslaught from him, only for Gillespie to gain revenge for his mauling the night before. Third ball, he found a good line just outside off-stump and Ponting at third slip did the rest, making a fast, head-high catch offered by Hicky look easy.

Corky came in and continued to give Ramps support, even surviving after hooking Fleming into his eye between the peak and grille of his helmet.

The end came with real speed thanks to Gillespie, who blew the tail away with sheer pace. His figures of five for 88 looked strange from just 15.2 overs, but they looked a damn sight better than nine overs for 69 at the start of play.

There was no way I or anyone else could have a go at the tail for folding so quickly, after all we'd picked seven batsmen and if they couldn't do the job then it was unfair to expect the others to do it instead. But there was a bit of a heated debate in the dressing room towards the end of our innings surrounding Ramps' tactics.

Gillespie was flying in and had taken three wickets in his previous over to leave Ramps alone with Al. Ramps began the over on strike and, with the field spread, pushed the ball into the covers, setting off immediately.

Very quickly it was obvious they couldn't get back for two, and it left Al exposed to the strike.

'That's pisshole,' said Goochie, who felt that even though the situation was hopeless, Ramps should have done more to protect the number eleven.

I could see what Ramps was trying to do, and when Goochie and I chatted it through with him later he genuinely reckoned there was two there when he set off. But there wasn't, and the whole thing went pear-shaped next ball when Al, expecting a bouncer, was stuffed by an outlandish slower ball.

That was lunch, with our last four wickets falling in six Gillespie balls for just one run. They wanted just 64 to win, and had eight sessions to get them.

Deep down I knew we needed something out of the ordinary to win, to say the least. I think we all did, but we still had to make them work for every run.

'We're up against it,' I said before we went out, 'But I don't want to see anyone giving up, and if worst comes to worst let's at least make sure we ruin a few averages.'

We did just that, even though yet another catch went down as Al dropped Slater off his own bowling, and the way we made them fight told me another 100 runs would have made us at least evens to pull off a win.

I opened up with Al this time ahead of Corky, who was on the field, but not feeling great after his blow to the head. I'd stuck with Corky through the series so far as I reckoned the new ball was his best chance to get some swing. But Al's efforts so far had taken him ahead, and he responded by bowling well again.

That was small consolation though. The fact that we were at least that number of runs light at the end was the fault of the batsmen, no one else, and I said so to the press. Maybe I was a bit over the top in suggesting it was one of our worst batting performances in my career, but I still felt it was time for a few home truths.

After a quick drink with the Aussies in their dressing room – something we really felt we had to do whether we wanted to or not – that theme was continued in our team meeting that evening back at the hotel.

The meeting would have taken place anyway as our mid-match chat, but given there was no match left to chat about, it seemed as good a time as any to chew the fat.

First things first. We decided the next two days would be for resting, not naughty boy nets. They would serve no purpose, especially after back-to-back Tests, and by having a break before the next match, I hoped it would mean everyone came back fresh for our next outing, against Victoria in Melbourne.

I tried to look on the bright side of what was a crushing loss. 'Right,' I said. 'Let's be clear on this. Yes, we are 1–0 down, but we were in this position against South Africa last summer. We came back to win then and we can do it again now.'

Bumble agreed, but was keen to see players stand up and be counted a hell of a lot more, and I couldn't argue with that.

'People have got to be honest with themselves and ask if they are doing enough when it really counts. Everyone has got to put even more into the team from now on, and we *must*, repeat *must*, build partnerships when batting or bowling,' he said.

The one good thing about the early finish was that it gave me a chance to spend some time with my parents. I hadn't seen them socially since they arrived before Brisbane, so we went out for a family meal at Coco's in South Perth, a favourite haunt of mine.

The chat strayed onto cricket, but it was more about life back home, including a progress report on how Judy was coping without Butch as she neared the end of her pregnancy. It was just what I needed to bring some sense of reality back after a shattering three days. Defeat was tough to take, but it was a game of cricket, not life and death.

Tuesday 1 December

I think everyone was left with a strange, empty feeling, as we should have been in the middle of a Test; instead, everyone was left wondering what to do with themselves.

I thought the time off was good for two reasons. First, it gave the squad the chance of a break after a hectic start to the tour that had seen us have just one day off since we arrived. And second, I wanted everyone to use the time to think where we went wrong and how we could improve. In fact, I told them so at the team meeting the previous night. If we could come up with one idea about how we could do better next time, then the period of contemplation would be worthwhile.

The players used their free time in different ways. Some had a lie-in; others played golf, while some just took advantage of the unexpected free time to do some Christmas shopping. Certainly everyone was flat, but that was a relief given that we'd just lost a Test.

Thorpe was one of the players who spent the day relaxing at the hotel, and before I went to lunch, I took the chance to have a word with him. He'd had some treatment from a specialist during the Test, and although he still said he felt stiff, he was hopeful of being back sooner rather than later.

I said I wanted him back quickly too, but he had to prove his fitness first. 'You broke down on us at Old Trafford last summer and we can't afford for you to do that again. In order to play in Adelaide, you'll have to play in Melbourne against Victoria first.'

Thorpey agreed, but before he could do that he had to prove he was fit enough to be picked in the first place. That test would begin tomorrow in a net session at the WACA and continue after another air trip across the continent, the start of his latest problems in the first place.

On the face of it, an optimistic chat, but I think we both knew in the long-term things were more hopeless than hopeful. Even if we got him back on the field for the remaining Tests, it would be hard to make a man with a bad back hop around the continent in a plane through the one-day series to follow and expect him to be fit for each match.

And if he wasn't fit then, it would be a tough call to pick him in the final World Cup squad, to be named at the end of March. There was always a Sharjah tournament in April for him to prove his fitness after that, but with his wife Nicky expecting their second child at about that time, I didn't hold out much hope of him wanting to go there.

All in all, it was difficult to see Chalks playing much part in the rest of the winter, but all we could do was take one step at a time, beginning with that first net session back at the WACA.

I went to Cottesloe Beach Café for lunch with some friends from M-G, but it wasn't the pleasant day I'd hoped for. The weather matched my feelings – it was overcast and drizzly – but at least I got away from the hotel; if I'd stayed there I would have just moped around feeling sorry for myself.

A low-key day for everyone ended with dinner with my parents and more M-G friends. A relaxing evening, but a flat day all round.

Licking our Wounds

Wednesday 2 December

Anyone wondering how dedicated this bunch of players is should have been at the WACA this morning. Despite the fact it was a day off, seven of us – me, Chalky, Gus, Tudes, Ramps, Suchy and Nass – turned up for a session in the nets, along with Bumble and Fizz.

Most of the attention, at least at first, focused on Graham Thorpe. It was Chalks' first workout since two days before the Test, and he batted for twenty minutes against Gus and Suchy, as well as being put through his paces by Riddler.

He seemed to come through okay, which was a relief to everyone, and providing he suffers no reaction to the trip to Melbourne tomorrow, he'll have another workout at the MCG before we see if he's fit enough to play against Victoria.

The media were there in force to see his net session, but once they saw he was fit, they switched tack to another story that they found far more interesting, the appearance of dad, who watched me bat.

In order for us to be competitive, I know my batting has to fire, but so far I just haven't hit top-form, and I'm at a loss to explain why. The odd small thing might be wrong, like my head being in slightly the wrong position, but I don't think it's anything major.

No offence to Bumble, our coach, but dad knows my game inside out, so I asked him to come along and see if I was doing anything wrong. He watched me have a net, then fed the bowling machine for 20 minutes.

At the end of the session, he gave me the thumbs-up, with one exception. He said: 'I think the only thing wrong with the way you're playing is that you're getting out!' At least I know the problem now, so I can try and put it right.

Of course, afterwards the hacks were pestering us for a quote about the session, but we're both too wise to say too much in that sort of situation. A quote like 'I've got this or that wrong with my game' would be just what Mark Taylor would want to read, so I restricted it to simply saying how much dad knew about my game and what a good net it had been.

Thursday 3 December and Friday 4 December

Our latest internal flight, to Melbourne, went pretty uneventfully, and I managed to sleep through most of it. The Melbourne hotel where we are staying is pretty swish and all rooms are suites with washing machines and dish-washers (not that I'll be using either piece of equipment). But for those of us with families arriving here for Christmas, it might not be the best spot. The pool is tiny, and it is indoors, so there is nowhere for people to sit outside and get some much-needed sun. I might need to look around for alternative places to relax or else the credit card might take a bit of a hammering from eight days of Christmas shopping by Lynn when she gets here!

The chance of a decent net session was ruined by some typically unpredictable Melbourne weather. It rained just after we got to the MCG, but the groundstaff were caught unawares and the nets were left uncovered.

There were still some indoor nets to be had, but they were far from ideal, as were the dressing rooms, which are far too small for a touring team with 18 large cricket cases. At least the nets saw a return to form for my personal thrower, Wayne Morton, who has now recovered enough from his dislocated shoulder to serve up his usual array of half-volleys, long hops and good length balls – all to order.

After all that, it was back to the serious business of picking the side for the match. It was a tough one, as originally I wanted to play just as a batsman to give Warren Hegg an outing, but that was shelved when almost all the batsmen either wanted or needed to play. That included Thorpey, who seemed okay, but needs another fitness test in the morning after the rain stopped him having a net. We rested Butch, a move I later found out surprised the press, who thought he needed time in the middle after two failures in Perth. But we reckoned he would be able to use the time to net instead, and as that had done him no harm before Brisbane, we hoped for the same this time too.

The bowling choices were easier as we rested Tudes, Gough, Corky and Mullally after Perth so in came Fraser and Headley. Also included was Ben Hollioake, for his first four-day match of the tour after recovering from the groin injury he picked up back in November.

It's going to be a big game for 'Pelly'. He's come here without much form last season because we backed his ability to rise to the occasion, but there comes a time when potential has to stop and performance start, and the hope is that will be sooner rather than later. He has all the attributes to become a top-class cricketer: he is a clean striker of the ball, can bowl a seriously quick ball and is brilliant in the field. But he needs to start producing that regularly, especially for England, as we desperately need someone to fill a hole at number seven.

The toughest call of all was the spin option, but we went for Crofty. That was partly because we need him to bat because runs from the lower order are looking more and more important, and partly because we know we can call Suchy into a Test whether he's played or not as he's such a good trainer.

It was tough on Such and Hegg, as they will now have played just one four-day match between them in the trip. But that is the nature of modern touring, and thankfully they are two great tourists who will still knuckle down to help everyone else.

The team meeting was quite short, stressing the need to get back on the winning trail. We have a good chance to do that because the Vics have picked a pretty inexperienced side, without seven regulars, including captain Shane Warne, Matty Elliott, Paul Reiffel and Damien Fleming. The press are saying they are snubbing us by putting out a below-strength side but we can't really complain as counties back home do it all the time against touring sides. It's just up to us to go out and win, then get on our high horse afterwards.

The evening ended with a call to Grav, alongside Bumble and Goochie to try and finalise the one-day squad. Much as we'd like Thorpe to play, I think we all doubt whether he'll still be here by then. We decided Goochie should speak to him on Sunday night to let him know how important it is he plays in Sharjah, if not the Carlton and United Series, in order to prove his fitness for the World Cup. We can't afford to lose a key player on the eve of a big game next summer.

Saturday 5 December

I think it was Colin Cowdrey who used to say no matter how out of touch you feel, it's a different, much easier game after just 30 minutes at the wicket. I don't know about that, but I can vouch for the fact that it's certainly true after you've batted for four hours.

By the time I ran myself out, foolishly going for a second run to backward square leg just as I thought I could have batted forever, I felt like a weight had been lifted from my shoulders. I had 126 under my belt, and by the end I was timing the ball as consistently well as I had at Lilac Hill in the opening match of the trip.

I suppose I owe opposition captain Brad Hodge a drink for that one. He won the toss on what looked like a pretty good pitch, but armed with an inexperienced line-up, he opted to field first when I called wrongly for the third match in a row.

It was a cold, overcast morning, but already I was feeling pretty good. We'd gone down to the ground especially early to make full use of the nets after missing out yesterday and to allow for an early start. That early start, with 30 minutes extra time, applies to each of the first three days so we can fly to Adelaide on the last night of the match before the next Test. I had a really good ten-minute hit before play, as well as some throw-downs from Fizz and a solid keeping workout from PB. It might seem like a lot to cram in before a full day of cricket, but I, along with the rest of the lads, must feel happy about preparation before we start.

Down to come in at four, I got to the middle earlier than I'd have hoped after JC and Nass fell in the first 65 minutes. The pitch was a typical pre-Christmas MCG strip, slow and low, so that coupled with my lack of time in the middle made timing the ball tricky to start with.

The Vics attack held no real terrors either, but that wasn't ideal as they lacked the pace to make stroke-playing easy. So it was a case of grafting for runs early on, and that hardly made for riveting cricket for the few people who'd bothered to get lost in the massive stadium.

Ath was struggling for his timing too, but he looked set to post his first first-class fifty of the tour when he drove at a wide half-volley only to be snapped up in the gully. That left us in some trouble after lunch at 94 for three, but it was reassuring to see Chalks striding to the crease at that stage.

Despite his obvious quality as a player, he is one of those guys who needs to feel needed, so I was glad I was in the middle for his return, and I tried to build him up with a few words of encouragement every so often.

Having come through a fitness test in the morning, he looked pretty free at the crease with no obvious signs of discomfort, but the long innings he needed didn't arrive as he drove at the off-spin of Davison and was given out caught behind for 19. He hit the ground hard as he played the shot, but the umpire also thought he nicked it, so that was that.

I wish I could say that after reaching fifty I put my foot on the gas and cruised to a century in rapid time, but that just wasn't the case. In fact, my second fifty took 17 balls longer than the first one and included just four boundaries. But as I cracked Davison for four to reach three figures, that was the last thing on my mind. It was more a case of 'forget the quality, feel the size' as I savoured only my second first-class hundred of the calendar year after the 164 I made against South Africa at Old Trafford in July.

I only really opened out after getting past the hundred, and added 24 in just 18 balls before departing. Maybe I was greedy, but I suddenly felt so good I wanted to face every ball, and came back for a second only to find myself six inches out on the verdict of the third umpire.

Hicky and Ramps ended the day in control, and as the century-maker I had to face the press. Normally as captain I only speak to them before and after the match to allow me to concentrate on the game itself, but this was a good news story so I was more than willing to make an exception.

Sunday 6 December

There were some good aspects to our play today, but twice we failed to nail down the opposition, and ended the day frustrated by the inexperienced home side.

First up, Hicky and Ramps added almost 50 in the first hour of the day and at 356 for five we were in total command. But then, inexplicably, we lost our way and with it the last five wickets for just 17 runs in 45 minutes. I was especially disappointed for Pelly, who had waited the whole tour for a first-class innings, only to play across one and lose out on a marginal lbw decision.

Once Hicky, Ramps and Pelly had gone, there was no point in hanging about just prodding and poking as we needed to be bowling to take the game forward. Crofty couldn't understand that though, as he mucked about for nought not out in half and hour, and he got some friendly stick afterwards. Gus took it to the other extreme though, slogging the ball straight up in the air 13 minutes before the interval, which meant we had to go and field for one over before lunch. No one was happy at that as it meant we missed out on a major 'pig-out' session in the players' dining room as the MCG has easily the best food at an Australian Test ground. Pasta, chicken, fish, wedges – and jelly snakes if you're feeling peckish during the day!

We started well in the field with Dean Headley flying in and generating real pace and movement. Some critics think it's impossible to captain and keep wicket but in situations like this it is a real bonus. I could see exactly how all the bowlers were performing, and Headless was streets ahead of Gus who continued to labour.

I think Gus is a bit resentful at having to prove himself here after the year he's had, and it's true he's been a real rock for us. But at the moment he's lacking some nip and doesn't really look like getting anyone out. I could see that better than anyone from behind the stumps, especially comparing him to Deano.

We reduced them to 43 for four, with Deano even getting in on the act with a direct hit from mid-on to effect a run-out, but once the ball went soft, we lacked a little bit of something special to get them out on such a slow surface. We stuck to the task, but towards the end of the day we looked pretty ineffective.

Afterwards, the manager had more serious business to attend to, a chat with Thorpey about his immediate future. He held a blinding catch at first slip during the day off Deano which saw him dive low and to his right so all looked fine from that point of view, and he was in good, chatty form next to me all afternoon. But Goochie stressed he needed to play in the one-dayers here or in Sharjah to stand any chance of playing in the World Cup. We need the little man, but he has to prove his fitness first, especially as we'll name our one-day party for the series here in the next week or two.

Monday 7 December

After a sluggish first session when we failed to take a wicket and dropped a couple of chances, the rest of the day went well, bowling the Vics out in the hour after lunch, then batting positively. But all that was overshadowed by a recurrence of Thorpey's back trouble, and after a management meeting following play, we decided he had to go home.

Sending any player home is never easy, especially as an Ashes tour is the highlight of a player's career. But all the same, it's pointless hanging on to someone when they are just not fit. There's no way we could pick him for any match in this condition because there would be no guarantee he would get through without breaking down again.

I guessed all was not well even before matters came to a head when he retired hurt after batting for forty minutes in our second innings. Towards the end of the Vics' first effort, he dived to stop a ball at backward point with all the flexibility of a falling tree. He didn't say anything, but Nass and I looked at each other, and I could tell we were both thinking the same thing.

I dropped down the order to give him the chance of a long knock at number four when we batted again with a lead of 73, but even before he went out he was flexing his back as if it was stiff. Then, once in the middle, he began to get even more rigid rather than loosen up.

Thorpey called for new gloves, but that was his idea of getting a message to Fizz, and when Goughie, who was acting as twelfth man, got back to the dressing room he said: 'Thorpey's struggling, I think he'll be off at drinks.'

That was five minutes away, and when Morton went to meet him at the break, they had a quick chat before calling it a day. Off he walked, and that was that.

I didn't get the chance to talk with him then as I was next in, but we had a quick chat after play and I think we both knew it was hopeless. Goochie, Nass, Bumble, Fizz and myself then discussed things back at the hotel and we all had to hold our hands up and admit the gamble to pick Thorpe for the tour had failed. Medically he had been fit, but there was no way we knew how he would stand up to the play-pack-travel routine of cricket again after surgery and, apart from one match for Surrey at the end of the season, a three month lay-off.

In terms of playing ability, and his record against the Aussies, he had to be here. But there was no point keeping him with us in this condition in the hope we might be able to patch him up to play at some point down the line. That would be a short-term solution to the benefit of no one in the long term, not the player, his county nor his country.

Thorpey was called up to Goochie's room and we broke the news to him. He obviously guessed it was coming, but was still pretty upset. What can you say to someone at a time like that? Not much really, but he knew it was for the best, and after about ten minutes, once it had sunk in, he managed a smile.

By this stage it was 8 o'clock and Murgers and Goochie decided not to make any announcement to the press that night. All we'd told them at the ground was that we would be considering the situation over the next 24 hours. Making an announcement now would merely cause a media circus around the hotel and as it was getting late that didn't seem too clever. Instead, it was decided to put the arrangements for his return in place then make the announcement at the ground after lunch, with Chalks, Fizz and Goochie all facing the press to let them know what had happened.

All this tended to overshadow the rest of the day, which saw Suchy, Tudes and Heggy go off to get some practice in a club game and Ramps cop a mouthful from the Vics' opening bowler, Ashley Gilbert.

The non-playing trio joined Chris Schofield, the Lancashire leg-spinner who's playing club cricket here and spending his spare time with us, in a match to get rid of the cobwebs, but it had mixed results. Tudes bowled a rapid spell but didn't take a wicket, Suchy got clobbered for a couple of sixes, had a long bowl and then hit former Kiwi captain Jeremy Coney for a six himself, and Heggy managed to get out caught at cover first ball. At least they got some cricket.

Gilbert, meanwhile, lost his cool after getting rid of Ramps as we looked for quick runs ahead of an overnight declaration. Both Ramps and I had hit him for boundaries before Ramps top-edged a pull to be caught at mid-wicket. As the ball fell into the fielder's hands, Gilbert turned to Ramps and said: 'F*** off. Go on, f*** off.'

It all seemed a bit rich, especially as Gilbert is making his first-class debut and is hardly in Ramps' league as a player. Ramps managed to maintain his cool and walked off without responding, but I know he was upset the umpires said nothing. I'm all for playing it hard with a bit of chat in the middle, but that was out of order.

It was mum's birthday today but she's flown home to be with Judy in the final stages of her pregnancy. I'm relying on Lynn to make sure there are some flowers and a card waiting for her when she gets home.

Tuesday 8 December

Despite our best efforts, the game drifted to a draw, but not without some 'handbags at ten paces' from those two good friends Ramps and Gilbert just before the end.

We'd declared overnight in an effort to push for the win, and with eight wickets down in the last couple of overs we fancied our chances. Deano was bowling to Gilbert, and given his performance the previous evening, he could hardly have been surprised to get a lifter first up.

Gilbert swayed out the line of it, and Deano was just turning at the end of his follow-through when he thought he heard our friendly batsman say something.

He didn't say a word, but Deano turned back and said: 'What did you say?' And that was all that was needed for Ramps to fly in from cover point and get involved.

He and Gilbert stood at the crease toe-to-toe and it looked pretty funny as they exchanged expletives, Ramps at 5ft 7in and Gilbert at least a foot taller. The umpires were just getting interested too when I trotted up to get Ramps back to cover, and that was that.

Just to add to the pantomime, we set a couple of short legs in an attempt to intimidate Gilbert, but the pitch was slow, the ball was old, and Deano had bowled his heart out so they hung on for a draw.

I had to defuse the issue with the press afterwards, but still a few hacks hung round outside the dressing room hoping for a hint of scandal after comments by former Australian batsman Dean Jones. He'd gone to the press area and claimed something racist had been said, despite the fact that nothing of the sort was uttered. Where he got his information from, I don't know. It was just a case of a few choice expletives, but Jones' claim got everyone going.

It wasn't the first time he'd caused trouble during the match either. On the first day he'd arrived just before the start of play and then had a go at us on television when the non-players did some sprint work with Riddler on the edge of the field. Far better we work on our catching as we've dropped so many chances in the series already was the tone of his criticism. As Bumble was quick to point out to the producers of the television coverage when he heard the criticism: 'If Jones had arrived at 8.15, he would have seen us doing a full-scale fielding work-out before play, as we do every morning.'

I like Dean Jones, but maybe his comments were ill-timed and ill-advised to say the least. I'd never condone over-the-top aggression on the field, and Ramps was close to going too far in my book then, but at least it showed a sense that we are a team, with one player keen to look after the interests of another. That is the sort of side I'd like to promote.

The day still had loads of plusses, despite our failure to win. First there was the appearance of Abdul Qadir in the nets before play. He may be over 40 and just playing club cricket now, but he's still a master, and all the lads had some top-class practice against him.

Deano also bowled well again, and I think he will play now in the next Test depending on the pitch. The same can't be said for Crofty though, despite the fact he picked up three wickets, and six in the match. In the second innings he had one man out edging a cut and the other two caught on the boundary. He's not bowling people out, and it means Suchy must be in the frame if he's bowling anything like well in the nets.

With Chalks on his way home in the evening, we needed a substitute fielder and I was keen to get Chucky Hegg into the action behind the stumps. I wasn't injured so it needed a bit of persuading on my part to get the umpires to agree to it, although Hodge and Tony Crafter, the ACB's umpiring manager were happy to go along with things. As it turned out Chucky kept well too, with two catches and a stumping in a neat display.

Our flight to Adelaide wasn't until 8.25 pm, so we stayed at the ground after play for a meal, and Chalky, having faced the press for the last time, alongside Fizz and Goochie, said his goodbyes. There was also a small ceremony to perform as he handed over his role as official first slip to Ath – the Chairmanship of the Office. All it involved was a handshake and a speech, but it brought some humour to basically a sad time.

Shane Warne joined us during our meal. He'd been in the nets that afternoon and had spent some time at the ACB. Why that was only became apparent later when Murgers gave me a shout as we were boarding the plane. A story linking Warney and Mark Waugh to bookmakers in the sub-continent was about to break and he stressed we should avoid getting sucked into any controversy if asked about it. Warney said nothing during the meal and seemed quite relaxed. I wonder if he and Mark Waugh will feel the same in 24 hours?

Wednesday 9 December

The newspaper under my door this morning certainly made for interesting reading. Mark Waugh and Warney have been linked to a bookmaker, who gave them money in exchange for information on pitch and weather conditions. It all happened four years ago, but with an enquiry surrounding betting, bribery and match-fixing going on in Pakistan at the moment, this will only add fuel to the fire. For my part, having played against both men more times than I care to remember I can't believe they would ever be involved in match-fixing.

It certainly caused a fair bit of interest at practice today, with the England squad very much down the list of attractions. Top billing went to Waugh and Warne, who read prepared statements on the matter before handing over to the ACB's Chief Executive Malcolm Speed to handle an avalanche of questions.

After practice it was my turn to face the press, and it was the biggest gathering I'd ever seen, twice as many cameras and reporters as there were for the press conference to announce I was captain!

It was certainly fun and games early on as several reporters, including one woman from ABC TV, climbed into me on anything but the Test to be played in two days time. 'How can you be sure none of your team are involved too?'

She kept hammering on at me about betting, and I almost lost my cool with her. In the end Murgers, alongside me, said: 'Any questions about *the cricket*?'

When no one said anything at first, we got up to leave, but then someone at the back piped up: 'What do you think about the pitch?', and the whole thing assumed a bit of normality.

To the best of my knowledge, the England dressing room is free from the sort of stuff that seems to have affected the Aussies. And I suppose one of the reasons for that is the fact we've spent so little time in the Indian sub-continent, where most of this seems to be happening, over the past few years. We haven't toured India or Sri Lanka since 1993, and we were hammered by both of them, and we haven't had a Test tour of Pakistan since 1987. And as for Sharjah, England has toured there just once in my whole international career.

Yes, there is some interest in betting, and a few of the lads had a flutter on the Melbourne Cup. One spread betting company even sent us – along with all the press boys – its odds for the series when we were in Adelaide last time, which caused a bit of fun in the dressing room.

But it's fair to say that a flutter on the horses here and there is a world away from accepting money from bookies for information, and I'm as sure as I can be that none of our boys have done that.

Back to the more important matter of the Test we needed to win, and the pitch had been flooded first thing and was too wet to walk on.

But that was because it was a roasting hot day, with another one to follow before the Test, and the groundsman is confident it will dry in time. If the pitch does dry properly but the weather stays hot, it could be a good time to win my first toss of the series as it might crumble a bit towards the end of the match.

Despite the hot weather, Corky has 'flu and although he warmed up, that just about finished him off judging by the way he started coughing afterwards. He's ruled himself out of contention, although with Deano bowling well, it might have saved us an awkward selection poser.

The nets didn't go all that well despite the fine weather. Everyone seemed off colour, and that didn't impress me one bit as I told the lads afterwards.

'Remember, we're 1–0 down in the series, not 1-0 up, and if we're going to turn it around we'll need to show a bit more commitment than that,' I raged.

'You know what Bumble says,' I added. ' 'Practice hard and win easy'. Well, I didn't see too much of that attitude today. Let's make sure when we get down here tomorrow you're up for it, because you can be sure the Aussies will be, come the start of the Test.'

Maybe it was a tough ask for everyone to practice straight after a four-day game and an evening flight, and in that heat too. But we must be up for it, or else there's no point in being here.

Thursday 10 December

Thankfully, my little chat with the troops after yesterday's session had the desired result, and despite another roasting hot day with the temperature touching 40 degrees, everyone was full on at nets ahead of what will be the biggest Test of most of our careers. Win, and The Ashes could be coming home; lose, and we can only draw the series.

I had a great net first up, very happy with the way I was striking the ball and everything felt right. It was good to have dad there too, and he was able to confirm I was looking okay.

The media were at the ground in force again today and once more they were looking for stuff on the bookmaking saga. The papers were full of the story and, perhaps not surprisingly Warney and Mark Waugh didn't get a very good press out of the whole thing. Waugh was followed from pillar to post during the Aussies' session, and I'll be surprised if this whole business doesn't affect him.

The pitch had dried out a hell of a lot from our inspection yesterday, and it looked fairly flat now, although there were some bare patches here and there. With that and the hot weather forecast for the first day, it must be a good toss to win as it should spin more and more as the match goes on.

After a good lunch of pasta, and lots of it with Tudes, Ramps and Chucky, it was off to the longest and toughest selection meeting I've ever attended. It took almost 90 minutes, and when you consider we're only picking from 17, that is a long meeting.

There was so much for Nass, Bumble, Goochie and me to discuss. Which spinner should we play? Should Tudor play again after impressing in Perth? Should Fraser or Headley play? Six or seven batsmen?

At the end of all that, there were bound to be some disappointed players. We went for seven batsmen because to win Tests, or at least compete in them, you need a big first innings score. We hadn't got a really big one in the two Tests so far, and as the number seven position has produced so little when we've played an all-rounder there, it seemed more sensible to go for a specialist instead.

That meant we would go in with four bowlers plus Ramprakash and Hick, a tough call given the very hot weather expected on the first day. But if we were going to do that we needed our most reliable men and the bowlers we thought most likely to get us 20 wickets.

Mullally and Gough picked themselves, but it was then down to a choice between Such or Croft, and Fraser or Headley, as Cork was unfit. Suchy had impressed everyone with his attitude and he's been bowling particularly well in the nets despite his limited opportunities. My look at the pitch in the morning convinced me we needed a spinner, and as Crofty had struggled to bowl players out against Victoria I was keen on Suchy. In fact, I told him he was in the frame during nets and made a point of keeping to both him and Crofty during the session. So, Suchy got the nod.

The decision to leave out Gus was the hardest one I've ever had to make as a captain. He had done so much for us this year and you knew you would get one hundred percent from him no matter what. But the fact remained he has struggling, while Deano charged in with real pace and rhythm on a slow MCG track and really held his hand up. Against Deano was the fact that he didn't always keep it as tight as Gus, but with Al capable of doing that job, we went for the bowler that on current form was more likely to bowl the Aussies out. It was a close call.

Once we'd finished that meeting, it was time to tell the squad, and I wondered what they thought of the side. It had been tough, but as I stressed to everyone after I'd read out the eleven names: 'This is our chance. They may be affected by the business with the bookie and if we can win here, The Ashes could be coming home. It's up to us lads. Let's do it.'

Wayne Morton stressed, as he had in Cairns, the need to keep fluid levels really high in the hot weather, although thankfully a cool change was promised for the second day. Then, as the meeting broke up, it was up to me to speak to those not playing on a one-to-one basis.

Gus was quiet but that left me in little doubt he was really pissed off. Crofty was also very quiet, but I hope both of them will take the decision in the right way and battle to get back for the next Test. That sort of competition for places is what can really lift us as a side.

Official duties over, I watched a few videos of my batting against Victoria, had a meal – with plenty of water – and headed for bed.

Australia v England, Third Test, Adelaide, 11–15 December, 1998

Friday 11 December, Third Test, Day 1
Australia 266–4 (Langer not out 108, Taylor 59, S Waugh 59)

Almost ten years after my Test debut, and there's still a wonderful mix of excitement and nerves when I wake up for the first morning of a match, and today was no exception. I woke a little earlier than normal, maybe understandably given the importance of this Test, but I still slept well.

In addition to the normal food and drink at breakfast, there were also huge glasses of water that we were all basically ordered to drink by Dean Riddle and Wayne Morton. The temperature outside was as hot as the forecasters predicted and although it wasn't as humid as Cairns, it was still roasting. I didn't need reminding it was a good toss to win.

The pre-match warm-ups and net practice were intense without being too taxing, as everyone appreciated the need to conserve some energy. As we jogged around the outfield though, it was unusual to see some carol singers serenading the members sat in front of the dressing rooms with 'White Christmas'. I'm all for getting into the festive spirit but that was ridiculous!

The ground itself looked in great shape. All the building work they've done since I first played a Test there in 1991 has been in keeping with the original character of the place, with the Bradman Stand at the City End a great looking building. Floodlights are now in place, although apparently they are having a few problems with them as they are meant to be retractable, and we're set to play under lights here when we come back in late January.

The only slight blot on the place is the positioning of a couple of temporary uncovered seating areas in front of the Victor Richardson Gates opposite the dressing rooms. They look ugly, and in this heat they would be no fun at all to sit in all day.

I think Mark Taylor and I both thought the pitch would turn later on, partly because of the heat, and partly because of some bare patches on the surface. It certainly had a bearing on both our final selections with our inclusion of Suchy, and their decision to make Gillespie twelfth man on his home ground, with Miller and MacGill both playing.

It meant that the toss was vital, but once again I was out of luck and lost it with a call of heads for the fourth Test in a row. There was little of the moisture of the previous two days in the pitch now, but we still had to make the new ball count if we were to avoid a really tough day at the office.

Once again though, we dropped catches. Hicky offended first, in just the third over, when he couldn't quite cling on to a low edge from Taylor off, you've guessed it, Goughie. The poor sod keeps running in and getting the edges, but we just can't hold them.

Slater got a life too when Ramps, like Hicky another normally safe pair of hands, totally misjudged a back foot forcing shot to cover point off Dean Headley. Thankfully though, that wasn't too costly as he got his man with a lovely leg-cutter four balls later.

The number of catches we've shelled on the tour has been amazing. When you think of some of the fielders we have in our side, players like Hick, Hussain and Ramprakash for example, you'd think we'd never miss a thing. But we have, and even I've been a culprit with the gloves on. It's not as if we don't practice enough. When we get to the ground, we work on high catches, reflex catches, running catches, flat-hit catches and slip catches, and Hegg and I do a fair amount of glove work too. But right from the time we played in Perth at the start of the tour, we've not clicked, and I wish I knew why.

We've even done work catching tennis balls to help ensure our hands give with the ball; if you try to catch a tennis ball with rigid hands, it will usually bounce out. But still they've gone down, and I reckon that's been a major factor in our failure to hold the Aussies so far on the tour.

Everyone knows it's an area we have to improve in, but unfortunately that also means players start to get up tight about it. If you're worried you'll drop the ball if it comes to you, you're less likely to catch it. Just look at the Aussies: they expect to catch everything, and usually they do. In fact, I can't think of a chance they've missed in the series.

The Aussies don't do anything radically different to us; after all there are only so many ways you can practise catching a cricket ball. What we need is a day or an innings where we catch everything: the simple ones, the half-chances, and the diving ones. Then we'll be right.

It was hot work out there, especially with catches going down, but we bowled with discipline for the most part, although Deano was expensive early on. We guessed he might be, and Bumble has spoken to him about the need to string some maidens together. On a flat pitch, if nothing is happening, that is the way to build pressure and get to a batsman. Deano's first ten overs either side of lunch cost 50, but thankfully Al, Goughie and Suchy all hit a groove and we kept them in check.

Suchy did especially well, just as I thought he would. It was his first Test bowl since July 1994, and even an experienced county pro like him will get nervous. But he bowled 18 overs in a spell either side of tea for just 43 runs, and the wickets of Taylor, caught at slip – hooray! – and Mark Waugh to help keep a lid on things.

Waugh got a very mixed reception from the crowd after all the bookies business of the past few days. I expected him to cop the boos and the flak he got from the Barmy Army up on the Hill below the scoreboard, and was quite pleased about it as I hoped it might get to him.

But what I hadn't expected was the reception he got from the members' area. Some clapped him to the crease, as they would any new batsman, but others just sat there with their arms folded, and some even booed him. That would have got to him, I'm sure, because he must have fond memories of this ground having smashed us for a Test hundred on debut here in 1991.

Even though I say so myself, I was pleased with the way I responded to his arrival. In that heat he was the type of player who could really have given us the run-around, but I got Goughie back into the attack straight away, and he and Suchy just strangled him.

Goughie gave him a cracking bouncer first up which really flew past his left shoulder, and although it was Suchy who eventually got him, miscuing a drive to be caught and bowled for just seven in 35 minutes, Goughie's efforts were also vital. He kept it tight and the pressure eventually told. It was just as Bumble had said after Perth: bowlers must work in partnerships, just like batsmen.

That was our last success for some time though. Langer played as well as I've ever seen him, compact in defence and always looking to work the ball around or capitalise on anything short. And with Steve Waugh growing in confidence after a shaky start against Suchy, it was difficult to see where our next wicket was coming from.

Suchy began cramping pretty badly after tea. That was no real surprise as it was his first bowl in first-class cricket since 9 November, but he still kept going, helped by the fact we had two drinks breaks every session, and a regular flow of water to fine leg from Tudes, the twelfth man.

Into the last hour and the new ball became due, but I was in two minds whether to take it. We were keeping things relatively tight with the old one, and I didn't want to waste it if the bowlers felt too tired to give it one last big effort before stumps.

Typical Goughie though, he was keen to get his hands on it, even after 18 overs, and he convinced me to give it a go. He didn't let me down either, forcing Steve Waugh first to inside edge just past me, and then getting the edge to second slip.

It was a carbon copy of the delivery he found for him on the first evening in Brisbane: around off-stump, bringing Waugh forward, and finding a fast, low nick. But unlike in Brisbane, when Nass shelled the chance, Hicky held on. It was a great catch, and an object lesson in what slip catching is all about. He'd stood there all day to the seamers with just one dropped chance to show for his efforts. But he kept his concentration, and gave Goughie some reward at last. It certainly left us in reasonable spirits at the end of the day. We all trooped off to be greeted by Fizz, Riddler and the non-players who handed us drink after drink to keep up our fluid levels after one of the most unpleasant days in the field in a Test I could remember since playing in Colombo in 1993.

We didn't hang around either. It was straight back to the hotel and I joined the bowlers in a pool session with Riddler. We all cramped up at some stage, Suchy quite badly, but the warm-down was vital and we all came out feeling much easier.

I then went for a massage and a long soak in the bath, before room service and an early night. It would have been pointless to trail around town looking for a restaurant when rest was far more important.

Saturday 12 December, Third Test, Day 2
Australia 391 (Langer not out 179, Headley 4–79); England 160–3 (Hussain not out 58, Ramprakash not out 45)

Everyone pitched up in pretty good shape after the toils of yesterday, and thankfully it was cooler, although a little bit humid thanks to some cloud cover.

I didn't mind that too much as I hoped it would help the ball, just four overs old, to swing. I stressed to the lads before we went out: 'They'll be looking to weather us early on and then try to make hay after lunch so let's hit them hard in the first session and get into them.'

And we did just that. In fact things couldn't have gone much better in the first two hours, as we nicked five out for less than 100 in the session with Langer the only long-term problem.

Goughie got Ponting early, playing a flashy drive at a good length ball in the corridor outside off-stump, then we gradually chipped away the remaining resistance. Suchy was again excellent, and Deano found some good rhythm from the City End, generating pace as he had in Melbourne last week.

On paper they have a pretty weak tail with Fleming, who's just a slogger really despite his fifty in Brisbane, coming in at eight. But the one thing they all do down the order is to try and sell their wickets dearly, especially with a front-line batsman at the other end, and we had to work for every success. I hope our lower order can learn from this.

That was pretty well illustrated in a frustrating 40-minute spell after lunch that turned it from being a good effort with the ball into an average one. They were 354 for nine when McGrath, who's got no real idea with the bat, joined Langer. They added 37 with Langer farming the strike well, but McGrath still faced 27 balls in the stand. We managed to drop Langer at square-leg to increase the frustration, although he clipped the ball like a shell through Ramps' hands, and it took one of my best catches to end the innings just as they looked like reaching 400.

Goughie pitched short outside off-stump to McGrath, who fenced at the ball but edged it down. I had to throw myself forward and to the right and just got my glove under a pretty rapid edge. I enjoyed that one.

I enjoyed their score of 391 a lot less. The pitch, which started dry, had begun to dust a little, and now resembled a late-third day surface rather than just after lunch on day two. So we needed to bat well to get up somewhere near them on first innings to stay in the match.

Taylor knew the score, and had Miller on as early as the twelfth over to try and exploit the rough outside Butch's off-stump. Butch had struggled against MacGill in Brisbane and he looked equally ill at ease here with men around the bat. Fifth ball he padded up to a ball that appeared to straighten a bit, but umpire Steve Davis thought it would still have hit off-stump.

Ath was looking good, as good as he had done all tour, and with Nass they played really well. They punished Fleming for sixteen in one over, and also kept rotating the strike against Miller, who was getting bounce as well as turn.

The pair had added 65 at almost four an over, when Ath went in controversial circumstances. MacGill had come on from the City End, and got a leg-break to bounce sharply as Ath came forward.

Instinctively, Ath dropped his hands as the ball bounced and tried to steer the ball down. The edge still came though and Taylor, who had stayed in the crouched position at slip threw the ball up. As soon as he did he said: 'I'm not sure it carried'. Healy was sure it had. Ath was equally sure it hadn't, and after the umpires conferred, they referred it to the television official.

By this stage, I'd moved from the viewing area square of the wicket on the members' side of the ground into the dressing room behind it to get ready to go in. That wasn't because I necessarily thought it was out, but because if it was I had to be ready to go in.

I made sure I had everything in place, and by this stage the replay was being shown. The viewing area has a television and I heard a few shouts saying: 'It's bounced'. But then, there was a huge roar and I knew I was in. I picked up my bat and gloves and off I went.

Ath was clearly seething as he passed me, but I had to put that behind me. I played the last two balls of the over from MacGill with the crowd still bubbling from the wicket – they'd seen the replays on the big screen, like the third umpire – then Nass got a single off the first ball of Miller's next over.

I took guard with men hemming me in on either side of the pitch, and a large patch of rough in front of me caused by Al's follow-through. I was confident I could cope with the situation, but Miller found the perfect first ball for me.

I do tend to push out at the ball early in my innings, and that can leave me vulnerable to the turning ball. Miller pitched it on a length just outside off-stump, it turned and bounced as I pushed forward, took a thick inside edge before hitting my pad and looping in a gentle arc to Slater at short leg. A simple catch, I was gone and from 83 for one and cruising, we were now 84 for three and on shaky ground.

I got back to the dressing room and there was no sign of Ath. He'd already gone to the nets to get out some of his frustration at getting out in the way he did. In fact, it was all happening in our little room.

Bob Cottam, a good friend of Ath, had gone to the Australian viewing area to have a go at them for even appealing for the catch, but as they were all out on the field their manager Steve Bernard, whom Bob has known for years, copped an earful instead.

Goochie, meanwhile, had said Ath was all ready to storm up to the third umpire's room when he came off and ask him what he thought he was doing. With the match referee John Reid's room next the umpire's area, that wouldn't have been the best thing to do, and thankfully Goochie persuaded him not to do that. Instead Goochie wanted to write a letter of complaint about the decision to Reid. That wouldn't change the decision, but it would register our unhappiness about how it was reached, so the manager and Murgers got together to draft something, which is worth repeating here.

Dear John Reid,

I am writing to you in my official capacity as Tour Manager of the England cricket team to express our disappointment at the decision concerning the dismissal of Michael Atherton.

In our opinion, it is clear from television replays that the ball bounced before being caught by Mark Taylor.

We must stress our complaint is not aimed at Mark Taylor, but instead at the third umpire, Mr Paul Angley, whose responsibility it is to come to the correct decision.

On this occasion, we feel he has made a glaring error. In our opinion, we believe the decision was made hastily, and he did not allow himself the opportunity to view the incident from every possible angle or with the benefit of frame-by-frame replays.

The laws of the game state that any benefit of the doubt should go to the batsman. We would like to ask whether this took place on this occasion. Could Mr Angley be 100% sure his decision was correct in the short space of time that elapsed between the incident and the verdict he gave?

We are also given to understand this is Mr Angley's first Test match as a third official. Given his inexperience, should he not have deliberated longer before arriving at a decision?

We believe this grave error of judgement could affect the outcome of this Test match as the incident took place when we were building a solid second wicket partnership in response to Australia's total.

I respect your position in this matter and look forward to your earliest response.

Signed
Graham Gooch
Tour Manager, England Cricket Team

Goochie took the letter up to Reid just before the close, and he read it and said he would forward it to the ICC along with his match report and those of both captains. I have to fill in a form at the end of every Test commenting on the performances of the officials, and the comments I make, along with those of my opposite number and the match referee are taken on board by the ICC when they confirm the international panel.

Our letter wasn't going to bring Athers back, but it did make some key points about the role of the television umpire, and that had to be useful with the ICC meeting set for Christchurch next month. We could have left it until my report, but Goochie felt the issue was so important, it needed to be dealt with straight away.

While all this was going on, Nass and Ramps managed to put everything else out of their minds and play really positively up to the close, adding 76 in just 22 overs. Ramps never missed a chance to score, and after the passive way he'd played in the first two Tests, his effort was a revelation.

At the close, Goochie and I called everyone into the dressing room for a quick chat. Goochie said: 'Just to let you know, we've sent a letter of complaint about Ath's decision to the match referee. That is the way we are handling the situation, and no one else should pass comment on the matter. If you do you'll be in breech of the ICC's Code of Conduct, so just be aware of that, especially if any of you are doing columns with newspapers tonight.

'Anyway, what's done is done. Well played Ramps and Nass, that was top batting, and we're still in this game big-time. It's up to us to get up to and past their score tomorrow and then we can put them under some pressure.

'Well done today lads, and let's keep it going.'

We didn't hang about at the ground, and I once again headed straight back to the hotel for another early night and some relaxation. Alone, I could reflect on a day that had gone okay for the team, but I'd failed again. I needed runs in the second innings for myself as much as the team.

Sunday 13 December, Third Test, Day 3
Australia 391 & 150–1 (Slater not out 74); England 227 (Hussain not out 89, Ramprakash 61, MacGill 4–53)

We knew the first session would be crucial, and it was. We collapsed like a pack of cards, and by the end of the day we were staring right down the barrel. It's difficult to explain why things went so wrong. Ramprakash and Hussain started confidently with Ramps again playing much more positively than he had in Brisbane or Perth. Twice he swept Miller for six into the members, and although we weren't racing along, we still looked in control.

Then, all of a sudden it went wrong. Like I said, explanations are tough, but the appearance of McGrath was a huge factor. He is one of the key differences between the sides as he is a world-class performer. Whenever Taylor needs a wicket, he can throw the ball to him and there's a chance he'll get him one. I've got lots of very good performers at my disposal, but if we had McGrath as well as, say Goughie, who'd be in a lot of people's world XIs, we'd be a noticeably better side.

Despite the fact the new ball was only 12 overs away, Taylor brought him on after fifty minutes and he struck in his first over, with Ramps failing to get over a lifting ball on off-stump and steering it straight to second slip.

That brought in John Crawley, but apart from a glorious cover-drive off McGrath to take us past the follow-on, he never settled. We needed him and Nass to build another stand, but he played all round a quick ball from McGrath, and all of a sudden we were still almost 200 behind with our last two recognised batsmen at the crease.

Hicky began positively with two fours off MacGill, but then fell looking for a third, edging a drive at a well-flighted leg-break, and now our tail was exposed. Tail-enders will always struggle against wrist-spin, and Headley and Gough disappeared at the hands of MacGill as quickly as they arrived before Fleming cleaned up Mullally and Such in successive balls to complete our slide.

We lost seven for 40 in 14 overs, and it meant lunch was a very quiet affair. Nass had watched the whole thing from the other end, and felt desperate about not being able to farm the strike more, but with a collapse of that speed it was difficult enough for him to know what to do. And the Aussies were still trying to bowl him out as well so he had to think of survival too.

So, less than a day after we'd hauled ourselves off the ground having bowled Australia out once, we were back into the field again. It was much cooler now, and overcast, but the whole situation was just like Brisbane, with the Aussies batting again with time on their side and a huge lead. To make things worse, the pitch was really starting to wear now, and looked more like a fifth day surface than one after lunch on day three.

'All we can do is give it everything we've got,' I said. 'If we can get among them early on we're still in this game. We've got to aim to bowl them out.'

There was no lack of effort from the bowlers, but Slater and Taylor looked very comfortable as they built steadily on their lead of 164. Taylor fell in similar fashion to Butch, playing no stroke to an off-spinner, but that was our only success of the day.

Slater again cashed in, going for his strokes and hammering Ramps for a massive six. The straight boundaries at Adelaide are among the biggest in the world at around 100 yards, but Slater cleared it easily at the Cathedral End.

At the other end, Langer was happy to play a supporting role, although he had two lives by stumps. First he miscued a drive at Suchy but Butch couldn't latch onto a looping ball at mid-off, then Ramps induced a thick edge that I could only parry with my left glove. That was a tough one, but we just had to latch onto those sorts of nicks to stay in the game.

At the close the 'Go Aussie Go' anthem was blasted out over the loud speakers and appeared on the big screen, as it does at the end of every day's play. It's a video that lasts about two minutes and is full of images of Aussie cricketing heroes doing well. It's great marketing, but I think it grated on most of us as we walked off, but the only way we could shut it up was to bat better than we did today.

We had our usual mid-match team meeting back at the hotel and it started off in pretty subdued mood, although I urged: 'We've got to put this behind us and make the last two days of the match ours. If we can't win, then we must get a draw because if we don't The Ashes have gone. I doesn't get any more vital than that, but we can do it.'

At least the meeting ended with a laugh. Riddler is heading home first thing tomorrow to work with the A team who are off to South Africa and Zimbabwe in the New Year, before going to his native New Zealand with the NatWest under-19s, and that means no more of his jokes.

Riddler is the worst joke-teller in the world, as he proves every morning as he leads our warm-ups. He always either forgets a punch-line or even the joke itself, but he is so bad it is funny anyway. Needless to say, he tried to leave us with a joke, but true to form forgot it, and that had everyone in stitches.

Some players might jokingly grumble about what he does, making sure we're eating and drinking the right things, and putting us through new routines to improve out strength, fitness and stamina, but we'll still miss him. He is a former track athlete who came to England in the early 1990s and was introduced to cricket by Fizz after working with the Leeds and Great Britain rugby league squads.

He is part of the revolution in our preparations that began with Bumble's appointment as coach in 1996, and the way we kept going on the first day was thanks in large measure to him. I also think it's no coincidence that the injury toll has gone down over the past few years since fitness levels have improved.

There aren't many days left on the tour without cricket now though, so Riddler would only have a small role training the non-players if he stayed. Fizz will take that on now, with the Glamorgan physiotherapist Dean Conway coming out to ease the burden when the one-day boys arrive.

Monday 14 December, Third Test, Day 4
Australia 391 & 278–5 declared (Slater 103, Langer 52, M Waugh not out 51); England 227 & 122–4 (Ramprakash not out 43, Hussain 41)

Things went about as well as they could have done today until 5.52 pm. By then, chasing 443 to win, or more realistically needing to bat for almost five sessions to save the match and keep alive our hopes of winning the series, we were 120 for two, and Nass and Ramps were batting brilliantly.

But in the same way Brian Clough always said it only takes a second to score a goal, it only takes one ball to take a wicket. Or, in this case, two balls to take two wickets, and the whole picture changes.

We went from 120 for two to 122 for four in those eight minutes up to the close, and ended the day with a mountain to climb.

By now, the ball was spinning big time, so much so in fact that Miller was bowling round the wicket to bring lbws into play. Still though, Nass and Ramps were handling everything the Aussies could throw at them, even with three and four fielders round the bat.

The pair had come together just before tea when Butch and Ath were out in successive overs. At that point we could have folded, but I like to think this group of players is better than that, and so they proved, fighting like alley cats to get a foot-hold at the crease.

The fact I hadn't gone in at number four was a source of interest to all the press and television, and Charles Colvile of Sky Sports was quickly around to find out if I was injured. The honest truth is that I needed a bit of a break after keeping wicket. Through the series, Ramps or Chalks had often got ready to bat at four when we came off while I had a rest for half an hour or so, but up until now, our first two wickets had lasted the course until I got the pads on.

This time it was a bit different. By the time we started our second innings, I had been keeping for around eight sessions out of ten and after the heat at the start of the match, I just needed some time to compose myself. I would have gone in at four if the second wicket had fallen after tea, but the fact it fell 14 minutes before the break meant it was Ramps who went in instead.

It was all fuel to the fire for the critics who insisted I had too much on plate with the three roles of captaincy, keeping wicket and batting in the top order, but I managed it well enough last summer, and to me it isn't an issue. This is a unique situation, with the match being played in heat the like of which I haven't experienced since playing a Test in Colombo almost six years ago. I did all three roles then too, and it was tough, so I recognised the signs this time.

Sat with my pads on in the viewing area throughout the last session, I had a chat with Bumble with about 40 minutes to go. We agreed Deano, our usual nightwatchman, should get the pads on and go in with either six overs or twenty minutes to play.

He's a great bloke to have around because he'll die for the cause, and he also thinks about the game an awful lot. As he got ready to go in, he asked Bumble what he should do if he went in.

'If I just prop forward with all those men round the bat and the ball spinning like it is I'm bound to give a catch sooner or later,' he said.

Bumble agreed. He was a great player of spin and once got a Test double hundred against Bedi and Chandra, so he knows what he's talking about. 'Lap them,' he said. 'Get your pad in the way and hit hard and down. It's less of a risk than just pushing forward hopefully. It also rotates the strike, and that has to be good for upsetting the bowlers' rhythm.'

The clock kept ticking and with just eight minutes of play left there was a real chance we could get through the day with just two wickets down. Miller had other ideas.

Going wide of the crease from round the wicket, he pitched the ball on a length on middle stump and spun it back sharply. With the bowler coming from that angle, Nass, who was on strike, knew what to expect, but he just missed it. Up went the appeal, and, after what seemed like an age, Steve Bucknor raised the finger and mouthed 'That's out'.

Bucknor is a good umpire, one of the best in the world, but it's torture when you're facing an appeal and he's the man to make the decision. If you're not out, he'll let you know pretty quickly, but if he takes his time, there is a fair chance the news is bad. It's not often he takes his time and then says 'Not out'.

As the wicket fell, Deano looked at me and I said: 'Off you go'. Out he trooped.

Despite what he and Bumble had discussed before he went out to bat, it's one thing talking about it and another putting into practice in the middle. Miller bowled a teasing line and length and immediately got Deano feeling for the ball. He edged his second ball through slip for two, but fourth ball, propped forward and fell bat-pad at silly point. Bucknor's finger went up again, and now it was time for me to face the music.

The most frustrating aspect of my trip to the middle was that I didn't have to face a ball before walking off again. Miller had struck with the last ball of his over, and after one more set of six from MacGill it was 6 o'clock. That was how close we were to making it through to stumps with just two men out. But that is the mark of how good the Aussies are. Like the New Zealand rugby union team they keep going right up until the final whistle, with no let-up, and that approach brought them reward tonight.

We'd stopped them declaring until forty minutes after lunch, which was a pretty good effort given that they'd started the day 314 ahead with nine wickets in hand.

We began still trying to bowl them out as that's the best way to slow the scoring rate, but we were also realistic. By delaying their declaration as long as possible we would have less time to bat to save the match, so that meant fairly defensive fields and tight bowling, and the lads did their best.

Goughie was outstanding. He was helped by the fact the ball began to reverse swing, and he got Slater and Ponting either side of lunch, but by then Slater had reached yet another century – cue the celebrations – and Langer had added 52 to his earlier 179 not out.

I ended the day still believing we could save the match, as we still had Creepy and Hicky in the pavilion after Ramps and me. But one of us needed to play a really big innings with the others offering good support.

Tuesday 15 December, Third Test, Day 5
Australia 391 & 278–5 declared beat England 227 & 237 (Stewart not out 63, Ramprakash 57, McGrath 4–50) by 205 runs

All the planning, all the preparations, and all the cricket we've played over the past seven weeks was with one aim in mind: regaining The Ashes. And at 2.04 this afternoon, our chance to do just that went up in smoke.

That was the time Suchy was trapped plumb lbw to McGrath, and I had to watch it from the other end. I knew it was out straight away without even looking at the umpire, and I'd already began to walk off before the cheers of their players and the crowd confirmed the fact.

I'm sure the critics will enjoy that one, the captain on the deck of his sinking ship, but it is a feeling I can do without too many more times in my cricketing career. I felt empty. Everything I'd worked for on the trip gone with two Tests still to play.

The day had begun positively enough, with the lads whistling the theme from 'The Great Escape' as we headed to the ground on the team bus, and for the first 50 minutes Ramps and I coped pretty well. But Fleming then broke through, and we lost our last five wickets in just half an hour either side of lunch.

Fleming has looked a great bowler since Brisbane. There he looked distinctly ordinary off a really short run and must have been lucky to hold his place for Perth. But, picked there as an into-the-wind bowler, he was superb and has added a yard of pace since the start of the series. His rise has taken some of the pressure off McGrath and has given us less breathing space.

Here he bowled very well with the old ball and got Ramps with a jaffa of a reverse-swinging yorker that plucked out his leg-stump. He tried something similar on me but couldn't find his range and the ball slipped down the leg- side for four byes.

Even when Ramps was out I still thought we could save it, but I knew it would be bloody hard when Creepy followed in the last over before lunch. By this stage McGrath had been brought back, and even though he was under the weather with a stomach bug, he gave him a severe test armed with the new ball.

That test included some choice sledging – 'Nice shot for your last Test innings' was about the only one printable. I don't think it got to Creeps, who's normally pretty cool, but suddenly, at 12.58 and lunch beckoning, he pushed the ball into the off-side and set off for a suicidal run.

'No!' I screamed and he dived back just in time, immediately holding his hand up to apologise. He took his time, dusted himself off and settled again, but McGrath was soon on his way again and got him playing at a ball six inches outside off-stump next up. Creeps edged low to Mark Waugh at second slip, who took it without a flicker, and we were six down at lunch.

I had some chicken in the dressing room, having been very happy with the way I'd played in the morning session, especially given that these were my first runs in Adelaide on the tour at my fourth attempt! The ball was turning for the spinners and the pitch was more like one you might find if a game ever went into the sixth day, but my feet were moving well and I felt I could bat all day. Now though, I knew I would have to, and I needed Hicky to do the same.

First ball after lunch and that hope was shattered as Hicky squeezed a full-length ball straight to third slip. He hit the ground at the same time as the ball, so wasn't clear what had happened. The umpires called for television evidence, and that showed he was gone, something I suspected straight away. And from then on it was a case of waiting for the end.

That came really quickly, and I began to know how Nass had felt in the first innings. There was little point in trying to shield the tail too much as there was so much time remaining they would have to do a fair amount of batting if we were going to save the game. But even the few balls I allowed them to face were a struggle and we offered very little resistance against a pepped up fielding side.

At the end, there were the usual handshakes out in the middle, and I sought out Taylor and McGrath in particular. Taylor has done a great job as my opposite number, and I reckon McGrath has been the major difference between the sides.

Then, as the Aussies came off the field, our lads came out of the dressing room to greet them and offer some congratulations. The Aussies were buzzing, and rightly so because they had done us again.

But as they went inside to crack open the bubbly and celebrate, we all filed back into our dressing room and just sat there.

There was champagne in our dressing room too, a bottle of the stuff had been presented to Butch that morning before play for winning the 'Test Match Special' Champagne Moment in Brisbane when he reached his century. But it just sat there on the table in the middle of the dressing room, and no one looked in the least bit ready to drink it.

For what seemed like ages, the room was completely silent apart from the noise of Suchy and I removing our batting gear. Players just sat there staring at their feet or looking aimlessly around the room.

Just a few yards away, the music was blaring out of the Aussie dressing room and their players were singing their victory anthem 'Under the Southern Cross', led, as usual, by Ian Healy.

There was nothing to say at that stage, and probably rightly so. Everyone knew we'd lost, that didn't need repeating, and the main aim of the tour had gone. But for now it was good to let everyone mull over their own efforts and we could revisit things when people had some time for reflection.

Being positive, I stressed to the media afterwards that there was plenty to play for. 'There are four matches left in this part of the tour before the one-dayers start, and we now have to be looking to win all four. If we can do that, and share the series, then it will have been a good tour.'

The media seemed to accept this, and I went back to the dressing room to pack my stuff. Normally we would have gone into the opposition dressing room for a drink, but it didn't seem right. They were far too busy celebrating and their room was still full of cameramen and reporters trying to catch the mood, so most of the boys had already gone back to the hotel on the team bus, and only Nass and Goochie were left. We chatted about what I'd said to the press, but none of it was too deep, and after we'd packed, it was back to the hotel for us as well.

That empty feeling continued, but I had to pack for the flight to Canberra tomorrow. That done, it was up to the team room for a drink with the boys with all of us still digesting what had happened, before we headed to the hotel bar. I drank tea, and just made small talk with the lads, but although some of them went out for a meal, I just headed for bed. I didn't really feel like going out.

'We've got a bit of work to do'

Wednesday 16 December

Breakfast was a pretty sobering experience today as every newspaper was covered with Ashes news, none of it particularly good to read for us. A lot of the articles seemed keen to ask if The Ashes had any future as a five-Test series given that Australia have won every meeting since 1989. I was quizzed about that too, and I gave the same answer as Mark Taylor: if you ask any of the players on either side, they will tell you it is the contest they want to play in, simply because of the history and tradition involved. The public seems to like it as well, so why change? I know there has been a lot of talk about a World Championship of Test cricket and I don't know how that will work, but I would hope The Ashes series stay as they are. I know that is what both Boards want.

Dad joined me for breakfast as he was heading back home after watching three Tests while we flew to Canberra. The flight was a bit of a struggle for quite a few of us as Corky's flu is now doing the rounds with Ramps, Suchy and I worst affected. With sinuses blocked, the changes in pressure as the plane goes up and down can be pretty unpleasant, and Suchy's ear drum started bleeding which was none too pleasant.

We had picked the side for tomorrow's one-dayer with the Prime Minister's XI while we were in Melbourne, and gave Ben Hollioake, Hegg, Cork, Croft and Fraser an outing after all of them had missed the Test. It meant another outing for me, although I wouldn't keep wicket, but I felt I had to play as it was vital to lead from the front and get a win after losing the Test and The Ashes.

Thursday 17 December

We did our best to throw things away today, but in the end the lads came through with a show of character, and there haven't been many matches I've been happier to win than this one.

To the outsider, all the ingredients were there for it to go pear-shaped for us. Here we were in the middle of a Test series, having just lost The Ashes, and now we were facing a bunch of young hopefuls led by Mark Taylor, all of them keen to make a name. The match was billed as a festival game, and if we won you could be sure everyone would say we should always come away with a win in these sorts of games. But if we lost, you could be equally sure the critics would use it as another example of a tour in crisis.

You try to put all that negative thought out of your mind and just go and do your job, but I left no one in any doubt before the start that I expected a victory. 'Four games to go before the one-dayers and we must aim to win all four, starting today,' I said.

We batted first, but 26 for four wasn't the best of starts, even though I felt in good form. We batted as if we were still asleep for the first half an hour and it took Nass and I to steady the ship.

I was very happy with the way I hit the ball, especially through the covers off front and back foot, but Nass and I both fell in the 40s and at 107 for six we were back in the mire. Thankfully at that point Chucky and Corky showed why they are such respected county pros with a sensible stand that mixed common sense and aggression.

Those two, Crofty and Gus took us past 200 and gave us something to bowl at on a pitch that was helping all the bowlers. Gus did especially well, but he did get most of his runs off Taylor, who bowled the last over. He hit two sixes in an over of leg-spin which cost 16 runs, but only after he was bowled by a ball which bounced twice. He was ready to troop off, only for umpire Simon Taufel to call no-ball and save him.

While the rest of the lads had lunch in the dressing room, Goochie, Bumble and I joined the PM for a meal. He'd not seen much cricket in the morning as there was the small matter of the UK and USA bombing Iraq to get up to speed on, but he was back for our meal, and for another block-busting speech full of pleasantries by me. I had to pass on the wine and stick to coke and then it was back to the dressing room to get ready for our spell in the field.

Al Mullally set the tone with a great opening spell and Corky bowled well too, as if to prove we were wrong to leave him out of the one-day squad. But from 122 for seven in the 31st over, they almost got up to win thanks to Daniel Marsh, son of Rod, who smashed 74 in 72 balls, most over wide mid-wicket.

It got very tight, and I was wondering about whether to copy Taylor by bowling the last over if it meant we could lose the match. Thankfully, Hicky wrapped things up in the 49th over, perhaps inspired by seeing me whirling my arms around at short cover, and we'd won by 16 runs.

I wasn't exactly in the best of moods when we came off though and took it out on the players. I don't get angry very often, and even now I didn't lose it, but by being calm most of the time it means when I do want to make a point, the players take notice.

'We were diabolical in the last 20 overs of that innings in the field,' I said. 'The throwing was poor, there was no backing up and there was no energy in the field. That was simply not up to the standard you would expect from an international side.

'We won, and let's enjoy that, but we are going to have to be a hell of a lot better than that to compete in the next three games.'

On the positive side we'd won the first of our four matches left, but I think a few players thought we had won when they were seven down. As if they don't know it already, Australians never lie down.

A good-ish day then, made a hell of a lot better when I rang a Melbourne Airport hotel when we got back to our digs and found Lynn, Andrew, Emily and our baby sitter Jo had all arrived safely from home.

They, along with a few of the other families are heading down to Hobart to meet up with us tomorrow, before the main group of wives and girlfriends arrive in Melbourne when we get there for the Boxing Day Test match. I don't know how the other lads with families coming out feel, but I can guess their thoughts are the same as mine: I can't wait to see my family again for the first time since 16 October. And who said touring was glamorous?

Friday 18 December

I was in great shape to see my family for the first time in over two months: the flu bug which has been troubling a few of us refused to give up, and my ears, which have been blocked for two days, were very painful on the flight to Hobart.

We arrived at the hotel soon after lunch and Lynn and Emily were there in the lobby to meet me. Emily had grown a fair amount in two months, or so it seemed to me, but for the first five minutes she didn't seem to recognise me at all. Hardly surprising I suppose when you think how long I've been away since she was born in September 1996. In that time I've spent four months in Zimbabwe and New Zealand and another four in the West Indies, with two English seasons thrown in as well. Once she did remember me though, she wouldn't let me out of her sight.

Andrew was fast asleep when I arrived, but once he woke up we had a family trip to the local Burger King for their favourite chicken nuggets. Jet-lag bothers young and old alike though, and both children were ready to go to sleep just after 5 o'clock.

That was handy timing as we then had to pick the side for the Australian XI match that starts tomorrow and is being billed by the media as a sixth Test. Their side is very strong and only one of their players – Corey Richards of New South Wales – doesn't have international experience, so it's important we put on a top show.

Nass and I both decided to rest as we're certain starters for the last two Tests, so we made Ath captain. We also decided to give Pelly another outing, and rested Goughie, Al, and Deano, all of them almost certain to figure in Melbourne.

At the team meeting in the evening, I opened things up by stressing the importance of the next four days and everyone accepted that. We'd all had the chance to think about what had gone wrong so far and I said it was now up to each person to make sure they put it right.

I also said: 'I may be tour captain but Ath is the man in charge of this game. He'll captain it as he wants. He is the man who makes the decisions over the next four days.'

Ath had nothing to add, and that was that. Just the odd bit of training and twelfth man duties to look forward to over the next four days, plus, of course, some time with the family. But any thoughts of a wild start to things quickly came to nothing as I discovered everyone was asleep when I got back to my room!

Saturday 19 December

Quite a relaxing day away from a direct involvement in things, about the first day I can remember that on this tour. And the lads didn't do too badly without me as they reached 298 for three with Ath getting a morale-boosting hundred.

The children were awake by 6 am, but Jo did a good job and kept them at bay for an hour, so I got a fairly good night's sleep. Then it was breakfast with Andrew, who was desperate to bring me up to date with all the news in his life over the past two months. He managed to do that over a bowl of Rice Krispies!

I went to the ground with the rest of the lads, but after warming up I took a back seat, as I said I would. My activity was confined to a net session, some fielding practice with Goochie and a couple of interviews with Sky Sports and BBC Radio for their Christmas programmes.

While I was doing all this, Ath and Ramps took advantage of an Australian attack that looked more like General Hospital as the day went on. It began before we'd even started when spinner Gavin Robertson showed up with a back spasm. It was too hard for them to fly someone else in so we allowed them a substitute until Robertson's back improved. Then, after they'd lost the toss on a very flat pitch, Paul Reiffel broke down with a hamstring injury after only nine balls. Then Kasper broke down with another hamstring twinge after tea. It all meant the team's coach, Allan Border, had to make a couple of trips out of retirement while they hunted for some substitute fielders, and it was good to see the Aussies struggle as we piled on the runs.

Their injury crisis made me smile even though you never like to see fellow professionals injured. We've now got a great programme of fitness for all our players which means they break down less than ever before, but just four years ago, when we were last here, it was all so different. Then, at least half a dozen players, including some replacements, got injured.

I was really pleased for Ath. He came on this tour desperate to win The Ashes after two lost series as captain, but he's struggled with his fitness and his form has been mixed. And when he was starting to find his touch in Adelaide, the third umpire sawed him off.

While he spoke to the press after play, I went back to the hotel and had a swim with the children and then had to be content with a quiet room service meal. I'd planned a romantic dinner for two with Lynn, but she was still struggling with jet-lag. All in all, though, a relaxing day after all the pressure of the last few weeks.

Sunday 20 December

Typical isn't it! You get some time off and what happens? It rains. I threw back the curtains this morning to reveal lead-grey skies and there was immediately no chance of play before lunch.

After consulting with the umpires, the lads didn't even go to the ground in the morning, and most of them went back to their rooms to rest. All except the card school that is. Cork, Headley, Crawley and Hegg have become inseparable at every airport, meal-break or delay of any sort as the cards come out. I'm no card shark myself, so I don't know what they play, but it certainly seems to take up lots of their time, with Chucky the new boy among them, joining the group after Thorpey headed for home.

I spent my morning taking Andrew to the local cinema to watch the cartoon 'The Prince of Egypt'. I'd like to tell you that it was really good, but I slept through a fair amount of it, although I was woken every so often by Andrew's digs in the ribs.

We eventually headed for the ground for lunch, and after a few of us demonstrated some soccer skills on the outfield, the rain stopped and we began at 4 o'clock with an extra hour to play. Hicky and Ath made hay against their depleted attack and the ball went everywhere. Ath reached the first double hundred of his career, which surprised a few of us who are used to him batting for long periods, before declaring to give us forty minutes bowling at them.

That caused a few of the lads to raise eyebrows. On a pitch as flat as this, unless one team suddenly bowls brilliantly or the other bats very badly, the only way to get a result would be a couple of declarations and a run-chase on the last day with them the favourites to get those runs. Bumble, Butch and Pelly were three people definitely against giving them even a sniff of a chance and they wanted us to get 650 and then try and bowl them out twice.

Ath and Goochie were more in favour of making a game of it and putting our bowlers under pressure, and as Ath was captain that won the day. I favoured the grind-them-down approach more, but as I was keen to try and win the game, I was all in favour of positive cricket.

As it was, our lads had just as little joy on the surface as they had, and when the bowlers came back to the dressing room after play they were all blowing their cheeks out at the prospect of some hard labour in the middle.

In among all those runs though, spare a thought for Pelly, who picked up a first-baller at the hands of our old Surrey mate BJ, Brendon Julian. The tour couldn't have gone much worse for Pelly thanks to injury and a lack of opportunities, but this must have put a tin lid on it for him. At least, being an all-rounder, he has his bowling to redeem matters.

The day ended with all of us going to a pre-Christmas drink with the press. A few years ago we boycotted the event in Zimbabwe, and even now some of the players wouldn't cross the street to say hello to a few of the hacks. Bumble just didn't want to go at any price and I think some of the lads felt the same way, but Goochie was keen for us to remember it was the season of goodwill, and in the spirit of all for one and one for all, everyone pitched up. For my part I thought it was all a bit hypocritical to have them slag us off on one hand and then have a drink with them on the other. But they did pay for it all, including some delicious seafood snacks, and Christopher Martin-Jenkins of the *Daily Telegraph* and I each made a short speech to wish the other side festive greetings. But it still felt a bit like that Paul McCartney video which re-enacted German and Allied troops playing football against each other at Christmas, as you can be sure some of the writers will be sharpening the pencils again tomorrow.

Monday 21 December

I went to the ground with the lads as usual today, but was away by 12.30 for an afternoon with the family. Everyone who doesn't play in a game is allowed a half-day off away from the cricket, as just sitting around at the ground all day over the course of a four-month tour can send you stir-crazy. I did have a good session with bat and gloves before I left, but as soon as I was out of the gates of the Bellerive Oval, I switched off and put the cricket out of my mind.

Looking at the scores later, it seemed I missed a pretty forgettable day's cricket anyway, with Greg Blewett racking up another hundred against us to go with his 143 in Adelaide before they declared and we piled on more runs against their under-strength attack to set up the possibility of a run-chase tomorrow. The pitch is so flat though that it will be difficult to set them anything too generous so Ath will have to get the slide-rule out.

One thing of interest that I found out when we got back to the hotel was that the Australian selectors have dropped Ponting for Darren Lehmann, the Australian XI captain in this match, for the Melbourne Test. Ponting's axing was no surprise as we've kept him quiet through the series so far, but although Lehmann has slapped county attacks everywhere for Yorkshire, I think a few of us expected Blewett to get the nod instead. Not that we should be complaining as we scored an important little point over Lehmann this afternoon when Corky got him for just four. It shouldn't matter come the Test as that is a completely different game, but if we can get him cheaply again tomorrow, it can't do us any harm.

Tuesday 22 December

If only my afternoon off had been today, I could have missed the most disappointing display I've ever seen by an England side as the Australian second XI thrashed us.

It was a flat pitch and Ath set them a generous target of 376 in 76 overs, but we didn't just lose, we fell apart as they made mincemeat of an attack containing seven bowlers who've operated in Tests.

They got off to a flying start with Blewett reaching his 50 in just 38 balls, and in the process passing 1000 runs before the end of December, only one of a handful of Aussies ever to achieve the feat, and from then on we were fighting an uphill battle.

By lunch they'd already reached 124 for one in only 18 overs, and it needed a tight spell from someone after the break to try and tie them down and force them into a mistake. But we didn't manage one maiden over in the entire innings, and Blewett and Corey Richards were never put under any pressure as a result.

It was David Lloyd I felt most sorry for. Bumble had never wanted us to make a game of it in this way, preferring us to grind them down, scoring 650 and then trying to bowl them out. His attitude was that this was a game we just couldn't afford to lose, it was all about coming out of it strongly and taking plenty from it, even a win ahead of the Test.

Ath and Goochie thought slightly differently, wanting to put the attack under pressure and see how they responded. Well, they achieved the first aim, but the response wasn't good, and we lost without a murmur.

A few of the lads certainly disagreed with the decision to set them anything like a gettable target, but regardless of that, we should still have done better than we did. The bowling was both sides of the wicket, and Blewett and Richards did as they pleased.

At lunch, Bumble went into the dressing room and tried to rally the lads: 'Right then boys, we've got a bit of work to do out there this afternoon, but let's get stuck in and make them work for this.'

By tea though, after they'd added 197 runs in the session in just 29 overs without losing a wicket, his tone was slightly different. He stormed into the dressing room and said: 'Thanks a lot for your efforts lads, it's not your bloody jobs on the line. Thanks a lot.' Then he left. There was silence.

Even though he didn't show it, I know Ath was devastated at the loss, and Goochie was furious too. He had to go and face the press afterwards, and I know he resented that because he felt he was carrying the can for the players. But the press wanted blood, and Bumble was liable to blow a gasket if he'd gone to speak to them while Bob Cottam, quite rightly, wanted to have a chat with each of the bowlers individually before he passed comment on their efforts.

It was painful to watch, but I decided not to say anything to the lads afterwards. After all, I'd said at the pre-match meeting it was Ath's side. Better to say something after we'd all had a chance to have a think about things once we'd got to Melbourne.

There was some talking to do before we got there though. Bumble was in a state of shock at the way we'd played, and Goochie and I had a long chat with him at the airport before we left that evening. I'm not saying he was ready to quit there and then, but he was as low as I've ever seen him, and this is a man who is usually as bubbly as a bottle of champagne.

I said to Bumble, 'Yes, this is bad, but it doesn't affect the Test that's coming up. That is what we have to focus on now. Dwelling on this will just drag everyone down and we can't afford to do that with two Tests left.'

He seemed to accept that, and we all got on the flight a bit less tense than when we arrived at the airport.

Stuart Law, Essex's Australian player was generous enough to admit in the departure lounge that the boot may well have been on the other foot if we'd bowled first because the pitch was so flat, but that was no consolation now. The lads knew they'd let themselves and the support staff down, and when the cricket came on the television news, everyone stopped to watch it in silence, almost like they were paying their respects at a funeral.

Wednesday 23 December

Today was always going to be a day off, even after the defeat in Hobart. I've never been a fan of what the press call 'naughty boy nets', as practice should always be work you want to do rather than what you feel you should be doing to please others, particularly the press.

In any case, we only arrived in Melbourne late last night, and rest is just as important as practice at this stage of the tour. By the time we get to the end of the Sydney Test there will be some tired bodies around, so the chance to take it easy for a day is exactly what the boys need.

On top of that, several of them were out at the airport late last night as the Emirates flight with wives, girlfriends and families came in. Christmas can be a lonely time for players if close relatives aren't around so it's good they're here, but I reminded all the lads as we arrived at the hotel last night that we're still here to win two Tests. That must be the priority.

Hopefully this winter, we've got the arrangements with wives and families about right. When we went to South Africa in 1995, there was little provision for them apart from the fact they travelled on the same flights as us, and I know Ath felt the resulting chaos helped send the tour off the rails. A player isn't going to be at his best if his wife or girlfriend is nagging him to look after the children when he should instead be gearing up for a Test match. And having to get up in the middle of the night to look after children is hardly ideal preparation.

On the basis of what happened in South Africa, there was a total ban on wives and girlfriends when we went to Zimbabwe and New Zealand the following winter, and that didn't work either. A lot of the players disliked Zimbabwe anyway, maybe because the itinerary gave them no chance to have a look at the place, and the fact we weren't playing very well didn't help either. But not having relatives there at Christmas didn't do much for morale.

Last winter in the West Indies, the families came out when we were in Barbados and we stayed in villa-style accommodation. The Board also employed a secretary to help tour manager Bob Bennett co-ordinate family requirements.

I had to speak to the press at 5 o'clock. Normally out here I talk to them two days ahead of a Test for publication the day before the match, but as there are no papers on Christmas Day today was the day.

It was a pretty full-on conference lasting about 25 minutes with plenty of questions about yesterday's effort, which I said we had to improve on – no surprise there. I was also quizzed on the make-up of the side, with the balance – six or seven batsmen, and four or five bowlers – an issue. I had to be honest and say I had no idea as we wouldn't be looking at the pitch until tomorrow morning when we went down to practice.

I did hint we would look at five bowlers as an option though, and I gave Tudes a big plug. He's a young cricketer who's impressed everyone with his attitude and willingness to get involved in hard work, and if he keeps going the way he is I think he could go a long way. He's no mean batsman either, and we could take a risk and play him at number seven as one of a five-man attack.

The old chestnut about whether or not I'm going to be keeping wicket came up courtesy of Christopher Martin-Jenkins and I had to smile. Whenever we're losing, the question of my keeping surfaces, although it has a slightly different spin on it this time. In past years when I haven't had the gloves on, there's always been the call for me to keep as that allows us to play an extra specialist – batsman or bowler. Now I have got the gloves on and we're losing, there's an equally strong call from sections of the media for me to give up those gloves and go back to open, the position I'd always choose.

There is logic to both arguments, but they are still flawed for one simple reason: they both work on the basis that we would make the change in order to put out a stronger side, better equipped to win the Test. But as far as I'm concerned every Test is a must-win match, and the only basis for selecting any side is getting what we believe to be the best combination to do just that out on the field. If that means me keeping, then so be it, but if it means me playing solely as a batsman then I'm equally happy to do that instead.

I came on the tour as the first-choice keeper, and unless something happens to affect that thinking – and it hasn't so far – then I expect to stay there, although I did concede to Christopher that the subject 'may rate a sentence' at our selection meeting.

Australia v England, Fourth Test, Melbourne, 26–29 December 1998

Thursday 24 December

Back to business after the day off and before we began our build-up to the Test with a net session, we had a team meeting in the MCG dressing room with events on the last day at Hobart top of the agenda.

The first part of the meeting included the management, and Bumble said some pretty forthright things about our effort against the

Australian XI. 'Whether you agreed with the decision to set them a target or not', he said, 'our effort in the field on that last day was simply not up to standard, and if we play like that in the last two Tests we'll get hammered.'

Goochie also said we had to up our game if we were going to compete with Australia starting on Boxing Day, but both he and Bumble said they believed we were capable of doing that.

Once those two had said their pieces, they and the other non-players in the party left, and the seventeen players had an open chat about what had happened in Hobart and what we had to do to put things right.

There was nothing sinister in the coaching staff going out of the room. I just thought it was a good idea, because what I had to say related directly to Bumble.

'We didn't just let ourselves down the other day,' I said. 'We let down Bumble, Goochie and all the support staff too. They are the ones who keep having to make excuses when we perform badly, and if we keep doing badly they will be out of here. If we play badly we'll be dropped, but we can always come back; they can't.

'We've got to start to take some responsibility for our efforts. I know we can compete with Australia, we've shown it in this series already, but we've got to do it far more consistently through a Test if we're going to win.'

After that, a few of the other lads chipped in and not just with thoughts about Hobart, but about the match coming up too. I don't know why, as we're all in this together, but chats like this are always a lot less inhibited when the management aren't there.

Nass, as usual, was blunt but full of common senses about what had to be done: 'Lots more commitment and effort from everyone.' And Goughie was his usual self: 'For f*** sake, we can beat these, so let's go out and do it.' He was also very helpful about how we should bowl to Lehmann, his team-mate last season at Yorkshire. 'Don't give him any width' was the general message.

Meeting over – it lasted about 30 minutes – and everyone threw themselves into a fairly lengthy net session, which again included Chris Schofield, as well as Gavin Hamilton, the Yorkshire all-rounder, who's also playing club cricket here this winter.

The pitch itself looked pretty good. It had an even covering of grass but it also appeared basically dry. We'll have to wait and see if the groundsman takes any of that grass off before the start as that may well affect the balance of our attack.

Australia have had their hands exposed a bit at this stage by the news that Gillespie has pulled out with an injured knee. With Reiffel and Kasprowicz also out of action, they've gone for Matthew Nicholson, who took eight wickets against us for WA at the start of the tour. I think he's only played about six first-class matches, but that is the speed you can rise in this country. He's struck me as a pretty cool customer when we've seen him so far, but I'm sure he will never have played in front of the size of crowd he'll find at the MCG so it will be up to us to make sure he doesn't settle.

Friday 25 December

Not much chance of a lie-in on Christmas Day with the children up and ripping open their presents at 6.15 am. It might not be as restful as I would have liked ahead of a crucial Test, but seeing the looks on their faces as the wrapping paper came off more than made up for it. It makes you appreciate the chance to be with them at this time of year, despite missing so much of their growing up. Being the man about the place it was up to me to help put the batteries in toys and make sure they worked, but being hopeless with anything electrical I needed to get Andrew to help out on that one!

Fun and games over for a while as it was off to the MCG for a Christmas Day fielding session. Before we went out though, Fizz had a surprise for everyone, having spent the last few days buying gifts for all the touring squad. Everyone had a 'goodie bag' (actually it was a hotel laundry bag) with something in it, including a CD of their choice.

The 'somethings' were hilarious as each item was related to the recipient's character. I can't remember them all but the funniest were probably Hicky, who got a joke book (he's not known for his sense of humour), Goughie, who got two pictures of his favourite cricketer (Darren Gough) and Corky, who got a can of Boddington's. 'Why have I got a can of Boddy's?' he asked. 'Because you're a bitter man,' said Fizz, and that just about brought the house down.

If you're wondering what I got, well, it was a jar of anti-wrinkle cream. I know people think I like to look smart, but removing the creases from my face might be going just a bit too far.

Joking over, I was delighted with the way the lads went in the fielding session, they looked really sharp ahead of the Test. Goughie, as always, injected a bit of fun into proceedings by wearing a Santa hat, and we ended the session with a penalty-taking session. Crofty, always keen to show how Welsh he is, hammered his kick way over the bar, then announced that was where penalty kicks were meant to go in rugby union.

It was roasting hot during our session with barely a cloud in the sky and a blazing hot sun as temperatures touched 37 degrees C, apparently making it the hottest Christmas Day in Melbourne for over forty years. But, true to form in this city, where they say you can have every season in one day, it was cool and cloudy by the evening, with the chance of rain.

We all had another look at the pitch after practice and decided not to name a side until the morning of the match when they've finished preparing it, as there is still a fair amount of grass on the surface. All the same, I'm pretty sure we'll go in with six batsmen and five bowlers. Our seventh batsman has done nothing so far in two Tests so we might as well take a positive step of including a fifth front line bowler.

That would mean Tudes batting as high as seven in the order, something he won't have done for anyone except his club side back home. He's a talented lad and I've got faith in him, but it does mean the top six will have to do the business.

All those thoughts were put on hold in the evening when Fizz rang me to say Tudes had a slight niggle in his thigh, but we'll have to wait until the morning before making any decisions on that one, and I'm still confident he'll play.

I was in bed by 8.30 at the end of an enjoyable but tiring day. It's the 14th out of the last 18 Christmases I've spent away from home and it still feels strange to be overseas apart from all my family. My routine in the build-up to the match has been different from usual, but I still think I'm ready for the next five days.

Saturday 26 December, Fourth Test, Day 1
No play, rain

A day packed with action, frustration and quick-changes for us – and there wasn't a ball bowled as the first day was washed out by rain.

That rain, which kept sweeping in every time a start seemed possible, managed to ruin one of the great days of sport, Boxing Day at the MCG, as 75,000 fans were left with no cricket. But it did give us a chance to catch our breath after just about the most frustrating and unsettling build-up to a Test I've ever known.

When we arrived at the ground, I had it in mind to play just the six batsmen with me at four and keeping wicket, and Tudes at seven as part of a five-man attack including Suchy. But Tudes arrived still feeling his thigh and we needed to give him a full-on fitness test to see if he could come through.

If Tudes wasn't fit, it would mean a complete re-jig of the plan, as there was no way we could have Gus, his likely replacement, at seven, followed by Headley, Gough, Mullally and Such.

As far as I was concerned, playing Tudes was a positive move and a statement of intent that we wanted to win the match. He'd roughed the Aussies up in Perth, and on a pitch that was expected to have some pace in it here I was hopeful he could do something similar now.

But if he couldn't play, I was still keen to make that positive move. Swapping Tudes for another batsman was hardly that after the way seven batsmen had gone as a plan in the last two Tests, so the next best thing was for me to play as an opener.

Butch and Ath as an opening pairing had done really well against South Africa last summer, and their success was one of the reasons for us winning that series. But now, apart from Butch's hundred in Brisbane, they'd done nothing together, and changing that had to be a good move.

The partnership between Ath and I had been one of the strengths of our cricket over the past four years, and although it meant reverting to a four-man attack I felt if we could get us a good start, then that would compensate for us being a bowler light.

Of course, if Tudes didn't play and I did open, it meant Warren Hegg would have to play, so when we arrived at the ground I told him to prepare as if he was playing. He looked a bit startled, but he is a good pro – that's one of the reasons we brought him along in the first place – and I knew he wouldn't let us down.

It can't have been easy for him to get ready though, hoping he was playing, but knowing him as I do, also hoping Tudes was okay. But to be honest, it wasn't exactly a bowl of cherries for any of us with all the uncertainty about the team.

The big man did a lap of the ground – a test in itself given the size of the MCG – then he had a bowl in the middle under the supervision of

Fizz. I went out and watched, and although he could still feel the twinge, he wanted to have another bowl in the nets as well.

Off we all went, with me trying to cram all my preparation in, batting and keeping, as well as monitor the situation with Tudes. He had another bowl at me, but at 10.20 he came to me and said he didn't think he was fit.

'I think I could get through the first innings without a problem,' he said. 'But if I stiffened up and wasn't able to bowl in the second dig I'd be letting everyone down, wouldn't I?'

It was a brave decision for the young man to make and I admired him for it. His parents and girlfriend were over from England to watch the Test and it would have been easy for him to say he was okay and try to play through it. But he took the wise course of action and admitted he just didn't think he was up to it.

From there, it was a quick chat to Bumble, Goochie and Nass to confirm my thoughts, an even quicker word of commiseration for Suchy and Creepy, who both missed out after playing in the last Test, then it was off to the dressing room to get ready for the toss.

Chucky was there and it was a pleasure to let him know he was in, even though it wasn't quite as I had planned it. He wasn't expecting to play so hadn't brought his blazer down for the presentation of his cap and he had to borrow Murgers'.

So 10.30 came around and off I went with Mark Taylor for the toss. It was an overcast morning, but as we reached the middle it began to spot with rain and the covers were brought out. After we hung around for a couple of minutes, it hadn't eased, so off we came again, past Chucky, who by this stage was getting a bit nervous. I knew he was thinking that if it rained all day, maybe Tudes would be fit tomorrow and we'd go back to plan A, that didn't include him!

To his relief, the rain eased at 10.45, and off we went again. I was keen to bat first, although with the overcast weather I wouldn't have minded if we'd bowled, but the decision was taken out of my hands when I called heads wrongly for the fifth Test in a row. Taylor put us in.

As the toss was taking place, the ground announcer said the start was set for 11.10, and by the time I'd done the Channel Nine and Sky interviews, time was marching on. It meant my cap presentation to Heggy wasn't exactly something he'll treasure, but I needed to go and get ready, and he knew that.

I rushed off but by the time I'd got my batting gear on, the rain had returned. Ath and I sat around for five minutes in our viewing area above the dressing room, but we soon realised there was no chance of a prompt start so we switched off for a while.

And that was basically that. During the day it brightened up a couple of times, and a few of us had some throw-downs in the indoor nets from time to time to get the feel of bat on ball while the card school swung into operation. But just before 5 o'clock, the umpires gave us the nod that it was off for the day and we headed back to the hotel.

I had a quiet dinner with Lynn to end the day and then went to bed early to look forward to a return to the top of the order.

Sunday 27 December, Fourth Test, Day 2
England 270 (Stewart 107, Ramprakash 63, MacGill 4–61); Australia 59–2

After all the worries, all the frustrations about a lack of runs, it all came right for me today with my first Test century against Australia. But even though it will rank as one of the best feelings in my career, it was still a mixed day for us as we failed to press home an advantage after having them on the ropes.

When Ramps and I were together, we had them rattled. We added 119 for the fourth wicket and the score was scorching along at four runs an over with the ball flying everywhere off the middle of our bats.

But suddenly I got careless and was bowled round my legs sweeping at MacGill. Ramps went in the next over, miscuing to mid-on, and we had two new batsmen on nought, one of them a debutante, the tail was exposed, and the Aussies smelt blood.

How many times has it happened that we have got ourselves into a good position against them only to lose our way as they then pounce and steam-roll us? Quite a few I would reckon, and if you ever wanted an example of what was meant by the line 'We must learn to win', then this was it.

Put simply, when the big points come along the Aussies produce their best cricket. We have done that too recently against South Africa, but we must learn to do it more often.

I'm as much to blame as anyone. After a nightmare start when we lost Ath and Butch in McGrath's first two overs, I managed to gain a foothold and began playing as I know I can.

When you've been out of touch, little things can make a massive difference. The second innings in Adelaide gave me renewed confidence, but the old saying is you're only as good as your next innings and by the time I was taking strike on a freezing cold morning, we were already nought for one wicket.

Fleming bowled me a good ball first up on about off stump and I was drawn into the stroke. The ball took the edge, flew through the slip cordon – along the ground – and went for four. I was off the mark, and immediately felt more relaxed.

McGrath's opening spell didn't exactly help my condition as he didn't concede a run off the bat until his fifth over, but I felt in good nick almost straight away. With Nass digging in at the other end, I took four more boundaries off Fleming's opening spell, and we both tucked into Nicholson, with his first three overs costing 26, determined not to let him settle.

Nass fell to him before lunch, but the arrival of Ramps only served to up the tempo even more. There was a stage when I went from 19 to 78 with eleven fours, and I don't think I've driven the ball as well as that on the whole of the trip.

Ramps settled quickly, and for the first hour after lunch we really made hay, adding 73 at five runs per over. Every stroke we tried came off, and Ramps seemed to be really enjoying himself, playing with the freedom he'd shown in Adelaide.

I'm not normally one to hang around in the 90s and today was no exception. I got to 99 thanks to a three off Fleming which took me to MacGill's end for the start of the next over.

He knew I was looking to get after him, impatient to reach my hundred so I think he tried to second-guess me by pitching a bit short. I stayed at home though, and rocked back to cut him backward of point and as soon as I'd hit it I knew it was my hundred.

I would have liked to celebrate there and then, but the boundaries at the MCG are among the biggest in the world so it was a case of getting the running spikes on and setting off. As I turned for the fourth, I began to raise my bat, and as soon as I reached the safety of the crease off came the helmet and I saluted the crowd.

Then I kissed the three lions on my shirt. It wasn't meant to be for show, just an expression of what it meant to me to score a hundred as England captain in an Ashes Test. It's difficult to put that feeling into words, but it meant a hell of a lot.

What made it even sweeter was that it was my first hundred against Australia. I know a lot of Australians have a lot of respect for the way I play the game, something that comes from my record against other countries, especially the West Indian quicks, and the time I spent playing cricket in WA.

But all that respect means very little if your record against Australia is poor, as I accept mine is. Let's just hope this is the start of something good.

One consolation for me is that Graham Gooch saved his best against Australia for the second half of his career, and he is someone I look up to as a batsman and a man. It took him ten years to get his first Test hundred against them, although thankfully I've managed it in around eight!

I've never blamed my keeping for my batting failures, but it is worth pointing out this is only my sixth Test against Australia as a pure batsman. I like to think I can bat as well as I did today with or without the gloves and I think my record over the past two years shows that. But maybe I have to admit that it wasn't always the case.

Anyhow, at 200 for three, we were cruising and I really thought that, with Hicky to come, the sky was the limit. Maybe that was my problem, a bit of over-confidence, because I got careless and paid the price, bowled round my legs by MacGill sweeping.

Our leg-spin coach Peter Philpott hasn't got much hair, but he must have pulled it out watching this dismissal. Right from the start of the tour he told us to get our front pad in the way of the ball when we sweep, but I disobeyed that rule and lost my leg-stump, hitting over a full-length ball.

And from there it was the usual pack of cards collapse. Maybe Ramps should have railed himself in when I got out, but he felt confident enough to keep attacking, only to miscue in the next over, and then, apart from Hicky, who did well considering he was batting with the tail, that was more or less it.

From 200 for three with them on the ropes it was a let-down, but before we went out I stressed we still had a competitive score. The new ball had moved around for them, and we had to go at them hard in the time left that evening.

Goughie certainly did just that, with one of the quickest spells I've seen from him. He had great rhythm, and bowled a great line to both the left and right handers. He hit Langer in the chest, and Taylor on the right arm, and one of his deliveries was timed at around 91 mph on the speedster at the ground – that is quick in anybody's money.

I brought Ramps on just before the close as the light was fading fast, but after an over from him the umpires still reckoned it was too dark to go on, and they closed at 59 for two. A good day's work, and we were still in the game, but it could have been so much better, despite my personal pleasure at a hundred.

Monday 28 December, Fourth Test, Day 3
England 270 & 65–2 (Stewart not out 43); Australia 340 (S Waugh not out 122, Gough 5–96)

Yet again we lost our way at a crucial time, and although we are still well in this match, they showed us once more how to play the big points, with Stephen Waugh a thorn in our side for the umpteenth time in my career.

He is just so good at shepherding the tail and he did it again today, coaxing good performances from blokes who don't really look like batsmen. His partner today was Stuart MacGill, who played and missed at a whole over from Goughie when we took the new ball, then helped Waugh add 88 for the ninth wicket to give them a lead of 70.

Waugh really is the ice-man. He likes to get off the mark quickly to settle himself, and he managed that first ball today, much to bowler Gus Fraser's annoyance, then he just settles in and waits for the bowler to bowl at him.

He has tremendous self-discipline, and won't fret if he's not scoring. He just waits and waits until he gets something he can go for, then he gives it everything he's got. His areas are the drive at a full-length ball in the arc between extra-cover and mid-on, the clip off the toes or the hip, and square of the wicket off the back-foot. He rarely plays the hook, preferring to defend or duck, but even that one came out off the locker today to take him to three figures.

His method with the tail is interesting and the statistics make even more interesting reading. He and MacGill batted together for 18 overs, but although he was the senior batsman, MacGill took the first ball of the over 12 times. If the tail folds quickly, he can leave himself open to charges of batting for himself, but he's done it so well over the years it's hard to question his methods.

The one thing about his play is that it seems to inspire his partners,

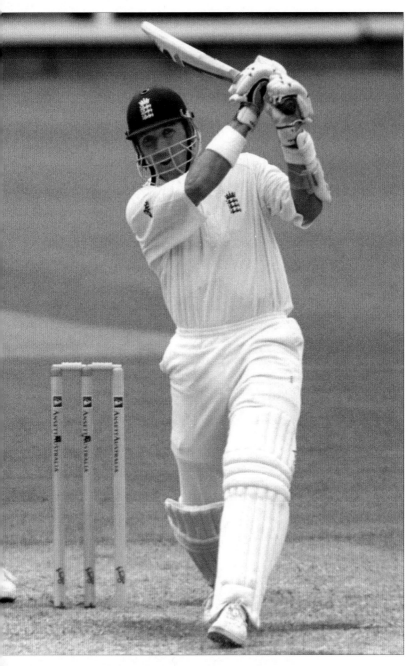

Back at the top of the order in Melbourne, I scored my first Test century against Australia. Here I am driving Stuart MacGill for four.

Above: Keeping fit on the tennis courts in between the cricket. Tim Henman needn't worry, I won't be challenging at the top of the British rankings just yet.

Above: 'Deano' Headley, whose phenomenal stamina helped us win the fourth Test, appeals against Matt Nicholson as the match reaches an unforgettable climax.

Right: 'You beauty!' The celebrations begin after Goughie traps Glenn McGrath to win the Melbourne Test, a fabulous effort by our bowlers spread over four hours.

Right: 'Take that!' Our only chance to get 287 on a Sydney turner was to be positive. Here I am putting that idea into action.

Above: Coach David Lloyd faces the media. I have enjoyed working with 'Bumble' and hope that can continue for a while yet.

Left: Stuart MacGill exposed our failings against leg-spin. With 12 wickets in Sydney and 27 victims in four Tests his performance was crucial to Australia's success.

Left: Goughie fully deserved his hat-trick in Sydney, and it capped our first-day fightback. Victim number two was Stuart MacGill, comprehensively castled.

Below: Spin-twins Stuart MacGill (left) and the returning Shane Warne helped Australia make the most of Sydney's turning pitch to end our hopes of squaring the series.

Above: Mark Waugh put the bribery controversy earlier in the series behind him to score an all-important hundred in the fifth Test in Sydney.

ECB Chairman Lord MacLaurin looks on as Mark Taylor holds up the new Ashes Trophy. MacLaurin's support for the players since he became Chairman has been superb.

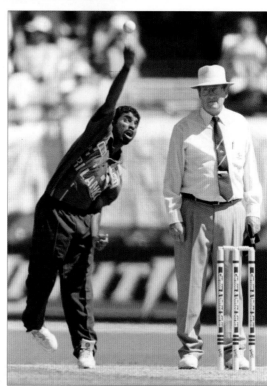

Muralitharan bowls in Adelaide, watched by umpire Ross Emerson. Sri Lanka's failure to accept Emerson's no-balling of him started the ill-feeling that wrecked the match.

Goughie and Mahanama exchange words after their barging incident in Adelaide during the Carlton & United One Day Series. It was the most unpleasant game of cricket I have ever played in.

Three of the central figures in the controversial Adelaide match: Sri Lanka captain Arjuna Ranatunga, Muralitharan and umpire Emerson.

Hicky cuts towards a century against Australia in Adelaide. Hicky made three limited-overs hundreds on the tour, but we won just one of those matches.

Shane Warne has words during the first of the one-day finals matches in Sydney. The Aussie captain had the last laugh as he had Nass stumped in the 43rd over – and the batting collapse began. How we lost this opening match after needing just 35 runs off 7.5 overs with six wickets in hand defied belief.

Left: Out of the 1999 World Cup and my England captaincy at an end. Victory here over Zimbabwe preceded a disastrous loss against India, which meant we were eliminated from the tournament by virtue of an inferior run rate.

Below: On my way to 95 in the first innings against South Africa in the third Test at Durban during the 1999/2000 tour. After losing the first Test, we felt we had improved as the series wore on.

Below: Dropping Jacques Kallis off Chris Silverwood in the first innings of the fourth Test at Cape Town. This was one of my rare errors in the series – but Kallis went on to make 105.

and by the end of his innings, MacGill was swiping our tired bowlers through mid-wicket with glee. Once again though, we failed to deliver the killer punch, and that is worrying.

We lacked a bit of aggression with the ball during their stand, although there was a slight excuse that the four-man attack had put in a huge effort up to that point. But all of a sudden we seemed to be running on empty and everyone switched off.

We went off the boil in the field too. Nass and I got in each other's way and failed to run out MacGill when the two batsmen should barely have crossed, and it wasn't until Al got rid of the tailender that we pepped up. He bowled McGrath two tasty bouncers, and bowled him off the body with the second of them.

Up to tea, we'd done well. We'd worked our way through their batting, held some good catches, especially Nass's one in the gully to remove Langer, and had really looked on the ball. Once again though, their tail sold their wickets dearly, and we have to learn from that.

So, from tea, when Goughie yorked Nicholson to get a 'Michelle' (having earlier passed fifty Test wickets against Australia) to leave them on 252 for eight, we were suddenly batting again for an awkward hour trailing by 70.

Poor Ath. He was on a pair and took strike to his old enemy McGrath, but it was Fleming who handed him the first set of spectacles of his Test career. He just survived a big appeal for lbw the ball before thanks to a nick, but next ball lost his off-stump to a ball that pitched and held its line.

Technically, he's struggling. His bat seems to be coming from around second slip, and though he knows it's not coming down straight, he can't seem to correct it. The middle of back-to-back Tests isn't really the time to be making major changes to your technique, but it's something he'll have to look at before the start of next summer.

Some of the press have suggested his back is one of the reasons for his technical problems, but even if it was he'd never say. He's one of life's non-complainers, and given the way he's performed with the condition over the past few years I don't believe it's a major factor now. In fact, I've every confidence he will put this behind him, if not in Sydney, then next summer. He's had problems like that before, way back in Zimbabwe in 1996/97, and then again last winter in the Caribbean. Both times he came back strongly, and I'm sure he'll do it again.

We may have lost that early wicket, but I felt in great touch again. I took eleven runs from McGrath's second over, and with Butch looking as good as he had since Brisbane I thought we'd make it to the close with just one wicket down and on terms.

Unbelievably though, he swept MacGill straight into the body of Slater at short leg and the ball stuck. Butch had decided that was the way he would play against the leg-spinner having failed when he just prodded about, and he couldn't have timed the shot any better. But stick it did, and that was a body blow for us, if not for Slater just before stumps.

When the close came I had 43 and we trailed by five. And family or no family, it was time for an early night with the need to play another big innings tomorrow.

Tuesday 29 December, Fourth Test, Day 4
England 270 & 244 (Hick 60, Stewart 52, Hussain 50) beat Australia 340 & 162 (M Waugh 43, Headley 6–60) by 12 runs

There are some moments that will live with me forever, and the instant Daryl Harper put his finger up to give Glenn McGrath out at the MCG at 7.33 will be one of them.

To win any Test is special, but to win this one, which we'd gone into as total under-dogs and which, even 75 minutes from the end we'd looked set to lose heavily, made it one of the greatest moments of mine, and I would think, every other players' careers.

All series I have wanted us to show a never-say-die attitude and really try to put the Aussies under the cosh. And for a magic afternoon today we managed it.

The real heroes were the bowlers. At the start of the tour everyone had questioned whether we could bowl Australia out twice, but this evening they answered that question with an emphatic 'yes' thanks to an unbelievable effort less than 24 hours after giving it everything to bowl them out first time round. And the way they did it was truly inspiring.

They were all heroes, with Goughie finding the energy from somewhere to mop up the tail, while Al bowled a brilliant, tight spell that put them under pressure before that. That spell was even better because his boots were broken, and he spent the whole time in the field in a pair he borrowed from Theo King, a school teacher from

Wolverhampton. He doubles as our dressing room helper and general good bloke in his holidays with no job too big.

But the other bowlers won't mind me saying Headley was the star. He was magnificent. He had bowled with pace in the first innings, as he did in the state game back at the start of December, a game which kick-started his tour. In that first innings he only had a dropped catch by Hicky off Fleming to show for his efforts; now he had the man of the match award, and six wickets.

The Aussies were only chasing 175, far fewer than the 250 I'd wanted to set them at the start of the day. Every time we'd looked like putting a partnership together, we lost wickets, and although three of us – Nass, Hicky and me – passed fifty, no one could go on and get a big score.

We got a bit of boost at the end when Al and Gus added 23 for the last wicket, riches given our earlier tail-end effort, and Al really got under McGrath's skin by carting him for three fours. But we didn't realise how vital those runs would be until much, much later.

We took heart from the fact that so many of our players had got in and then got out, because although the pitch was dry, there was still some seam movement. And the dry conditions were also helping the older ball to reverse swing.

The fact that I didn't have to get ready to keep wicket meant I could give a slightly longer team-talk than normal, and there was plenty I had to say, with Bumble chipping in too.

'Right,' I began. 'We've got the runs on the board, not as many as we might have liked, but they're there and now they've got to get them.

'We know their recent record of chasing targets in the last innings isn't great, so it's up to us to put them under pressure. Their record says they can choke in run-chases and we've got to make sure that happens today.

'Remember that choking goes back to Botham and Willis in '81 when they lost time and again looking for fourth innings scores, so they'll be nervous. And don't forget The Oval last summer either. Or Adelaide on the last tour.

'Let's make sure they stay nervous. Sharp in the field, give them nothing, support the bowlers and plenty of noise out there too.'

We also reminded the lads, especially the bowlers, to keep taking liquids whenever there was a break in play, as this was going to be a very long session.

Because we'd been bowled out within half an hour of the scheduled tea break at 3.40 (Mullally was out at 3.11), tea was taken straight away, so that immediately made the last session almost half an hour longer. Add to that the extra half hour which we were playing at the start and end of every day to make up for the washed out first day, the fact that we had no front-line spinner and the chance of the extra half-hour if a result was possible and it could be a very long session indeed!

As I suspected, they went after us first up with Slater really going for his shots. There's nothing like a quick start with runs on the board to settle the nerves when you are chasing a small score, and it can also send the heads of the fielding side down, which adds to the effect.

Slater really did climb into us and Deano, in particular, suffered. His first over cost nine, and his third had gone for ten when he found a break-back to trap the opener in front. It's not often you see an Aussie walk, least of all for an lbw, but Slater was on his way before Steve Bucknor's finger went up.

That wicket came at just the right time for Deano and for us. I have to say I would have taken him off at the end of that over if he hadn't struck as we couldn't afford to go at that rate defending such a low score. But it brought Langer in, and as he and Taylor are similar players, more accumulators than hitters, it allowed us to regain control.

I wouldn't pretend to be a great captain, but there are times when you look that way and my move to bring Al on for Goughie just after Slater's fall certainly suggested I had the Midas touch.

Goughie couldn't quite find the inspiration he had at the start of the first innings, but Al did the job in his first over. He'd tied Taylor down for the first four balls of the over before dropping short, and the Aussie captain went for the pull. It was a top-edge, but it went up miles into the air with Deano having plenty of time to think about things at long leg.

He got under it and held it neatly, but that was the prelude to what looked like a crucial miss.

The batsmen had crossed so Langer was on strike for the next ball from Al, and the ball seamed away from him and bounced, catching the outside edge. Hicky tumbled forward and to his right, got his finger-tips under the ball, but couldn't hold on.

And that was our last success for a long time. Al bowled two successive maidens to Mark Waugh, but Gussie, who'd replaced Deano at the Southern End, wasn't at his best.

Normally I'd want a long, tight containing spell from him and that would have given me the chance to rest Headley and Gough while Al kept things nailed down at the other end. But Gus went for 23 in four overs, and it meant I had to bring Goughie back much sooner than I wanted.

Even that didn't work though, and he'd bowled two overs for 11 to take the Australian score past 100 when a moment of magic from Ramps helped set us on our way.

Al pitched short again, as he had to Taylor, but this was his ninth over and he could be forgiven for being a bit tired. Langer saw it early and nailed it in front of square, right off the middle of the bat.

Then, out off nowhere, came Ramps. He took a moment to sight it, pushed off with his left foot and clung on to a blinder a few inches off the turf in front of Bucknor.

He was up straight away, waving his arms, high-fiving everyone, and shouting as loud as he could 'How about that then? Let's get into it boys. Let's nail 'em boys.' Butch, who'd been at cover point so had a great view of the whole thing, raced over and was whooping and laughing. It gave everyone a lift, and we were going again.

That brought Steve Waugh in, and I had some juggling to do. Al was tiring, and Gus had been costly, so I brought Deano back from the Southern End, and after one more over from Al, sent Goughie on from the Members' End.

Things didn't exactly go according to plan straight away either. The second over of Deano's spell went for ten, and the fourth had cost seven, bringing the target down below fifty, when he struck to get rid of Mark Waugh.

The ball was a good length just outside off-stump that may have just held its line. Waugh was looking to play it through mid-on, but closed the face of the bat too early, it took the edge, and Hicky took a good, tumbling catch at waist high.

Deano was fired up and bowling with real pace at this stage, but I think we all thought deep down, even though we wouldn't admit it, it might be a case of too little too late. But I knew we just had a chance as long as we could start to exert some pressure.

The ball was now 34 overs old, but it had begun to reverse swing. Rather than swinging away from the shiny side as balls usually do, this one was swinging towards it. This effect is achieved by wetting the shiny side to make it heavy while leaving the dull side rough and dry.

It's all perfectly legal and the in-swing it allows can be devastating. Deano and Goughie are masters at using a ball in that sort of condition and they began to weave their magic.

Deano began to Lehmann by staying over the wicket and Lehmann responded by getting off the mark with a clubbing off-side boundary. But with runs precious, it was a case of now or never so straight away he decided to switch his angle of attack and go around the wicket.

That made sure Lehmann had no width outside off stump, just as Goughie had suggested before the match, and once again it came off, as he drove hard at the last ball of the over. The batsman definitely hit the ground, but Bucknor judged he'd got a fine edge as well, and suddenly they were 140 for five.

I now thought we had a real chance, but to keep up our momentum we had to get rid of Steve Waugh or new batsman Healy as soon as possible. They've taken the game away from us so often before, but if we could pick up one more wicket we would open up an end, exposing their tail.

By this stage, the Barmy Army, based in the far corner of the Southern Stand, were really making themselves heard. They'd been brilliant throughout the tour even when we had been struggling at various stages of the past three days, and now they really got behind us and gave us a real lift.

I love playing with vocal support behind us and I know the rest of the lads do too, especially when we are away from home. Playing in Australia used to be really intimidating because of the noise their crowds make, but with the level of support we've had on this tour, it's sometimes made us feel like we're at home.

It would be great to get that backing in home Tests too, even though I know flags and even fancy dress are banned. But maybe there should be a place for all the types of supporters in England, so long as the vocal ones don't over-step the mark.

Deano responded to the support he got here alright. Heals was batting with a broken finger after he'd mis-gloved a ball from Fleming, but he's batted through pain before. He loves to impose himself straight away and to his second ball he went for an expansive drive. It caught the edge and Hicky took another tumbling catch at second slip.

That brought drinks out onto the ground, and I gathered the lads around for a pep-talk. 'We're into them now,' I said. 'Just stay sharp, give them nothing and we can win this.'

And importantly, Deano told everyone: 'The ball's reversing now boys. Make sure you don't wet the wrong side, or better still just get it back to the bowlers as quickly as possible so we can look after it.'

Fleming didn't stay long, just three balls in fact before Deano trapped him lbw, having for all the world looked as though he'd got him plumb the ball before. He'd now got four wickets in 13 balls and with the momentum going our way I thought we were favourites.

At that point there were 7.1 overs left of the 45 we had to bowl to the close, and I hoped we could win it there and then. But the bowlers were running on adrenaline and there was always the danger they could run out of steam if two players got a foothold.

That looked for all the world as though it would happen too, as Nicholson dug in with Waugh. The pair nudged, nurdled and scampered 21 runs by the scheduled close at 7.22, and they were beginning to look comfortable against Deano and Goughie.

I knew Steve Waugh would claim the extra half-hour at that point as they only wanted 14 to win, and we were looking tired. That was hardly surprising, as by this stage we'd been in the field without a break for almost four hours, longer than even a one-day international innings.

That was partly our fault with the over-rate, but they'd also been losing wickets, so I tried a bit of play-acting with the umpires. As Goughie finished his over, I picked up the bails at the Northern End and handed them to Harper. 'That's it then,' I said.

It was all done with a wry grin, because he then went over to Bucknor, consulted with Waugh and the bails had to be replaced. And how grateful am I for Waugh's decision.

That meant we were in for another eight overs if it went the distance, and I spoke to Deano, who was due for the next over. 'It's now or never, mate,' I said. And he responded.

Waugh had left Nicholson on strike and to the fifth ball of the over, he feathered the ball to Chucky, and we went bananas. Now I really thought we'd win.

Waugh now had to stay on even though he might have wanted to go off, and we had all the cards. The shadows were over the pitch, and for a new batsman, with the bowlers running through sunlight, that wouldn't be easy, especially as they were tailenders.

MacGill survived the last ball of the over, then Steve Waugh made the fateful decision to take the single off the first ball of the next over, from Goughie. You couldn't blame him in some ways. After all, in the first innings he and MacGill had added 88. But this was different, intense pressure at the end of a Test, and maybe he should have taken more responsibility.

I was all ready to take Goughie off before Deano had got rid of Nicholson. He was knackered, running on empty, and I signalled to Al down on the boundary to warm up. But once Deano had struck, it was no time for a new bowler, especially with Steve Waugh on strike, as a couple of ill-directed looseners could have gone for four and taken them to the brink of victory.

I asked for one last, big effort from Goughie – and showman that he is, he obliged.

In the fading light and against a new tailender Goughie knew what to do. Fast, straight and full. In fact, it was almost too full, and went through MacGill on the full toss, bowling him all over the place. He didn't even look back. Off he trooped, and now it was McGrath's turn to face the music.

It was a dream situation for us. Four balls to bowl at McGrath to win a Test in fading light. But we had to be aware what Waugh might do too. He might have been a helpless onlooker at the non-striker's end, but maybe they would try and run a bye to the keeper. 'Everyone *has* to be on their toes,' I shouted, although it didn't really need to be said.

Goughie almost got his man first ball as he played and missed, but second ball was bang on. Fast, inswinging, and full. It hit McGrath on the boot as he edged forward, but Harper was always going to give it out.

Pandemonium. Goughie grabbed a stump and started waving it above his head, and Hicky ran down from slip to try and gave him a bear hug. Bumble and Theo as well as all the non-players raced onto the ground and began hugging everyone, and stumps and bails were being grabbed by seemingly every player.

I tried to remain calm, although inside I was bursting. I went across to the umpires to shake hands, and also to Steve Waugh. 'Well played, mate,' I said. 'Doesn't matter, does it?' he replied, completely dejected.

Off we jogged, by now accompanied by the first battalion of the Barmy Army, and we raced into the dressing room with Deano almost in tears, as he had been after we'd won in Trinidad earlier in the year. It was a crazy place, with everyone screaming and yelling, but Murgers caught my eye.

He had a huge grin on his face, but still had to do his job and asked whether any cameras would be allowed in the dressing room. 'If we'd won the series, yes', I said. But we'd won a Test, and great though that was the main prize had gone. 'When we win in Sydney then fine, but not now,' I said.

Lord MacLaurin, the ECB Chairman, and Chief Executive Tim Lamb, both of whom had just arrived in Melbourne for the Test, came in to say well done, and then John Reid, the match referee appeared with a late Christmas present. 'You're eight overs down on your required rate for the match,' he said. 'But as you've won we'll forget it. Well done lads.' As an eight over deficit would have cost us 55% of our match fee (about £1700), that brought a cheer from everyone.

There was no Channel Nine presentation because the match had gone well beyond their normal off-air time, although I joked it had something to do with the fact we'd won. But Sky Sports were set up in our viewing room upstairs, and they wanted to speak to almost everyone, while outside the Barmy Army were banging on the viewing room windows, so we made a couple of appearances.

Then, it was the press and a slightly easier conference than usual, although they are always easy when you win. One question that came up was whether I'd keep in the next Test as my opening the batting had worked so well this time. 'I wouldn't have thought so, but we'll have to wait and see,' I said.

I'll be honest, the success of me opening again with just a four-man attack had surprised me a bit, but the end justified the means, and as it worked so well I was forced to admit it might be a good idea to stick with it for Sydney too. And the fact was both Butch and Ath had barely got a run again, so someone had to open!

My press conference in the players' dining room took place while the rest of the lads were singing and shouting next door in the dressing room and that meant I had to speak up a bit at times. But it brought a smile from the press as they knew how much the win meant for everyone.

Once I was back in the dressing room, it was a case of packing up, having a sip or two of champagne and then it was back to the hotel for some celebrations. Lynn was there to meet me, and we went to the hotel bar to be joined by a couple of hundred fans and most of the players.

I rang dad and the family at home with Murgers' mobile phone and they were all buzzing. Because the match had ended so late, it was breakfast time in England and they said the television and radio news was full of the win.

But by this stage the adrenaline had stopped flowing and I was exhausted. So was Goughie, and we both headed off to bed by midnight, long before the celebrations kicked in. I reckon I might not do that if we win in Sydney as well though.

Australia v England, Fifth Test, Sydney, 2–5 January 1999

Wednesday 30 December

It was a case of the morning after the night before for quite a few of the lads today, with many of them not getting up until lunch-time. I had no problem with that though, as everyone deserved a lie-in after the efforts of yesterday, and the celebrations that followed.

Apart from the relaxing, which I reckon is the most important thing we can do right now in the middle of back-to-back Tests at the end of a hard tour, there was also the need to turn our thoughts to the Sydney Test, which begins in just a few days.

The Australians certainly haven't been slow in doing just that, with news reaching us at lunch-time that Warne has been recalled to their squad. That's no surprise given the tales we've been hearing about the SCG pitch this season, with reports that it is turning an awful lot. Nicholson has been left out to make way for Warney, but with Miller also able to bowl medium-pace, they could go into the match with two leg-spinners plus Miller and Mark Waugh to bowl off-spin.

They wouldn't be thinking along those lines unless they thought the pitch will spin big, so Goochie, Bumble and I discussed what our options were. The one-day boys are flying down to Sydney tomorrow on their way to Bowral for a game against the Bradman XI on New Year's Day, so we decided we would take Croft, Giles and Crawley – one of our best players of spin – off them when they arrive. At least that way we're covered if we need an extra spinner or two, or a spare batsman. In return, we'll send a couple of our lads not playing in the Test up to Bowral by car on the morning of the game.

Thursday 31 December

A day off, the last of the Test tour, so everyone had the chance to spend some time with their families, or just relax.

I had the morning with the children, mucking around in the pool, along with others including Fizz and his family before I had some more serious work to do in the afternoon. I'm changing bat and kit manufacturers tomorrow, moving from Kookaburra, whom I've used for the past eight years, and going back to Slazenger, the company I began my first-class career with.

As such, I had to go through all my kit and kit bags and get rid of all the Kookaburra stuff, replacing it with Slazenger gear I'd been sent. Sponsors pay good money for players to endorse their products, so I had to make sure I had the correct gear as it will be something that is bound to interest the photographers when I pitch up at net practice tomorrow.

Once I had checked all my gear, it was time to see the press for my pre-Test media conference. I took Ashley Giles ('Splash') along with me as the fact he's been drafted into the squad was bound to cause some interest, and rather than bother him later it made sense to have him on hand to answer any questions now. That did cause some fun though as several of the Aussie media didn't know who he was and thought he was a physiotherapist there to take queries on fitness matters. I was asked whether Splash's call-up was an admission it was a mistake to bring two off-spinners in the first place, but I played a straight bat to that one. We picked what we thought were the two best spinners at the time, but with the prospect of a turning pitch and a left-armer in the country it made perfect sense to draft him in just in case the pitch was a complete dust bowl. We would have looked far sillier if he'd gone to Bowral and then been called back once we'd seen the pitch.

With official duties done, it was off to get ready for New Year's Eve on a boat. Goochie had arranged for us to have a cruise around Sydney Harbour to watch the traditional fireworks and most of the squad took up the offer. It was a relaxing evening for Lynn and I, with the only hiccup coming when, having left our berth, we had to go back for Suchy who'd gone to get a packet of cigarettes for his fiancee.

The fireworks were spectacular and very loud and there were an amazing number of boats in the harbour area. The atmosphere on the boat, which had plenty of non-cricket people on it as well, was very festive, as you'd expect and we got a good meal as well. Music played, everyone relaxed, and once we'd seen the New Year in, we headed back to shore and were back at the hotel by 12.45 am. It's not every day you get the chance to bring in a New Year like that and I think everyone was grateful we did it.

Friday 1 January

After a few days of rest after Melbourne, it was back to business today with our last session before the Test. It was satisfying from my point of view to see that everyone was fully focused on the job in hand, although that was hardly surprising given the importance of the match. After all, we have the chance to square the series and that would be a hell of achievement given all the stick we've taken over the past two and a half months.

Although Splash was with us as a new addition, we were without Cork, Fraser and Hollioake. They were driven up to Bowral by Malcolm Ashton first thing to play in the Bradman XI game alongside Ian Salisbury, who's playing club cricket over here, and Gavin Hamilton. Gav finished last summer strongly and has impressed Grav so much that he's pushing for his inclusion in our World Cup squad of 30, which has to be named by 15 January.

Splash bowled steadily in the nets and was then interviewed by the Australian media who have called him 'Ashley Who'. Meanwhile Goochie, Bumble, Nass and I had our first look at the pitch, which was basically what we'd expected. It looked pretty dry although there was a light covering of grass, and like Adelaide it could be a case of win the toss, win the match. Let's hope I call right for once.

We expected the ball to spin from quite early on, but that still left us with several awkward decisions. Should I go back to keeping allowing us to play a balanced attack of five bowlers, including two spinners? If I didn't keep, which four bowlers would we play – three seamers and one spinner or two plus two?

Well, I answered the first question pretty easily. My batting had been one of the successes of the Melbourne Test, and with Ath and Butch both struggling for runs I felt I had to keep opening. And if I was opening, I couldn't keep as well.

I suppose I could have kept wicket and opened if we batted first, dropping down the order if we fielded. But that would have caused too much uncertainty as players at this level do like to know where they are batting. And unless Crawley or Ramprakash moved up to open at short notice, it would have meant playing both Ath and Butch, something that we couldn't really justify given their lack of form.

John Crawley's inclusion meant one of them had to go, and it was an agonising decision. Apart from a few Tests in India, I couldn't ever recall Ath being dropped, but his form was poor as he would be coming into the match after a pair in Melbourne. On the other hand, Butch had barely scored a run in the Tests after his hundred in Brisbane, and would be counting the days to going home with Judy almost due, not that it affected our decision or his form if he'd played.

In the end we played a hunch and went for Ath. Even though he has been struggling, he is a big match player, and a much better player of spin than Butch, providing he gets through the new ball. Also, I hoped he might recapture a bit of form with me at the other end, as he and I have been a plus for England whenever we've batted together over the past few years. It was a tough one, but these are the kinds of decisions we have to make as selectors.

We kept our bowling options open by naming thirteen with Splash getting the nod ahead of Crofty simply for the sake of balance. If we'd wanted to play two spinners, it would be difficult to play Croft and Such, with both our back-up bowlers Hicky and Ramps, also off-spinners.

I'd like to bowl Hicky a bit more, but over the past three or four years he's bowled very little for his county Worcestershire. Maybe that's because he lacks a bit of confidence after the back injury he picked up in Australia in 1994/95. I've seen him bowl more than 50 overs in a Test match innings a few years ago and do a good job, so his bowling is certainly not forgotten at England level.

Incidentally, I don't see the inclusion of Splash ahead of Crofty as an admission we shouldn't have brought two off-spinners. With Al's footmarks a possible factor, we wanted both here as competition for each other, but we were never really going to play both of them in the same side. Splash's presence in the country gives us that extra option, but if he had come instead of or as well as the other two I think he would have had very little to do until this point in the tour.

By the way, I don't regard Phil Tufnell's international career as over. We picked what we thought was the best squad for the tour of

Australia, and Tuffers was one of those disappointed to be left out. But there's no doubt he can come again.

Tudes was now fit again and we went for him in the squad as he has shown he is a wicket-taker. We know the pitch is going to be slow, but if it gets uneven as the match goes on, we might want his extra pace and hostility, and it's likely he'll fight it out with Al for the last place if we go for three seamers.

Selection over, it was back to the hotel for a bit of relaxation and then the final pre-Test team meeting of the tour. It was pretty positive and constructive too: 'The Ashes may have gone, but this is the type of match we came here for,' I said. 'Win here and we'll end up with a drawn series, which would be a fantastic effort after all the criticism we've taken.'

Bumble took up the theme: 'We've hung in there and now we're bubbling. The win in Melbourne means we'll be the side flying in here. Let's take that confidence and use it. And let's win.'

There was some talk about Warney, and everyone expected him to play. After all, you don't pick someone with over 300 Test wickets just to carry the drinks. That would mean either Fleming or Miller missing out. We discussed how Warney was bowling from what we'd seen of him on the television. Goochie, who's seen more of him than most down the years, said he wasn't getting as much action on the ball as he used to and had barely bowled his flipper, the danger ball which pitches short then hurries on. But he would still be a threat, especially if the pitch starts to offer turn.

The tailenders have really struggled against MacGill in this series, and they would like to be told how to bat. Discussing methods is fine as far as I'm concerned, but it's then up to each player to put his own game plan into action. I said, 'It's not for me or anyone else to tell you "right, we're blocking everything," or "right, we're hitting over the top if it's pitched up." You must work out your best method against each bowler and how you'll look to score your runs. Then, once you've done that, stick to it.'

Meeting over, and after all the excitement of the previous evening, it was time for a relaxing evening. A take-away pizza and a spell in front of the television fitted the bill perfectly.

Saturday 2 January, Fifth Test, Day 1
Australia 322 (M Waugh 121, S Waugh 96, Headley 4–62)

I've played in some pretty memorable days of Test cricket, but today is up there with the best of them.

It had everything. A huge crowd generating an electric atmosphere, an amazing first hour when we got three wickets, brilliant batting from the Waugh twins, and then a Test match hat-trick by Goughie as we hit back superbly in the last hour.

First things first though. We had an injury crisis at the start of the day and I managed to lose the toss for the sixth Test in a row. I don't know whether that is a record, especially as I called heads each time here in Australia, but it was bloody annoying, especially as everyone knew batting last is going to be tough on a pitch which will spin more and more as the game goes on.

What made things worse was that I borrowed the coin from John Reid afterwards and spun it a few times once I was back in the dressing room. Can you believe it, I tossed five times, and each time it came down heads. At least it goes to show I'm not a useless tosser after all.

By then we'd lost Ath. He had been complaining in his own quiet way about stiffness in his back the previous day during a fielding session, but we expected him to come through okay. But after a net, he said he couldn't bend properly and in a match where we might need to take every half-chance, he would obviously have been a liability in the field. So he stood down after chatting with Fizz, and Butch, who 24 hours earlier had been making plans to go home once the match began to get back to Judy, was now in a Test match.

With our two back-up bowlers, Hick and Ramprakash, both offies, it made sense to go with three seamers and just one front-line spinner, and Such got the nod. Headley and Gough picked themselves, so the last place was between Tudor and Mullally.

Al has been our steadiest bowler in the series, but apart from his 'Michelle' in the first Test he has bowled really well without taking the wickets he probably deserved. Add to that Tudes' wicket-taking potential that we'd seen in Perth and I went for him. It was a gamble, but 2–1 down, we had nothing to lose.

It meant Al, Splash, Pelly and Crofty would be heading off to join the one-day boys in Brisbane, but they were still at the ground for the morning session, with the first seventy minutes one of the most amazing periods I can remember at the start of a Test.

By the time the clock had hit 12.10 we had three wickets, they had 52 runs, there'd been a wicket off a no-ball, a line-decision for the third umpire and the crowd were making enough noise for Wembley Stadium.

That crowd was superb. I think it was a full house, and someone said it was the first time they've had to shut the gates on the opening day of an SCG Test in almost 25 years. They made a real noise, and with the Barmy Army singing all day, it was a great atmosphere to play in.

The drama began as early as the fourth over when Deano got Taylor with a beauty, angling across him and forcing him to play. It took the edge and Hicky tumbled forward at second slip to take the catch. It was almost a carbon copy of the one he dropped off Langer in Melbourne, so straight away things were going for us.

That feeling took a bit of a jolt when I brought Tudes on, as within the space of three balls Langer had two let-offs. The big man replaced Deano, whom I planned to swap for Goughie, and immediately things began to happen.

From his second ball, Slater called for a quick single, but Langer was slow to respond. Ramps hared in and hit the stumps direct at the strikers' end.

Out on the field, you instinctively know when line decisions like that are close, and we all thought this was very close. Direct hits can make all the difference, and we all strained to see the big screen at the Randwick End of the ground. The oohs and ahhs of the crowd told us just how close it was, but the picture wasn't too clear from the middle. To be honest, it looked like a dead heat, the type you expect to be given in when you're batting and out when you're in the field so Langer got the benefit by the skin of his teeth. Stood near him as the green light came on I could see him puff out his cheeks so he knew it was close.

That may have been out of our control, but two balls later we blew the chance to bury Langer once and for all. Maybe he was affected by the delay, but when Tudes angled a wide half-volley across him, he threw the bat with no real movement of the feet and got a big nick through to Chucky.

We all went up behind the wicket, but straight away Tudes stopped dead, having heard Darrell Hair's call of no-ball. It's something he's worked on from the start of the tour with Bob Cottam and he and Deano have largely got rid of the habit, but of all times for it to come back, this was not the best to say the least.

Things like that can really break you in the field if you let them. After all, it was a hot day, two top players were at the crease, and in the space of three balls, they've had two let-offs. It was especially tough for Tudes. But the attitude in this squad has been top value, especially over the past two weeks, and we got back to it straight away.

Deano typified that, and he got his reward right on the hour mark when he tempted Slater into hooking a ball which got too big on him, flicked the glove, and gave Hegg a simple catch.

That was drinks, and already it was 52 for two in only thirteen overs, so there was no shortage of entertainment. Two overs from Tudes had played a big part in that, what with the run-out appeal, the wicket off the no-ball and 21 runs, but I told him at the break he was staying on.

I just felt the Aussies had gone after him, seeing him as a bit of a danger man. He'd been a bit leg-side too, but I wanted to give him the chance to find some rhythm, something that was vital as he was one of only four front-line bowlers in the side.

I didn't quite expect to be rewarded as quickly as I was for that move though. First ball after drinks, and Langer slapped a short, wide ball straight to cover point, Ramps held a simple catch, and they were 52 for three.

The two Waughs were in, our bowlers were still relatively fresh, and if we could break through again, we were really at the races. It's at times like that you need things to go with you, and this time they didn't. Steve edged Tudes past his leg-stump in the same over he came in, and Mark pushed forward to Deano, and the bat-pad just got away from Creepy as he dived forward at short leg. I suppose you could argue that those sorts of things go for you when you're a consistently winning side, but I prefer to think we just didn't have the rub of the green when it counted.

That's cricket though, and given their little bits of luck or whatever you want to call it, the Waughs did what they do best from then on, and gave a great display of Test match batting. They dispatched the bad balls and defended against the good ones.

If I had to be critical, I'd say we bowled a little bit both sides of the wicket, and their score of 101 at lunch was far too many on the first day of a Test. But on the plus side, the commitment of everyone was superb, and never faltered, even as the twins batted through the afternoon session without being parted.

By this stage Suchy had come on, and almost straight away began to turn the ball. Often the ball will spin on the first day as it grips on any remaining moisture in the pitch. Then, as the pitch dries completely, it stops spinning, only to start again as the surface wears on days three, four and five.

This surface was a bit different to the type of pitch we usually see in England though. It was really dry from the start, and it was dusting as the ball hit it even on day one, so every run Australia got in their first innings was a real blow to our chances of staying in the game.

By tea, I had Ramps operating in tandem with Suchy, and both were spinning the odd ball sharply. I suppose the fact that I had two spinners on by that stage will mean I'll be criticised for not playing two slow bowlers, but it still comes back to what I said before. We picked what we felt to be our four best bowlers to take 20 wickets and that only included one spinner.

In any case, that choice was made in the knowledge that Ramps could do a job for us, and he bowled steadily enough. He had Mark missed at short-leg, a reflex catch to Creepy, straight after tea, and now he is Middlesex captain I hope he will use himself more and more as a bowler. He has plenty of potential, and if even one of our top six can bowl it will give us so many more options, especially if I don't keep wicket.

Just when it looked like both Waughs would get hundreds, Suchy got Steve with a beautiful bit of bowling, drawing him down the pitch then beating him between bat and pad. It spun a long way, almost too much, but just clipped the stumps to give us all some relief.

At first though, that relief was short-lived. Lehmann came in, and Ramps and Suchy gave him far too much width. Both had bowled long spells by this stage, but he was able to take full advantage, and despite being unsure of his place in the side, got easy runs through a series of clubbing off-side boundaries.

The fact the Aussies were scoring so well left me in an awkward position. It had been a hot day and all the bowlers were tired, but I wanted to save Headley and Goughie for the new ball, as if we could get a breakthrough or two before stumps, six or even seven down at the close would be a fair day's work.

That meant Tudes was back in the firing line, and once again, he made things happen. He bowled a wide long-hop to Lehmann, who clubbed it like a rocket backward of square. It went straight to Nass in the gully and knocked him off his feet, but he held on, and they were five down.

Both sides knew the importance of the next forty-odd minutes now, and Healy and Waugh just looked to consolidate as we pushed for another wicket or two before the close. Both Goughie and Deano were tired, but with eight overs left I took the new ball. Both lads were determined to give it everything they had for the short time left in the day, and even if things didn't work out, I still thought there'd be enough hardness in the ball for another burst tomorrow morning. Thankfully though, that wasn't needed.

Although it was Goughie who eventually took the headlines for his hat-trick, it was Deano who got the first breakthrough with the new ball. With stumps just five overs away, maybe Waugh just went into his shell a bit, keen to be there the following morning. So when Deano found one on the perfect line just outside off-stump, he pushed at it a bit tentatively and feathered it to Chucky.

That was a key wicket and gave everyone a lift. Now we had an end open with the tail, and it gave us a chance to really go hell for leather to the close.

Confession time now. Goughie has Headless to thank for the chance to take the hat-trick, because if he hadn't got rid of Waugh, I was all set to put Goughie out to grass for the day.

He'd bowled bloody well on a really hot day, but the strain of the last Test, and his first five-Test series without a break in the whole of his career seemed to be telling on him. He seemed a bit tired, but the fact a new batsman, his old mate Warney, was coming in made me keep him on.

It was a similar position to the one at the end of the Melbourne Test. I was all set to pull Goughie off then too and throw the ball to Al when Deano struck, and after that you'd have needed a crow-bar to get the ball out of his hands. It was the same this time around.

'One more?' I said. 'No problem.' No captain could ask for any more.

The over began quietly enough, with a leg-bye to Warne, before Goughie set off for the fourth ball, to Healy. The hardness of the newish ball helped him find a little bit of extra bounce from somewhere and it also cut back as the batsman shaped to cut. It flicked Healy's right thumb and Hegg took an easy catch.

Heals started to walk, but being an Aussie stopped after a pace or two just in case he might get away with it, apparently making out he'd walked away because he had something in his eye. He didn't, or at least he didn't get away with it, and they were seven down.

To be honest, eight overs from the close when they were five down and Waugh and Heals were in, I'd have settled for both of them being out by stumps. But now I think we could all see a real chance of rolling them over quickly. And Goughie, being the showman he is, responded.

He couldn't have picked a better man to be coming in next than Stuart MacGill, whom he castled so completely in Melbourne. For a man who got 44 in the last Test, he didn't look as though he fancied it one bit and Goughie must have known it.

Both men must have known what was coming too: a fast, straight yorker. Goughie can bowl those to order, and he obliged now with MacGill nearer the square-leg umpire than the ball, which plucked out his middle stump.

Two in two, the crowd going wild and Goughie back at his mark with Colin Miller on his way. Corky came on as twelfth man with some drinks and Goughie tried to avoid him as he knew what he'd say. Corky was true to form too: 'Come on Darren, let's see you join the club.'

That 'club' is made up of bowlers who've taken hat-tricks in Tests, something Corky did in his first summer of international cricket, against West Indies at Old Trafford. Goughie's had a few chances to join too, but until today hadn't got there.

Last summer he had two in two against Sri Lanka at The Foster's Oval, and even on this trip he got two again in Perth before Miller stopped him, so there was a score to settle.

I put a bit of pressure on with a full array of slips in place plus men in front of the wicket catching as the last thing any of us wanted was for the chance to go begging for want of an extra catcher.

Goughie's last two hat-trick balls had been good-length deliveries, so I thought he might go for the fuller length this time, and he charged in, roared on by what seemed like the whole crowd.

It's a funny feeling as a fielder at that point. You always concentrate as the bowler comes in because that's your job, but it's also probably fair to say that at times like that you try to concentrate even harder if that's possible. After all, you don't want to be the man who drops a hat-trick chance if it comes your way.

Thankfully, it didn't come to that. Goughie produced a ball that would have got out most players in the world first-up, let alone a number ten. It started to swing in then straightened at the last second, added to which it was a yorker, so basically it was pretty unplayable. It cannoned into off-stump, and we all went bananas.

We all rushed towards him and he was shouting with joy, 'Yes! Yes!' Everyone else was pretty chuffed too. We were all jumping around, and there was even time for a funny incident when Goughie turned round straight into Tudes' mouth. It was open at the time as he was still busy shouting out his congratulations, and with the difference in height between the two of them, he bit the top of Goughie's head. That sent Goughie off to fine leg rubbing the bite mark, while the rest of us got a real laugh out of it.

It was a fabulous achievement and the reaction of the crowd was superb. Not just the Barmy Army, but the whole ground rose to him as he went back to his fielding position, and after the lack of luck he's had in the series, he deserved it all.

It was just a shame it was the end of the over because with McGrath coming in, I think we'd all have fancied Dazzler getting four in four. Now though they were nine down and Warne was left with a real dud at the other end.

His decision was to throw the bat and he slashed at the next delivery, from Headless, only for Nass to drop a hard chance in the gully. No matter, it brought McGrath onto strike, and we only needed two balls to clean him up, well caught by Hicky at second slip.

We all raced off the field as if we'd won the Test, and for a while the adrenaline was flowing as fast as if we had. All through the series our tail has been called paper thin, but here they lost their last five wickets for 3 runs in 15 balls. One of those runs was a leg-bye, and another came from a dropped chance. And all that after they'd lost seven for 33 in Melbourne.

Best of all, it was close of play so we didn't have an awkward over or two to face that evening which made things even better. Everyone was rushing around, patting Goughie on the back or shaking his hand, and I was delighted for him.

It all meant we'd bowled them out in a day too, which we'd have settled for at the start. I reckoned we could have bowled a bit better, with 30 fours too many in a day for my liking. But it was still a good effort and we now had the chance to build a big score while the pitch was reasonably good and then put them under pressure second time around.

Once Goughie had finished telling the press how he'd done it, we headed back to the hotel and the bus was bubbling and full of excited chat. I was buzzing too after a day like that, but I still made sure I had an early night knowing that bowling the Australians out was only half the battle. Now we would have to get the runs on the board as well.

Sunday 3 January, Fifth Test, Day 2
Australia 322 & 13–0; England 220 (Crawley 44, Hussain 42, MacGill 5–57)

Not for the first time in the series, we needed to get a good first innings score on the board – and we failed. They bowled with discipline, but too many of our top six batsmen got in and then got out again when well set and that could have cost us not only the game, but also a chance to share the series.

They've got some top-class bowlers: McGrath, Warne, and MacGill, who's got better and better as the series has gone on. Against blokes like that you have to cash in once you're established, because there's always a chance they can find a top-class delivery to get you out. But although seven of our top eight made it into double-figures, no one got past 44.

I was the exception to the double-figures club, becoming another landmark in McGrath's career into the bargain thanks to a good piece of bowling and a poor shot.

I was determined to try and dominate, as I like to do at the start of any innings I play. It was another hot day, the pitch was bound to be far harder to bat on if we needed another knock, and I reckoned if we could take the initiative it would put them on the back foot straight away.

Taylor and McGrath probably knew this though, and McGrath responded by bowling very cleverly at me, as Jacques Kallis had for most of last summer. He bowled a pretty full length, but well wide of off-stump, tempting me to go for the drive. That was basically all he offered. There were no easy tuck-aways off the hip to keep the scoreboard moving, so he was saying if I wanted to take control, I would have to go after the ball and risk bringing Heals and the slips into play.

Eventually I lost patience and went for the drive without being quite balanced enough. I edged it high to third slip, and Warney knocked the ball up, grabbing it at the second attempt and giving McGrath his 200th Test wicket.

I'm told his strike-rate is up there on a par with that of Dennis Lillee and there can be no better mark of what a fine bowler he is than that. I remember the first time we saw him, in Brisbane in 1994. I don't think he got a wicket against us in the whole match, and you'd have got long odds on him being where he is now four years later.

He's not express pace but is capable of bowling the odd really quick ball to keep you on your toes. He's got a high action, gets close to the stumps and bowls a great line on around off-stump, always at you. And with his height he can get the odd ball to really bounce at you from around a good length. All-round he is a real handful and he has been the major difference between the sides in the last two series.

On this pitch though, most of the bowling was going to be done by the spinners so any wicket the pace bowlers got would be a bonus. Miller opened up with his medium-pacers from the other end, but every so often he would throw in an off-cutter which would bite, turn and bounce sharply to let us know what we could expect when Warne and MacGill came on.

Taylor gave the ball to MacGill first and he bowled steadily without looking like he would run through us. It was pretty tense stuff with men around the bat and Butch and Nass battling for everything they could get, but they hung in there for over an hour together.

I was pleased with the way Butch played. Earlier in the series he struggled against the spinners, but here he seemed much keener to play positively and look to keep the strike rotating as well as cashing in on anything loose.

That was certainly the case when Warney came on. Butch was determined not to let him bowl and second ball slog-swept him over mid-wicket for four. But showman that Warney is, he bounced back to trap Butch on the back foot two balls later, plumb lbw. It looked like a leg-break, which Butch tried to force through mid-wicket, and it turned just enough to beat the stroke.

I remember Goochie once said he asked Ian Botham 'Who writes your scripts?' when he got a wicket in his first over of a comeback to

Test cricket, and the same was true of Warney here. Taylor had kept him waiting in the outfield for 90 minutes before bringing him on with the pitch already taking spin, and fourth ball he responded with a wicket. Love him or hate him, you have to admire him to be able to do that, and although I'd rather he didn't get any wickets against us, it's still good to see a fellow sportsman back at the highest level after career-threatening surgery.

If Butch's wicket was frustrating because it meant a player who was well-set was out, those frustrations grew after lunch. Ramps and Hicky both fell to attacking shots after they'd played themselves in, something you had to do on that pitch with the spin and lack of pace a real problem for new batsmen. Nass also played well, but he couldn't go on with it either, losing his way against Miller's off-spin and poking a catch to silly point.

Creepy justified his recall by looking our most comfortable player against the turning ball, but even though he got good support from Chucky and Tudes, the damage was done by that stage. And when the two lower-order players were prized out, Creeps fell changing his mind after setting out to sweep, probably a victim of his desire to farm the strike with Headless in and only Goughie and Suchy to come.

So less than a day after rushing off the field in triumph, we had to get back out there to do it all again, only this time we were 102 runs behind on first innings, and facing the prospect of batting last on a deteriorating pitch. The ball was turning a long way now, for both Miller and the two wrist spinners, and it was doing it off the business areas of the pitch too, not just out of any footmarks that had been made.

Privately I thought we needed to bowl them out for around 150 second time around to have a realistic chance of winning, but I didn't say that before we went out. I just gathered everyone in our viewing area as we waited for the umpires to get onto the ground and said: 'Come on lads. Let's see if we can get a couple of wickets tonight. We know they can crack under pressure so let's put them under some.'

And off we went. There was no lack of effort from Headless, Goughie or Suchy up to the close, but we couldn't quite find the inspiration of the previous evening and Taylor and Slater got through unscathed.

Maybe that wasn't all that surprising given the lads were bowling again so soon after last time and it was the second of back-to-back

Tests. Remembering the back-to-back matches we played in Trinidad last winter, they are great spectacles, but they are also incredibly draining to play in, especially if the weather is hot and the tensions are high.

I just hope the lads can find one last effort from somewhere tomorrow after a night's sleep as it is do-or-die day for us in the field. Two days gone, and already we're through two innings, so a draw is hardly likely on this pitch. The bowlers have been magnificent in this series for us, but they must be feeling really let down by the batsmen again, as we haven't posted a demanding first innings score in any Test. If they can give us a lifeline, it's up to us to take it.

Monday 4 January, Fifth Test, Day 3
Australia 322 & 184 (Slater 123, Such 5–81, Headley 4–40); England 220 & 104–2 (Stewart 42)

The odds may be against us, but we're still in the game at the end of another amazing day of cricket, which turned on a decision by the third umpire.

Michael Slater played the innings of his life to make 123 out of 184, but everyone tells me he was run out by a direct hit from Deano at long-on when he'd made just 35.

I say everyone tells me so, because I've only seen it on the big screen at the Randwick End and it wasn't clear enough on that for me to make a judgement. Once back in the dressing room though, I made a point of avoiding the television and just tried to get the whole business out of my head.

Why? Well, to be honest even if it was out – and enough people I know and trust have told me so to make me believe it was – watching it now isn't going to change the decision. What we've got to do for the remainder of the match is concentrate on the 287 runs we need to win the match, and let the administrators pick the bones out of the problem.

That problem seems to be that no one in authority in world cricket is prepared to grasp the nettle and insist that fixed cameras, square of the wicket on both sides are a must for every international match. And until that happens, situations like the Slater run-out are going to keep happening.

From what I could see on the big screen, the moment Deano's throw hit the stumps at the bowler's end with Slat's straining for his ground, Suchy was obscuring them by standing behind them waiting for the return.

No blame on Suchy there, but the problem would surely have been solved if there had been a fixed camera, level with the line, on the other side of the ground.

As it was, without conclusive proof of when the ball had hit the stumps, third umpire Simon Taufel, who had impressed us all with his performance up at Cairns in November, had to rely on a shot straight down the wicket instead.

Again, from what I could see out in the middle, that did show the instance when the stumps were broken, but the crease wasn't all that clearly marked beyond the pitch and it wasn't easy to see when Slater's bat was over the line.

Slats clearly thought he was gone, and as he completed the run he continued slowly in a big arc towards the pavilion for a good fifteen or twenty yards before stopping. By this stage the replays had been run several times, and every time they were run, I think he sensed there was more chance he would be given not out.

Everyone knows the law states that the batsman should always be given the benefit of the doubt in any decision, and Taufel applied the law when he gave Slater in. But when we got back at lunchtime PB for one was ready to strangle him over what he, and plenty of others thought was a real injustice.

I personally don't think you can blame the umpire too much for that one, and in any case I've always lived by the creed that you simply accept the umpire's decision whether you think it's right or wrong; if you don't then there's no game.

And you can't blame the television stations either. Their first job is to provide a product for their viewer and they pay a massive amount of money in order to be allowed to do that.

Their job is not to run the sport though. They might ask for certain playing hours to please schedules, or want more one-day cricket, but the job of running the sport is up to the administrators and it is their job to sort out this mess over line decisions.

The whole question of fixed cameras seems to have been around for a long time but no one seems to be answering it. The last time we were in South Africa in 1995/96 they had them, but three years on they are still not an accepted part of international cricket and I can't see why.

I know a lot of people go on about the cost of the cameras, and although I don't know how much they'd cost, I know they are expensive. But that problem was solved in South Africa by sponsorship, so they proved it was not an impossible mountain to climb.

In any case, cricket is being played for big stakes these days. We won £200,000 from Vodafone, Cornhill Insurance and the ECB for our series win against South Africa, and the latest ECB TV deal agreed last summer totalled over £100 million.

Those stakes are high, so we shouldn't have to risk losing them through a failure to embrace technology. That will be the point I will be making in my end of match report to John Reid and I'll make the same point to Lord MacLaurin. He'll be on his way to Christchurch at the end of the Test to attend the ICC meeting, and I hope it's an issue that is high on the agenda.

Whatever the rights and wrongs of the issue though, we still had a game to play, and we were superb all day. Before play started I stressed it was now or never: 'We've got to hit them hard and try and bowl them out as quickly as we can. We've done it at Melbourne and we can do it again.'

With the ball still only seven overs old I opened with Goughie and Deano and both responded with early wickets, Gough picking up Taylor in the first over of the day, thanks to a low catch by me at first slip. It's somewhere I haven't fielded all tour with Thorpey and Ath in the side, as well as my keeping duties.

Once the hardness had gone from the ball, I relied on Suchy at one end and a mix of Goughie and Headless at the other. Goughie was tiring now, but Headless just kept running in, and the ball he got Steve Waugh with was a beauty, holding its line to knock back his off-stump.

It wasn't too long ago that Headless was on the outside, but he kept plugging away and in the last three innings has looked top-class.

I gave Tudes just five overs, but that wasn't an admission he shouldn't have been there. It was simply that Headless was running hot and he showed amazing stamina to keep going, running in and generating consistent pace. As for Tudes, his five overs were tidy, and they still helped do a job, spelling the other bowlers.

Meanwhile Suchy wheeled away from the Randwick End. He bowled unchanged from there, starting at 11.51 and ending when he got rid of McGrath for his first 'Michelle' in Tests since his debut almost six years earlier. He bowled with real control and fully deserved his figures.

They would have been even better but for Slats' innings. Whether or not he was run out, it was a brilliant effort, especially when you consider that everyone else really struggled. What impressed me most was the way he played Suchy. He was down the wicket at every opportunity, and when he did come, he did so with real conviction, driving high and handsomely over the in-field. That meant the ball was back in Suchy's court, and to unsettle a Test spinner on a turning pitch like that was top-class.

When I caught McGrath 15 minutes after tea, we needed 287 and had over two days to get them. Time wasn't the issue; the state of the pitch was. By now, bits were coming out of it when the odd ball landed, and the occasional delivery was turning and bouncing really awkwardly.

I'm a big believer in having a game plan for any situation, and my plan in this one was to play my shots. That wasn't to say I went out swinging from the hip at everything, but if the ball was there to hit I'd go after it. Being positive just had to be the way to play because it was the sort of pitch where you were bound to get an unplayable ball sooner or later.

Butch had the same idea and took three fours off McGrath's first over to set us rolling. We knew that seam bowling was the lesser of two evils on this pitch so both of us tried to score off him wherever we could as it was only a matter of time before the spinners came on and there were men round the bat.

Sure enough, MacGill was on by the ninth over, and Warney followed five overs later, and it was Warney who struck first, once again getting Butch in his first over. Butch came down the wicket to a ball angled across him looking to drive but the ball didn't spin and Heals had an easy stumping.

I kept playing my shots, lofting MacGill twice to the fence, and was feeling really good when I took one risk too many. I went down the pitch but he must have seen me coming because he dropped it a fraction shorter. I still went through with the shot, but the ball turned past the outside edge and Heals had another easy job with me yards down the track.

As I walked off, I was struck by the reception I got. I hadn't even made fifty, we hadn't won the game, and my dismissal was a real hammer blow to our chances. But the crowd really gave me a great hand and I appreciated that. I took it as a compliment to the way we had played the match so far, fighting every inch of the way.

And we still did that. Nass and Ramps, easily our two best players in the series, battled it out to the close leaving us with still an outside chance of a famous win. Everyone was really up in the dressing room after they came off, and we decided to have our mid-match team meeting straight away at the ground while everyone was still really focused.

I began matters by telling the lads how proud I was of the way we've fought over the past two Tests. And I stressed: 'We are still really in this game. Bat well tomorrow, win the game and draw this series. That would be a great effort.'

Rallying cry over, Bumble and Goochie spoke about how we were going to get the runs. Bumble said: 'You've been dead right with your approach so far, really positive, that's the way we'll get the runs. Build partnerships and look to rotate the strike, make sure the bowlers keep having different problems to solve.'

Goochie was also keen on the idea of rotating the strike, and added: 'With the way the pitch is, I think the sweep is a good way to do it. When you play it, you're not always trying to hit fours but it can also be a shot to ease the pressure by picking up ones.'

There was a tremendous feeling of belief and togetherness in that dressing room tonight and I think everyone genuinely believes we can win. Let's just hope we do.

Tuesday 5 January, Fifth Test, Day 4
Australia 322 & 184 beat England 220 & 188 (Hussain 53, MacGill 7–50) by 98 runs

We lost. But at least in losing, we seem to have restored the pride in English cricket, and a belief in The Ashes series.

After we went down in Adelaide, there were an awful lot of people, it seemed to me, who wanted to knock English cricket and The Ashes. Thankfully our efforts in the last two matches have shown everyone that we can be a force in international cricket and the contest between the two oldest Test rivals is still alive and well.

The crowds for this match which, I think, topped 110,000 over four days certainly showed the public have an appetite to watch us compete with Australia, and at the end, when we had lost I thought it was only right that we showed our appreciation of them for that.

The fans here have helped make this Test one of the most memorable of my career, and also confirmed the fact that Sydney is second only to Lord's as my favourite ground in the world.

As we lost our ninth wicket just after lunch, I got Murgers to call through to the public address announcer to thank the crowd for their support while also urging them to stay off the ground. The presentation was due to take place on the field, so it might have been a bit chaotic if they'd been there with us, and in any case, there's a $5,500 fine for the public going onto the SCG at any time.

When we had lost, we all had to go out for the presentation. I made sure the eleven that played all went on in whites, that we looked a team right to the end, but once we emerged there was a delay while the presentation area was made ready.

The crowd, especially the Barmy Army at the Randwick End, was still singing away its support, so I led our boys down there to say thanks. It wasn't planned, but it just seemed like the right thing to do. They certainly appreciated it, as did the rest of the ground when we turned and clapped them too. They clapped back, and it was one of those moments that will live with me for a long time.

The Barmy Army have followed us all around Australia, win or lose, and given us fantastic vocal support. Believe me, when you're in the middle, and I can think of the climax to the Melbourne Test, that is a real boost, especially when all you can hear are English voices in an Australian ground.

And just one more thought about the Army: I wonder how many of their critics witnessed the reception they gave the Australians when they did a lap of honour after us. They gave them a standing ovation, and rightly so.

By then, Mark Taylor had been given the new Ashes trophy, a cut glass replica of the famous urn. I actually believe the urn should go to the country that holds The Ashes and it's a pity the Australians don't get the real thing, but I suppose these days it's more symbolic than anything else. You're not playing just for the urn these days but also the history and tradition it represents. And as MCC President Tony Lewis said before he handed over the trophy: 'The urn doesn't travel too well.'

The ceremony was also the time when Mark Taylor and I had to say a few words to Channel Nine. Both of us stressed how enjoyable the contest had been and how important Ashes cricket was to both sides.

I chose the moment to add a bit more. Of course, I thanked the players and the supporters, but ever since our defeat in Hobart, there have been a few pieces in the press about Bumble standing down after the World Cup next summer, before his contract runs out at the end of the season. I thought this was the perfect stage to stress my support for him and I did just that.

'As far as I'm concerned,' I said, 'I hope David and I are working together for a good while yet.'

Bumble has been superb for England. We still might not be a consistently winning side, but we are much better prepared than we were, even four years ago. We have more access to videos, both of our opponents and ourselves, we use a sports psychologist, have specialist coaching, work like hell on our fielding, and I believe we're fitter than any previous England side. A look at the number of players sent home injured from tour since our last Ashes trip in 1994/95 shows that.

Bumble was a huge mover in bringing all this in, and I think it has helped to make us a harder unit than in the past. The players want for nothing now, all we have to do is get it right on the field. It would be a shame to waste all the progress we've made just for the sake of change.

That said, we went down with more of a whimper than a bang as it turned out, and for all the talk of spin, it was McGrath who set us on the slide to defeat with a brilliant opening spell. It was fast, gave us nothing, and when the odd chance did come along to score their fielding was really switched on.

Ramps fell after 20 minutes without adding a run, caught low down by Taylor to give him a Test record 157 catches. He is up with Ian Botham, Mark Waugh and Graham Roope as the best slip-fielders I've seen and I can't remember him dropping one in this series.

The spinners then took over. Nass battled hard, but the rest subsided quietly, with Hicky and Tudes bowled behind their legs, enough to send Peter Philpott to an early grave after all he's told us.

After the media had their pound of flesh, it was off to the Aussie dressing room for a drink and a chat. This always happens at the end of the series, and usually lasts a few hours. It's always a really relaxed affair with players getting stuff signed for each other and some real camaraderie behind closed doors.

Back to the hotel by late afternoon, and away from the ground I began to feel a bit flat. All the work of the previous two and a half months now over, and only a lost series to show for it. Back with my family though, at least I was able to get some perspective on the whole thing.

Wednesday 6 January and Thursday 7 January

Just four days after The Ashes series and we were into the first of ten qualifying matches for the Carlton and United Series against Australia and Sri Lanka, so even though the Test finished a day early, it did have its plus points. For me it was the chance to relax, switch off for 24 hours and spend some quality time with the family before I flew to Brisbane and they flew home.

There were still official, or at least semi-official things to be done though. On Wednesday evening we had our last team meeting of the Test tour, which was basically just a signing-off by Goochie, who now hands over the reins to Grav, already in Brisbane with the rest of the one-day squad.

Nine of us, plus Bumble, Bob Cottam, Malcolm Ashton, Murgers and Wayne Morton will link up with those boys while it is bye-bye to everyone else. The meeting was a final chance to say our farewells to one and all as a group, have a drink or two and also to get autographs on anything and everything, from shirts to photos and even newspapers. Players can sometimes give the impression they don't care for autograph hunters, but behind closed doors they still get each other to sign. Some do it to remember the tour; others do it for benefit items.

It's been an enjoyable Ashes series, and I've relished the responsibility of being captain, even if I didn't score as heavily as I wanted. But there's no time for reflection; that can come at the end of the tour after a one-day series against the finalists in the last World Cup, Australia and Sri Lanka.

Carlton & United Triangular One-Day Series

Qualifying Matches 1–10

Sunday 10 January

1st one-day international, Australia v England, Brisbane. England 178–8 (50 overs, Fairbrother 47) beat Australia 145–9 (Bevan not out 76, Mullally 4–18) by seven runs. Target revised to 152 in 36 overs following rain.

A great start to the campaign, thanks to some top-class bowling by Mullally, and, it probably has to be said, a little help from the Brisbane weather.

Although Al bowled brilliantly, our total of 178–8 in 50 overs should have been well within Australia's range, but rain, which had done us a favour during the Test here in November, returned between the innings, and made their target a slightly harder 152 in 36 overs.

Australia got off to a flier through Mark Waugh and Adam Gilchrist, their keeper who is sent in at the top of the order to give it a slap in the first fifteen overs. Defending such a low score, we couldn't really afford that. We needed wickets and Big Al came up with the goods.

I brought Goughie back for the final over with 12 to win and despite his problems with control I had real faith in him. Dale was on strike, McGrath was next man in, and Goughie has experience of a host of one-day games behind him. The first ball of the over, a waist-high full-toss, did make me wonder a tiny bit, but Goughie came back superbly with a rapid yorker next ball, and with ten off four balls and McGrath on strike we just had to keep our cool to win.

It was a great feeling to win a game like that, and just the start we wanted after the way everyone had been building the Aussies up before the game.

One last thought: we have a new match referee for this tournament with John Reid being replaced by Peter Van der Merwe, the former South African Test batsman. He gave us the usual pre-series briefing, along with the Australians and Sri Lankans, and stressed one thing: 'I don't deal in fines, just suspensions'. After the way the tour has gone so far, I can't see him being too busy in that area.

Monday 11 January

2nd one-day international, England v Sri Lanka, Brisbane. Sri Lanka 207–7 (50 overs, Kaluwitharana 58, Atapattu 51, Tillekeratne not out 50, A Hollioake 3–32) lost to England 208–6 (49.3 overs, Fairbrother not out 67, Muralitharan 3–34) by four wickets.

He may be 35, with hamstrings as tight as a drum and a receding hairline, but Neil Fairbrother, 'The General', is still a top one-day player at any level, as he showed tonight when he steered us to a great win.

The heat was on in every sense as it was hot and humid, we were losing wickets and drifting behind the run-rate. We needed 18 in three overs and their spinners were strangling us when 'Harv' skipped down the pitch and lofted Jayasuriya for a straight six which immediately eased the pressure. All of a sudden we could push the ball around without the need to get a run every ball, and with Crofty again showing his value down the order we got home with three balls to spare.

It was a tough game though, as you'd expect against the World Champions, who still looked a bit ring-rusty after only arriving in the country a week or so ago. But whenever they asked us a question, we came up with the answer and after losing to them last summer that was important.

But it wasn't just The General who did us proud today. Goughie looked much more like his old self with the white ball and got the key wicket of Jayasuriya in the first over. Then, after they looked as though they would get away from us, reaching 99 without another loss in just the 22nd over, Smokey and Crofty combined to strangle the life out of their middle order.

One thing I noticed was that the Sri Lankans didn't come and shake our hands afterwards. I don't know why that was, but when we play Australia one side or the other always makes the effort to go to the opposition and say well played. I was disappointed it didn't happen here.

Friday 15 January

3rd one-day international, Australia v England, Melbourne. England 178 (43.2 overs, Hussain 47, McGrath 4–54) lost to Australia 182–1 (39.2 overs, M Waugh not out 83, Ponting not out 75) by nine wickets.

After the success in Brisbane it was back to earth with a bump today as we were hammered. We got our fingers burnt over-attacking when we batted, lost wickets far too regularly and managed to get bowled out with more than six overs in hand. Then, when we bowled, we dropped Mark Waugh first ball, and weren't really at the races after that.

It was as one-sided a game as you'll see, and the crowd got so bored with the whole thing they started pelting Mark Ealham with rubbish and even a snooker ball down on the fence. By that stage Australia only needed about 40 to win and no one wanted the game abandoned because of the problems, so I called Warney out and he calmed the locals down so we could get a finish.

It should never happen but at least if you're pelted with empty plastic bottles it doesn't hurt too much if you're hit. Snooker balls and glass bottles are different though, and we had to put a stop to that.

Oddly enough, something similar happened when we played Australia A in Melbourne four years ago. Then, someone started driving golf balls onto the field from one of the hospitality boxes, and he even managed to reach the square with a couple of them.

At least, with the match heading west a few of the lads managed to see the funny side of Ealy's problems. Crofty, who along with Ealy often gets stick for his love of food said: 'No wonder he's complaining. He thought the snooker ball was a pickled egg and tried to eat it!'

Sunday 17 January

4th one-day international, Australia v England, Sydney. England 282–4 (50 overs, Hick 108, Hussain 93, Fleming 3–64) beat Australia 275–6 (50 overs, M Waugh 85, Lehmann 76) by seven runs.

It doesn't get much better than this. After the thrashing we copped on Friday, we showed superb character to bounce back with a great win, holding our nerve as Australia closed in on their target.

We decided not to be so desperate in the first few overs. If there was a chance to get after the bowlers then okay, but there had to be a middle ground after some of the frantic play of Melbourne.

Hicky was the prime candidate to bat at three, and he has the track record to do it. In Bloemfontein a few years ago I saw him play one of the best innings you could ask for in the first fifteen overs of a game against South Africa. Batting at three he made fifty in 30-odd balls against Allan Donald and co just by orthodox cricket shots through the in-field.

It's a shame that he doesn't bowl much for his county Worcestershire these days, because I've seen him turn his arm over at international level before and do a good job. I still regard him as an option for England.

Pre-match plans are all well and good, but you still have to put them into practice, and thankfully we did, superbly. After Knighty and I got out early, Hicky and Nasser had a look at the bowling and got settled. In fact, we started pretty slowly by modern standards and were only 55 after 15 overs.

But once they were in, they played brilliantly. Hicky drove powerfully and also put Warney into the Bill O'Reilly stand at square leg with a flick of his forearms, while Nass kept the board ticking with lots of sweeps and deflections off their spinners.

They added 190 at almost a run a ball and when both fell late on to Fleming, who started to get some reverse-swing, Harvey and Smokey showed what you can do late on with some experience and wickets in hand. They blazed 37 in the last four overs and most satisfying of all was that Australia's big three of Warney, McGrath and Fleming all went for more than 50 runs in their ten overs.

A total of 282 was a great score, but the pitch was a belter, and Australia had already chased 260 to beat Sri Lanka here last Wednesday so we knew we still had lots to do. But thanks to our bowlers, especially Giles who we introduced into the side alongside Crofty and who bowled magnificently in the final overs, we got home by seven runs.

Once the game was over I started to notice a dull pain around the base of my right thumb. It's an old injury that started a few years ago when a ball knocked the thumb back. That stretched the ligaments and every time I take a blow there it's sore. It happened twice tonight with balls from Smokey and Crofty doing the damage, and although

I know it's not cracked I put it straight into a cup of ice once I got my gear off.

Our win over Australia in Brisbane might have been a bit lucky with the weather playing a part, but this win, in front of a full house owed nothing to luck. They should know they are in a contest now.

Tuesday 19 January

5th one-day international, England v Sri Lanka, Melbourne. Sri Lanka 186 (50 overs, Ranatunga 76, Chandana 50, Gough 4–28) lost to England 189–3 (45.2 overs, Hick not out 66) by seven wickets.

This was probably our easiest win of the tournament so far, but there are still some parts of our game we can improve on.

Their final score was never going to test us if we batted well, but although we won with more than four overs in hand, it was frustrating that Knighty and I both got starts again without going on with the job. As we did against Sri Lanka in Brisbane, we added over 50 easily enough, but then both of us got out in the same over hitting attacking shots straight to the fielders.

With The General resting his hamstrings that could have spelt a bit of a flutter, but although Nass got out with 72 still needed, Creepy and Hicky got us home without any further problems.

When Creepy hit the winning runs, I made sure our lads went out onto the edge of the ground straight away to shake their players' hands as they came off. That hadn't happened in Brisbane, but I wanted to make a point here of saying that is the way we do things at the end of a match.

That makes it four wins out of five, and with Sri Lanka still looking for their first points we are starting to get to the stage where another victory against them could knock them out. That's a nice thought to have just halfway through our qualifiers, but that's all it is at this stage.

Saturday 23 January

6th one-day international, England v Sri Lanka, Adelaide. England 302–3 (50 overs, Hick not out 126, Fairbrother not out 78) lost to Sri Lanka 303–9 (49.4 overs, Jayawardena 120, Jayasuriya 51) by one wicket.

'Your behaviour today has been appalling for a county country captain.'

My words, picked up on Channel Nine's stump-microphone, came during the most bad-tempered and incident-packed match I have ever played in. And even though a stutter meant they didn't come out quite right – where 'county' came from I don't know – I really meant them.

The words, aimed at my opposite number, Arjuna Ranatunga, came out at around 9 o'clock in the evening during Sri Lanka's run-chase, and were a culmination of the frustrations building up inside me since 3.21 in the afternoon. It was then that bowler Muttiah Muralitharan was no-balled for throwing by umpire Ross Emerson, and the game ground to a halt for 14 minutes. Ranatunga had a finger-wagging argument with Emerson, then took his players to the edge of the ground while Sri Lankan officials emerged from their dressing room to meet them, and started further chats, both with a mobile phone, and Ranatunga. While all this was going on, Knighty and Hicky just waited in the middle of the ground, and eventually the match re-started.

In all fairness Ranatunga did approach our batsmen before he went to the side of the ground, to let them know what he was planning to do. Hicky said later that Ranatunga told him: 'I am taking my players off the field'.

If he had done that, I think the umpires would have had grounds to call the match off and award it to us, but thankfully sense prevailed and they did at least stay on the ground, albeit near the boundary fence.

It's not for me to get into the rights and wrongs of whether Murali should have been called. As I've said before, that is up to the umpires and, beyond them, the ICC's advisory panel on suspect actions, to decide upon.

But what really upset me was that the stoppage that followed brought into question the whole fabric on which the game of cricket is based.

That fabric relies on one, main premise: the umpire's decision is final. Whether you like that decision or not, you have to accept it, because if you don't there isn't a game any more.

Goodness knows we had enough decisions go against us during the course of this match. Television replays showed Jayawardena was run out on 33 but survived to make 120 and win Sri Lanka the game when Emerson gave him not out without referral to the third umpire. There was also a four that was signalled six, again without referral to television evidence, and a seven-ball over.

All these things went against us, but at no time did we go up to the umpire, start wagging our fingers and stop the game for 14 minutes. You just can't do that as far as I'm concerned.

I thought the tactic of stopping play was all wrong and towards the end of the stoppage I even went down to the gate as captain of the batting side to find out what was happening. Splash had taken some water out to Hicky and Knighty, but I didn't want them standing out in the hot sun forever if this situation was going to last a while.

Jut as I got there, Van der Merwe, who had headed down from his box behind our dressing rooms as soon as he saw what was happening, was just on his way back to his hideaway and their players were returning to the middle. It seemed the situation had been resolved, so I went back to our rooms.

That wasn't the end of the fun and games though. Murali, who had been no-balled from square-leg, switched ends to operate from Emerson's end, the Southern side of the ground. But having done that, he and Ranatunga then wanted Emerson to stand right up to the stumps.

The last time Murali had been called, by Darrell Hair and then Emerson three years ago, both men had done it from the bowler's end, so switching ends might have been seen as an odd move at first. But, if they were concerned about Emerson seeing Murali's arm, a way around that could be to ask the umpire to stand as close to the stumps as possible. That way Emerson couldn't get a decent view of his arm and couldn't no-ball him.

Emerson, by contrast, was keen to stand a bit back from the stumps to get a decent view, and that could have given Murali the chance to run between the umpire and the stumps. But neither he nor Ranatunga wanted that, maybe understandably given the situation, and they told Emerson to stand as close to the stumps as he could.

Ranatunga seemed quite insistent, but Bumble, who used to be a first-class umpire, said he was completely out of order and read the Law to us: 'The umpires shall stand where they can best see any act upon which their decision may be required.'

Our position during this whole affair is easy to forget but you really have to give credit to Hicky, in particular, for keeping his concentration and going on to play a blinder. To stand out there for 14 minutes not knowing what was going on was one thing, but to then get back to batting so well speaks volumes for him.

I say that because I know it was bloody difficult for any of us to focus on the match in our dressing room for quite a while after play resumed. There was a mass of excited chatter among the boys and Crofty turned the television up in the back room to hear what the Channel Nine commentators were saying about events.

We knew there was a chance that something like this could have happened because the newspapers had been full of speculation about it in the days leading up to the match. Emerson had called Murali during a one-dayer in Brisbane in January 1996 and this was the first time he'd stood with him on this tour.

The matter was even raised in our team meeting on the morning of the match. 'What happens if he's called?' someone asked. 'Just get on with your game, that's out of our control and nothing to do with us,' said Grav.

That was easier said than done, and try as we might, people kept mentioning the incident as we sat watching the game. Will he call him again? Will he just bowl leg-spinners from now on? Will the Sri Lankans go home? All questions that were floating around as Hicky and Knighty began batting again.

I don't think the speculation did Nass's concentration a lot of good, but Harvey, who's seen it all before, took it in his stride. He and Creeps must have had some mixed feelings though given that Murali has signed to play for Lancashire next season, and Creeps, who's their captain in 1999, was spotted on a mobile phone in the back of the dressing room later on.

Hicky and Harvey put everything behind them and took advantage of a great pitch and fast outfield to butcher the bowling. In fact, they took 69 from the last five overs, sending poor old Vaas to all parts inside and outside the ground. A total of 302–3 was a great score, and, I thought, a winning one.

I was even more convinced of that after we got away to a flier in the field. Smokey ran out Kalu', at the non-striker's end with a direct hit, which made everyone happy after all the work we've done on hitting the stumps during the tour. Then Atapattu, who got a hundred against us at Lord's in August was caught by Harvey at slip off Al, despite my attempts to block his view when I dived but didn't make it.

Gradually though, Sri Lanka got a toe-hold in the match, first through Jayasuriya, who played as we know he can, then Jayawardena, Tillekeratne and Ranatunga, who all played like men who have had a lot more one-day international experience than most of our team. And I don't think we took our feet off the pedal when we had them two down, whether we meant to or not. They just played really well.

Whether Jayawardena should have been there to do that is a moot point. He and Tillekeratne didn't run very well together, and after a mix-up between the pair he was straining for his ground when I whipped the bails off.

Experience tells you when a run-out is close and as Jayawardena was running towards me I could see pretty clearly where he was as I gathered the ball and demolished the timber. I immediately spun round to Emerson and appealed, and was surprised to say the least when he shook his head and said 'not out' almost straight away.

Now I know it is a fineable offence under ICC regulations to ask for the third umpire to be called as that is viewed as putting unfair pressure on umpires. But that doesn't stop anyone dropping a playful hint, so when Emerson came to replace the bails I handed them to him and said: 'I'm not allowed to ask for a television replay, am I?' with a smile on my face.

Ross shook his head and said 'He was well in', and we all went back to our positions, but just before the next ball the replay on the big screen confirmed Jayawardena was short of his ground and a huge groan went up around the place.

After everything that had happened during the day even up to that point, Ross must have wished the ground would open up and swallow him. So, at the end of the over as he moved into position, I broke off from a chat to Crofty to put my arm round him. We players feel bad enough if we make a mistake, but it can't be any easier for umpires, and getting on their backs about things would do no good at all.

Sadly though, there was still plenty of drama to come, and some of it involved Ranatunga again. My outburst while he was batting was in response to a tactic he seemed to be using against us, and I followed it up by adding: 'A metre either side, that's all I'm asking for.'

That was a reference to the way I felt he was deliberately obstructing us as we tried to gather throws coming in from the outfield. He would get in their path, then at the last possible second get out of the way, leaving us badly unsighted. And occasionally his bat was left in the way, with the risk of the ball deflecting off it at all angles.

The tactic was completely out of order, even more so because of the conditions we were playing in. One of the floodlight towers had blown a fuse, and so we spent the whole of our time in the field operating in three-quarter light. That made the ball extremely difficult to pick up at the best of times, especially when it got older and its white colour was replaced by a dirty grey. Ranatunga's efforts could have given Sri Lanka some overthrows; or it could have meant one of us got badly injured by copping a ball in the face.

The whole floodlight issue was interesting in itself. When the tower packed in at first, and faced with our massive score, the Sri Lankans were keen to get the match called off. But as they started to play well, that issue seemed to slip off their agenda.

Faced with Ranatunga's actions, which were going on when he got to the non-striker's end as well, and as Sri Lanka got closer to our total, I think it would be fair to say we came close to losing our cool. That was especially true when Mahanama got involved in the action.

Mahanama is an experienced player who has often opened in Tests and is a handy man to have coming in at number nine as he did here, especially in a tight situation.

This was tight alright, with four overs left and 31 needed, and facing Goughie he dropped the ball down in front of him and he and his partner Chandana set off for a quick single. Goughie recovered quickly from his follow-through and scampered across to kick the ball onto the stumps with Chandana straining for his ground. In fact, Goughie may even have had time to bend down and pick the ball up before shying at the stumps – and I say 'may' because it was at that point that Mahanama took centre stage.

It is an accepted practice in cricket for you to run between the thrower and the stumps if you are in danger of being run out. It might hurt if you cop a ball on the back or the leg, but that is the price you pay. But this seemed to me to be slightly different looking at it from my position behind the stumps, Mahanama appeared to run into Goughie as he was preparing to gather the ball, and the big screen replay appeared to confirm this.

It's not for me to say whether Mahanama was at fault and if so whether it was deliberate or not, but Goughie was incensed and appealed for a wicket on the basis he had been obstructed. As it was, I think Emerson believed Goughie had run into Mahanama, turned the appeal down and had a brief word with him about that.

Now Goughie is one of the few cricketers in the world who almost always seems to see the funny side of something. He is one of the game's nice guys and to get him upset takes some doing. But here he was furious, I've never seen him like that on the field before, and he made a gesture with his head at Mahanama as he walked back to his mark.

I would never condone a head-butt in any situation, but the fact was Darren didn't go through with it, and knowing Goughie as I do, I also know he would never do such a thing anyway, least of all on a cricket field representing his country. His gesture was just one of frustration, and I could totally sympathise with that.

By now though, we were rattled. We weren't thinking straight, and instead of looking for yorkers as we usually would in this situation, Goughie threw in a slower ball that Chandana picked, and picked up, for six.

That was the end of the over and I made my way to the other end of the ground to prepare for the next six balls. But as I did so, I brushed against Mahanama. Basically, he was talking to Chandana and strolling along one line and I was walking from wicket to wicket down that same line. Neither of us gave way and we rubbed shoulders. He started jumping up and down and flapping his arms, but to me it was pretty tame compared to what had happened during Goughie's over. This was a brush of shoulders; that was a full-blown collision.

They got home in the last over with Murali of all people, after everything that had happened during the day, slicing a full toss just over Smokey's head at point to score the winning run. On another day that might have gone to hand, but Smokey was so keen to be up for the single with the scores tied that even though it only carried 30 metres, it still went over his head.

We got back to the dressing room and the lads were as flat as pancakes. Smokey was first in and fly-hacked a plastic chair out of the way, but the rest of us just sat there for a few seconds, and for my part I was struggling to take in the events of the day. I had to pull myself together pretty quickly as there was a presentation ceremony to attend with Channel Nine. But before I went, Murgers did his best to brief me on what I might be asked in relation to the mass of events that had taken place in the middle.

One of those was the four that was signalled a six and I was furious when told about it. 'Why wasn't it changed, why wasn't anything done during the game?' I said to Murgers and Grav, only to be told they had already spoken to Van der Merwe on the subject. Apparently, things like that can only now be changed before the next ball is bowled and in some ways that is fair enough. It all comes back to accepting the umpire's decision and I do remember the habit of changing scores was getting silly. In a really tight Test against Australia at The Foster's Oval in 1997, the Aussies had two runs added on overnight, even though their innings had finished at tea the previous day!

I was ready to go and face the media when the Sri Lankans trooped in to our dressing room, led by their manager Ranjit Fernando, and that made my blood boil. They had made no effort to shake our hands when we beat them in Brisbane, and we had forced the issue when we won again in Melbourne. But here they were after beating us, in to shake our hands as quick as a flash. So I said to their manager: 'All I ask is that you're consistent. If you want to shake our hands make sure you do it after every game, not just when you win.'

Given what had happened out in the middle, I think a few of our lads did well to keep their cool when the Sri Lankans waltzed in, and I know some of them wanted nothing to do with any congratulations. But we shook their hands, and that was the end of it.

By this stage, Grav and Bumble were chatting with Van der Merwe in the doorway of our dressing room, and he now faced an interesting problem. After what he'd said at the start of the tournament about dealing in suspensions, not fines, how would he handle this situation? He decided to sleep on it.

I faced the television cameras and don't think I made too many gaffes, but then it was down to face the press, and David Graveney and Brian Murgatroyd came with me. Murgers always comes along to keep a watching brief, but after the events of the day, he and Grav felt having the tour manager along as well might be a useful exercise in dealing with some of the questions.

It's true to say things hadn't gone all that smoothly out on the field, and I said, 'That was the least enjoyable game of cricket I've ever played in.' I felt Ranatunga was largely responsible for that and said so, or words to that effect, to the media. Basically, the umpire's decision must be accepted. It all began with that being questioned, and things went from there.

As to whether any of us were going to be up in front of the match referee, it wasn't for us to decide. All Grav did say to the press was that the events on the field during the game were not what you would want to see at any level, and we would be seeking a meeting with Van der Merwe as soon as possible.

It was a fairly tough press conference with Peter Roebuck looking to pick me up on my brush with Mahanama. He liked to call it 'a collision'; I felt that was the term I'd use to describe Mahanama's clash with Goughie.

By the time we'd got back to the dressing room the lads had gone and it was left to me, Murgers and Grav to head back to the hotel. Most of us headed for the bar to try and unwind after an amazing day, but Murgers joined Grav in his room as the calls over the incidents started to fly in from back home and elsewhere.

Sunday 24 January

David Graveney, who I don't think got a lot of sleep last night, got hold of Van der Merwe first thing and the referee came around for a 10 am meeting to let us know what he had decided to do about yesterday's events.

He put our minds at rest straight away when he said he wasn't charging any of us with anything under the ICC's Code of Conduct. If I'm brutally honest I have to accept that we were lucky to get away with that, especially Goughie and maybe even myself, but we did allow ourselves to get sucked in.

Van der Merwe did stress that we shouldn't allow that to happen again. If we did, he said, he would have to suspend so many players the series would end up being an eight-a-side affair. That lifted the mood a bit, but we all accepted the message was deadly serious.

He did say he was charging Ranatunga under the Code of Conduct. I never like to see fellow players 'done', but after he had wagged his finger at and argued with an umpire I couldn't see how it could be avoided. There was a game in the afternoon though involving Sri Lanka and Australia, so I reckon it's anyone's guess when the hearing will take place.

Once the meeting was over, Van der Merwe headed off for similar meetings with the Sri Lankan and Australian management teams, and Grav and Murgers began to formulate a statement on the affair to give to the press. Already one newspaper back home had laid into our conduct, so they both felt we should make a fairly swift response to try and kill the whole issue.

That was certainly what I wanted to do. The last thing we needed was to be distracted from the business of playing cricket. We allowed ourselves to be sidetracked last night and paid for it with a defeat. We had to get back on track.

While they were composing the statement, Smokey and I started to watch the Australia-Sri Lanka match on the television, but I think the events of last night caught up with us as we spent most of the afternoon dozing. By late afternoon the statement just needed some form of remark from me, and it was ready to go after Grav had notified ECB officials back in London about its contents. That had to be done just in case anyone at home was rung up and questioned about it after release.

24 January 1999

MEDIA STATEMENT

'On Sunday morning the England tour management met with the International Cricket Council (ICC) match referee Peter Van der Merwe to discuss the previous day's match between England and Sri Lanka at the Adelaide Oval.

'At the meeting, attended by tour manager David Graveney, coach David Lloyd, captain Alec Stewart and media relations officer Brian Murgatroyd, Mr Van der Merwe said he would be taking no action against any members of the England team.

'He did, however, express his concern about the general atmosphere in which Saturday's match was played.

'The England management accepted this point, and has reiterated to both captain Alec Stewart and the rest of the England squad, the need to fulfil their obligations and responsibilities to the game of cricket.

'Tour manager David Graveney said: "I have stressed to Alec the responsibilities he has under Law 42.1, namely that the captain is responsible at all times for ensuring play is conducted within the spirit of the game as well as within the Laws.

"We all agree that events during Saturday's match have no place on a cricket field. We have accepted that and I have given clear instructions to Alec and all the players to ensure we are not involved in anything similar again.

From our point of view the matter is now closed and we are all keen to put the match behind us and return to winning ways by playing attractive and positive cricket in the remaining matches in the Carlton and United Series."

'England captain Alec Stewart said: "I would repeat what I said immediately after the match, that it was the least enjoyable game of cricket I have ever been involved in, and I know that is a view shared by all those in my team.

"I am fully aware of and accept my responsibilities as England captain, and will be doing everything possible to make sure myself and my team conduct ourselves in an appropriate fashion in the remaining matches in the series and beyond."

Grav read that statement to the press in the early evening, and then took questions. With Van der Merwe not pressing charges against us, Grav stressed that was an end of the matter from our perspective. All we wanted to do now was to get back to playing winning cricket, something the Aussies were doing a few hundred yards away at the Adelaide Oval. With McGrath finding a perfect length to unsettle the Sri Lanka batsmen, they were routed.

Sri Lanka aren't exactly top of most people's polls here for Australia's favourite visitors as there is some bad feeling which goes back a fair way between the two sides. As well as Murali being no-balled for throwing in 1995/96, they were also unsubstantiated claims made about ball tampering when they were in Perth. On top of that, Australia, along with the West Indies, refused to play World Cup matches in Sri Lanka in 1996 because of the threat of terrorist bombs.

Ranatunga got booed onto the field when he came into bat and then failed miserably. He'll have to be a strong character to survive this.

Tuesday 26 January

7th one-day international, Australia v England, Adelaide. Australia 239–8 (50 overs, M Waugh 65, Martyn not out 59, Lehmann 51, Lee 41) beat England 223 (48.3 overs, Hick 109, Knight 42, Warne 3–39, McGrath 3–40) by 16 runs.

No excuses. As Bumble said afterwards, 'We took the gas'. On a good pitch, we were 162–2 in the 35th over, needing just another 78 runs and with two established players at the crease only to lose the plot and suffer a really disappointing loss. Just like last Saturday it was a game we should have won comfortably, and if you add to that my three ducks in six innings in Adelaide on the tour, I won't be sorry when we leave this city, pretty though it is.

After the events of Saturday, I think we were all pleased to be playing Australia. We might have hard games against them, but there is rarely if ever any hint of a problem between the two sides, although I like to think we get on fairly well with most, if not all the sides we play.

The dressing room was a pretty sombre place again, though it wasn't quite as bad as it had been on Saturday. A few of us went in for a drink with the Aussies, and those that didn't joined Bumble in watching where we went wrong thanks to the videos of the match which Channel Nine always drop into us after every day's play.

To cap off an interesting day, we heard that Ranatunga's hearing with the match referee had been opened and adjourned before play. Apparently Ranatunga had arrived for the hearing with a group of legal representatives – something that is allowed under Code of Conduct regulations- and Van der Merwe decided he wanted to consult with ICC headquarters in London before going any further. Speculation among the press is that the hearing might now be postponed until we get back to Sydney next week.

Thursday 28 January

I'm not one to be bored easily, but this evening I endured almost four of the most boring hours of my life.

No offence to the company. It was Graeme Hick, David Graveney and Brian Murgatroyd. But we spent that time either inside or just outside the Multiplex hospitality box in the Prindiville Stand at the WACA ground in Perth, and frankly I can think of better ways to prepare for a one-day international the following day.

Hicky and I were there to give evidence in the Ranatunga hearing called by match referee Peter Van der Merwe in the wake of the England-Sri Lanka match in Adelaide. I was there to confirm what I'd said during the match – the remarks that were picked up on the stump-microphones – and then outline why I'd said it. And Hicky was to confirm what Ranatunga had said to him after Murali had been no-balled, that he was going to take his side off the field.

We'd found out we were to attend the hearing on Wednesday evening after flying into Perth from Adelaide, but it wasn't until this morning that we found out exactly what we would be doing there.

The one thing we were keen to avoid was to be dragged into the whole thing in a big way, especially as we all wanted to get on with the business of playing cricket again. We were also keen to make sure the goalposts hadn't changed and that suddenly we weren't being charged with something.

After breakfast, Grav, Murgers, Bumble and I met with Van der Merwe and a couple of lawyers from Melbourne he had brought over with him, Brian Ward and Sharon Hall, who often acted for the Australian Cricket Board. Hicky wasn't there as all he was expected to do was confirm what Ranatunga had said to him and he didn't need to be briefed to do that. My briefing consisted of going through what I might say if quizzed. The questions were quite straightforward: I had to confirm what I had said to Ranatunga after the 35th over, that I felt his behaviour had been appalling, and then outline why I had said it.

My one concern was that whatever Ranatunga may or may not have done, I didn't want to be seen to be telling tales on a fellow player. That's just not my style. Brian Hall said if the ICC process was to stand a chance of working, that might be necessary, but he added our testimony might not be required. 'You're there to show Sri Lanka that the ICC means business and can call witnesses if necessary so if Ranatunga is found guilty, it might convince them to accept a punishment rather than fight it.'

Van der Merwe also said that Ranatunga was being charged only on point one of the Code, namely 'The Captains are responsible at all times for ensuring that play is conducted within the spirit of the game as well as within the Laws.' There had been suggestions in the media he would be charged on four or five points, but that fell through on a legal technicality, something I didn't really understand.

From there, it was off to practice at 2.30 at the WACA nets. We'd originally wanted to practice much later in the afternoon, but with the hearing set for 5 o'clock, Grav wanted all the players not involved in that away from the ground to avoid the media circus that was bound to follow. Fair enough, but it did mean we netted at probably the hottest part of the day, which was tough on the boys with a game the following day.

I would love to write about the hearing and what was involved, but

I can't for two reasons. Firstly, ICC regulations don't allow me to do so; and secondly, apart from five minutes at the start, I was never in the hearing.

Grav and Murgers waited in our box while Hicky and I marched in, along with everyone else – and that included representatives of the Sri Lanka Cricket Board – at 5 o'clock. But after everyone was introduced, we all then trooped out while the legal teams of both the ICC and Ranatunga got to work.

There were four hospitality boxes set aside for use during the hearing, just outside the President's Box, where it was all supposed to take place. Van der Merwe and his legal team had one of them, the umpires, of whom only Ross Emerson turned up, had another, we had one, and so did the Sri Lankans, who were represented by their manager, vice-captain Jayasuriya, Murali and Ranatunga himself.

Once we were cleared out of the hearing, we just went back to our box to wait. And wait. And wait. It was novel for a while as we had a television set in there and could just relax, but after a while it got boring. And we got hungry too. We'd just finished a practice session at the WACA nets, so Hicky and I were a bit peckish and Murgers went down and bought some ploughman's lunches, crisps and fruit from the bar area a couple of floors below us.

Slowly darkness fell, and still we waited. Even Ranatunga wasn't involved in the discussions taking place between the legal teams, and, I assume, the match referee, but every so often one of those teams would come out of the President's Box and go into one of the hospitality boxes for a private meeting before discussions resumed.

After a while, we stretched our legs, went outside and stood out on the balcony, overlooking a massive group of reporters, photographers and camera crews that were waiting for the verdict down below. There was the odd smile from us and we even made small talk with Ross Emerson and the Sri Lankans, but basically we were getting more and more bored as time dragged on.

Then, at around 8 o'clock, the Sri Lanka squad showed up, and all of them headed into their hospitality box. If it was a show of support for their captain then it certainly looked impressive, and it got the dozen or so Sri Lanka fans outside the gate of the ground chanting and cheering.

By 8.30 we were desperate. We hadn't had a proper meal and both Hicky and I just wanted to get back to the hotel, which is only half a mile away from the ground, to rest up for tomorrow's game. There was even a suggestion we headed back there and came back if we were needed.

But just about then, Brian Hall came out and said it was over and all the people called to the hearing should head for the President's Box to hear the judgement. That judgement was that Ranatunga was found guilty as charged. He was given a ban of six one-day internationals, the maximum penalty available to Van der Merwe, but that ban was suspended. He was also fined 75% of his match fee, also the maximum available.

And with that, we left, with the thanks of Hall, who said our presence at the hearing, even though we had done nothing for almost four hours, had made a big difference. After reading this, you can make up your own minds on that one.

I'm not allowed to comment on the result of the hearing. But Murgers said he had been told by Chris Lander, cricket writer for *Mirror* newspapers, that if Van der Merwe had banned Ranatunga, the Sri Lanka lawyers would have gone to court tomorrow morning to overturn the judgement allowing him to play against us. As it is, he is going to play against us anyway, and I will be tossing up against him.

It has been a remarkable day, and I'll be relieved to get back to cricket tomorrow.

Friday 29 January
8th one-day international, England v Sri Lanka, Perth. England 227–7 (50 overs, Fairbrother not out 81, A Hollioake 46, R Perera 3–55) beat Sri Lanka 99 (33.3 overs, Jayasuriya 40, Ealham 5–32) by 128 runs.

I would never use the word 'revenge' to describe any cricket match, but it's fair to say everyone involved with our touring team got massive satisfaction from this result.

It all but puts us into the finals with two games still to play and, on top of that, all but knocks Sri Lanka out of the competition, barring a mathematical miracle and an amazing run of results.

That is pleasing in itself, as to come into a three-team tournament against the finalists in the last World Cup and win through shows the progress we are making as a side.

But after all the upset and disappointment of last Saturday in Adelaide, this result also goes a long way to making up for that loss.

It wasn't just the fact we won that pleased me, it was also the way we did it. First of all we got up from a real backs-to-the-wall position and posted a competitive score through Harvey, Smokey and Crofty.

Then, after they got away to a useful start, we did just what Steve Bull would have wanted: we 'nailed down the coffin'.

The bowlers all charged in, hit the pitch hard and found the perfect, aggressive length for Perth against a side that doesn't seem to fancy it one bit if the ball is bouncing up around the chest area.

The match was played without any of the problems of Adelaide, which I suppose is hardly surprising as the eyes of the cricketing world were on the WACA ground.

And it was great to see a man who usually never gets any headlines, Mark Ealham, finally get his place in the sun with a superb exhibition of bowling which earned him five for 32, especially as his wife Kirsty was here to see it all. Someone said afterwards that he's only the fifth England player to take a 'Michelle' in one-day internationals after Hendrick, Marks, Jarvis and Goughie, who's done it twice. In fact, come to think of it, it was Goughie who told me!

A score of 227 was good but not necessarily a winning one and we knew we'd need to bowl well and, just as important hold our catches and get any luck going. I wasn't sure we'd get that luck early on though, when Jayasuriya, who can take the game away from you at any time, glanced Goughie into my gloves only for the ball to be called a wide.

There are times when keepers appeal for leg-side catches on the off-chance that the ball has brushed a glove or bat, and often that can prevent a wide call. But I saw his nick all the way and was bitterly disappointed it went against us. But, as I've said before, you just have to accept the umpire's decision and get on with it as he's not deliberately trying to make a mistake.

That looked like a costly let-off as Jaya' waltzed down the pitch and slapped Ealy straight for six, but thankfully he then made a mistake and we had our vital breakthrough. He picked Ealy up easy as you like down to deep square leg, but straight to Smokey. All of a sudden we had a new batsman to have a go at.

We know Perth pretty well after all the time we've spent here on tour. And while it's a good pitch to bat on if you're in, it can be tough to get through the first half an hour or so and come to terms with the extra bounce here. So, if a new player comes in, you must get after him straight way and don't let him settle. We did that to perfection.

When Ranatunga finally came in at number six he was greeted by a hail of boos. He was listed to bat at five, but Jayawardena came in there and he copped boos as well as people thought he was Ranatunga. Interesting, as there's only a few kilogrammes and around fifteen years between them I think!

When Ranatunga got to the middle I went to shake his hand and he took it. I know a few people wondered why I did it after all that happened in Adelaide, but it wasn't planned as far as I was concerned. In fact, apart from the toss, I didn't even speak to him again during the day. It was simply I wanted to show that all that happened last week was over and now it was time to get back to cricket. Simple as that.

He didn't get many, only 11 in almost an hour, as he struggled with the extra bounce in the same way that most of his team-mates did. And even before he was brilliantly caught by Knighty, one-handed above his head at fly-slip, they were just playing for pride.

At the end of the game I made a point of going into their dressing room. I went round and shook hands with all their players except one – Ranatunga. But that wasn't a deliberate snub on my part. Apparently he was in the toilet and never came out.

There was even a nice touch as we were celebrating in the dressing room afterwards. Steve Davis, the umpire who'd given Jaya' not out over that leg-side tickle off Goughie came in with a beer for him. 'I owe you this for that one,' said Steve. Goughie smiled and replied: 'Ay, and I might have guessed it would be a free one from the WACA too!' They both laughed and it was great to see.

I took another blow on my thumb during the game but, believe me, despite that and Harvey's hamstring strain, we were all flying after this result. After all the fuss over the past week, it's been great to get back to business.

Wednesday 3 February
9th one-day international, England v Sri Lanka, Sydney. Sri Lanka 181–7 (44 overs, Kaluwitharana 54, de Silva not out 52, Alleyne 3–27) beat England 170–9 (44 overs, Knight 58, Sameraweera 3–34, Chandana 3–35) by 11 runs.

I think our feelings at the end of this one were best summed up by the way we held an hour-long team meeting in the dressing rooms straight after the match.

213

We may already be through to the finals, and Sri Lanka are on their way home whatever happens, but we were still desperate to establish a winning habit, and our failure to do that really hurt, especially when we should have won easily. That may have made us relax a bit too much, and Smokey, who captained the side while I rested, certainly felt that on the field, and said so afterwards.

But it was still a one-day international, with places up for grabs not only for the finals, but also for Sharjah and the World Cup, so there should have been no excuse for any lack of effort.

Sri Lanka's total of 181 didn't look a huge score, but by now we could see the pitch was starting to dust and break up and with their massed ranks of spinners we knew it would be tough. We all had a chat around the dinner table at the break and everyone agreed on one thing. If we were going to get the runs we had to take advantage of the first fifteen overs with the field up and get as many runs as we could, because once the ball went soft and the field was spread, hitting boundaries would be very difficult.

We knew we couldn't fall too far behind the rate, and there was also the threat of rain, so Ealy was padded up for the first fifteen overs. In the end he didn't go in because we didn't lose our first wicket until the seventeenth over, but even at that stage we were starting to get bogged down.

Ranatunga had played a neat card by opening the bowling with de Silva, a slow, low spinner who got a fair amount of turn straight away. Knighty and Vinny were taken a bit by surprise, and seeing how much spin he was getting, lacked a bit of confidence to get down the track and hit him. We needed to break the shackles but didn't.

Hicky went in at three but got a sharply turning grubber second ball, and from there it was a real tale of hard work as we died slowly. Knighty couldn't get the ball away and struggled even to keep the board ticking over. To justify batting like that – he took 97 balls to reach fifty – he had to bat through the innings and win the game for us, but when he and Creeps got out within eight balls of each other, the writing was on the wall.

Smokey was especially upset at the end, maybe thinking we should have batted first. But that wasn't the issue in mine or Bumble's books and we said so afterwards. 'You're never going to get 60 off the last ten overs on that pitch so we lost it before then,' said the coach.

Although there was nothing riding on the result everyone was gutted we had thrown away a winning position. The one thing we didn't need at that stage were players starting to bitch about others behind backs, so Smokey called a team meeting straight away to clear the air. 'If you've got something to say, say it now, because I don't want people bitching about each other in the bar afterwards,' he said. After all we'd said before the innings, getting lots of runs early on and staying on top of the run-rate, lots of eyes fell on Knighty and he was big enough to admit he lost the plot early on. 'I was surprised when they opened with de Silva and I have to say I didn't really have a game plan against him,' he said.

At least the meeting was open, with everyone having a say, and at the end Bumble said, 'Take this away with you, think about it, and let's be more flexible next time'.

By the time the meeting ended it was getting on for 11.40 at night and that didn't really please the press, who were still waiting to see us after the match. Smokey was still disappointed at the loss and hadn't even showered so I saw spoke to them. They obviously quizzed me about why we took so long to come out, especially as we had already qualified. I hope it shows them how much we want to win, and that will be the same on Friday when we face Australia in the last match before the finals.

Friday 5 February
10th one-day international, Australia v England, Sydney. England 210–8 (50 overs) lost to Australia 211–6 (47 overs, Ponting 43, Lehmann 41) by four wickets.

Not the best day we've had on tour. With the finals looming we lost our fourth match in the last five, missing the chance to score an important win over the Aussies. On top of that Goughie had to leave the field with a tight hamstring, and although Dean Conway thinks he'll be okay for next Wednesday, it's not ideal timing.

The subject of whether Goughie should have been playing at all with the finals so close was one that all the journalists wanted an answer to afterwards. Hindsight is a marvellous thing, of course, but there were several key reasons for his inclusion.

First, we wanted to win the game. We showed that in the choice of Al, Crofty and myself as well, after all of us missed Wednesday's Sri Lanka outing, as we really wanted to show we could beat them again.

That didn't work out, but it wasn't for want of trying, and as Goughie is our main strike bowler he was a natural choice.

Goughie's desire to play was also a factor, but not the main one, in our selection. As he said to me before the match: 'I've missed enough cricket over the last few years through injury, so I want to play every game I can for England. If I'm fit, I want to play.' My thoughts on that is if someone is on form you play him to keep that rhythm. It's as simple as that. He let us know his thoughts, but it was our decision to play him.

On top of that, of course, there are five days between this match and the first final, and we thought that was more than enough time for him to rest up. Goughie also gets bored very easily if he's just watching. If he's fit, he wants to play, so that decided us.

In the end it took some sensible hitting from Ealy and Mark Alleyne to get us past 200 after 180 looked about our limit at one stage. It was a competitive score, but we knew we had to bowl outstandingly well to win it from here.

We got the asking rate up to around five per over when Smokey broke through, trapping Lehmann lbw and they sent in Brendon Julian. They'd obviously watched our match with Sri Lanka two days ago and reckoned fifty or sixty off the last ten overs might be tough so thought if they could get quick runs now, it would ease the pressure later on.

I wanted to bring Goughie back for a couple of overs to try and nip that idea in the bud but when I asked him to loosen up he said his left hamstring was tight. I told him to leave it for a while and see how it felt in an over or two, but after he chased a ball to the boundary he came back to me and said: 'It feels too tight to bowl'.

With that and with the finals so close it made sense to send him off to rest and have the problem iced, but it left me hamstrung about getting rid of BJ. Without Goughie I needed the two overs I had left from Al for the death, so I had to mix and match with Crofty, Vinny, Smokey and Ealy. BJ took advantage, slogged 25 in 31 balls, and eased the pressure as he was meant to do.

We still gave them a flutter, getting rid of BJ, brilliantly caught by Hicky at mid-wicket, and Bevan, penned in by men around the bat and losing his cool by miscuing Crofty to mid-on. But that flurry by BJ had bought them time, I needed to bring the field in to save ones, and Martyn took advantage of the gaps in the outfield to finish things off quickly.

A frustrating night, especially as Goughie was lying on the treatment table at the back of the dressing room with ice on his hamstring when we got back inside. We had made a big, public play of trying to go into the final with two wins under our belts but now we were there with two losses. That is tough as Australia have now beaten us three times and will be bound to feel they have the edge on us. But I still think we can lift ourselves for one final effort. After all, no one remembers the qualifiers; it's who lifts the trophy that counts.

Finals Matches

Wednesday 10 February
1st one-day Final, Australia v England, Sydney. Australia 232–8 (50 overs, Bevan not out 69, M Waugh 42, Wells 3–30, Ealham 3–45) beat England 222 (49.2 overs, Hussain 58, Hick 42, McGrath 4–45) by 10 runs.

It's an easy thing to say while the events of this evening are fresh in my mind, but I can't recall being quite so upset or angry about losing a game as I was after we went down in this one.

They say there are lies, damned lies and statistics, but in this case the figures tell you everything you need to know. We needed 36 in 7.5 overs with six wickets in hand and two well-set batsmen at the crease.

You should win from that sort of position many more times than you lose, but we took the gas completely and didn't even get within a boundary of the game.

Nass, one of those well-set men, charged down the pitch to Warney, Smokey was given out lbw sweeping next ball and when Vinny, our other man with his eye in, was brilliantly caught at long off by BJ in the next over, we were on our way to oblivion.

I watched us go down the gurgler alongside Bumble on the dressing room balcony, and if I was upset, he was positively desperate. While I got up at the end of the match and went to congratulate the Aussies, he just stayed in his seat unable to comprehend how we had lost. Some punters gathered in front of the balcony, and began to wind him up a bit so Fizz had to shepherd him into the back room to avoid him losing his temper completely.

I can totally sympathise with Bumble. He can help me map out the tactics, discuss technique with the players and bring in all sorts of coaches and aids to help out. But even though he cops some flak from the press when we don't perform, he can't play the game for us. It is up to us to take responsibility to win matches, and this evening we just didn't.

The dressing room was like a morgue when I walked in after briefly seeing the Aussies. The lads were devastated. So, straight away I decided against a team meeting like the one we had after the Sri Lanka match. We knew we'd blown it big time and no amount of talking was going to change that.

I kept my post-match remarks short and sweet. 'Right, we've f***** up here,' I said. 'What I want you to do is go away and think about it. Think what we did well and think what we did badly and think how we can put it right because we've got another chance. It won't be easy to win back-to-back games, but we showed for 80 or 90% of the time here that we can compete. We just need to make sure that next time we compete all the time because we can't afford any more slip-ups.'

I looked across at Nass but he was looking pretty blank. He's an experienced player – we made our Test debuts in the same match in Jamaica in 1990 – and he knew he should have seen it through. He made 58 in 98 balls, but that tempo was okay as long as he was there at the end and we won. He was playing the right type of innings because he was holding one end up while the lads at the other end, Hicky and Vinny, were playing the aggressive roles.

But he had to be there at the end in that situation, walking off 75 not out with a win. We even sent that message out with Creepy when he took a pair of fresh gloves out for him at one stage.

It was more than disappointing when he was stumped off Warne trying to hit over the top when we were wanting less than five an over. But I got an idea of why he was trying to do that when Peter Van der Merwe popped in as usual after the match to pick up the form both captains always fill in on the performance of the umpires.

Peter said he'd spotted a fair amount of animated chat going on out there between Warney and Nass. And although he wasn't going to take any action over it because the umpires didn't have a problem, he just asked me to have a chat with Nass to make sure he kept a lid on it.

To be honest I hadn't noticed a thing out of the ordinary. There's always going to be a bit of harmless banter going on in the middle of a final, and that's fine as long as it doesn't go overboard. If Nass did allow himself to be wound up by Warney, I'm sure he regrets it now, with or without me telling him.

On top of that, poor old Nass was involved in the run-out of Hicky which was a key turning point in the match. Both of them were playing really well and we were comfortably on course to win when Nass dropped the ball out square on the off-side and took a couple of paces down the pitch before screaming 'No'.

By that stage though, Hicky had seen Nass's initial movements and was drawn into the run. The call made him turn on his heels and dive to try and get back, but by that stage Ponting, who's been superb in the field, had scored a direct hit at the bowler's end and there wasn't even the need for the third umpire to be called. Pieces of brilliance like that in the field can change a match and this certainly did.

Even after that though, we still should have won easily before we self-destructed. Once we lost those three quick wickets we were always struggling as McGrath came back at the death to bowl some devastating reverse-swinging yorkers that were far too good for new, tail-enders to get six runs an over off. In defence of Nass though, the way McGrath bowls at the death was one reason he went after Warney, but on this occasion the gamble didn't come off.

Although we should have won easily after getting into such a good position, it's also true to say that maybe they got ten or fifteen runs more than they should have. There was no Alleyne as he had flown home over the weekend after his father had died in a car crash – we wore black arm bands and had a minute's silence out of respect – and after his recent form maybe we missed him. But all the same, we did have Goughie and Harvey fit, which was a real plus.

We just seemed a bit off the pace early on. Perhaps that was because of all the rain they've had in Sydney over the past few days because no one expected us to play, but we could still have been a bit more switched on than we were.

Things didn't exactly start according to plan. The woman singing our National Anthem forgot the words, then when we got underway, in just the second over, Gilchrist top-edged Al high towards square leg and Smokey was there for what should have been a routine catch and a great early blow. It was the sort of catch you practice hundreds of times a week and would expect to swallow, but as he got under it the wind took it away from him, he ended up trying to catch it away to his right and barely got a hand on it.

Try as you might, that sort of thing can just set you back a bit, and I reckon it did, although we got back on terms thanks to a great spell from Vince Wells. He hasn't featured that much as a bowler so far, but after I brought him on in the 12th over, he settled quickly and strangled the life out of their innings. If you add his batting on to that – and apart from his dismissal, when he was undone by a slower ball, he did really well – he did his chances of World Cup selection no harm tonight.

Their final total owed a fair bit to Bevan, who played really well in the last ten overs. In Brisbane, and previously here in Sydney, he'd worked the ball around but hadn't found the boundaries. Now though, he hit the fence, although I found out afterwards he shouldn't have been there to do that.

When he'd scored six, Martyn pushed the ball to backward point and Bevan scampered through for the single as Nass scored a direct hit. It was close, a line ball, but on the pictures available third umpire Simon Taufel said not out, quite rightly giving the benefit of the doubt to the batsman.

After the match though, Malcolm Ashton said he'd had a call from Ross Dundas who operates the computer scoreboard at the ground. Ross also has access to pictures from a fixed camera square of the wicket and he said that showed Bevan was short of the crease. For some reason, they don't use that fixed camera for third umpire decisions, so Bevan stayed, and effectively won the game for them.

It all comes back to the point I made during the Test here when Taufel was third umpire again. On the evidence of this tour if nothing else, fixed cameras for run-outs and stumpings are a must, and the sooner the better.

At least I had some consolation from the game by finding the middle of my bat a few times and winning a joust with McGrath, although my fun was short-lived.

I started that fun by pulling Dale for six, which after the way he's tied us down gave me a lot of pleasure, then I really got stuck into McGrath in his third over.

After nine years at international level, I think most people know I love to hook and pull, and that I've got a few runs from the strokes down the years. But for some reason McGrath seemed keen to try me out with the short ball.

After Knighty took a single from the first delivery of the over, McGrath let me have four short ones in a row, and all of them went to the fence. The first I took off my hip through square leg, but although I caught it well, I managed to hit the second one even better.

This time it went in front of square, and although Bevan got a hand on it at short mid-wicket it still had enough legs to reach the fence. Bevan must have regretted it too, as he left the field straight away with a nasty looking finger injury.

I was winning the battle of wills but McGrath wouldn't back down by bowling a couple of good length balls to try and rein me in. He banged it in again, and I hammered him down towards the Pavilion for an all-run four.

I must admit the adrenaline was really flowing now, and when he dropped a fraction short with the next one, even though it was outside off-stump, I went for it again and had a bit of fortune, top-edging it over Gilchrist.

Four fours in a row and Warney began screaming from first slip. 'Pigeon, pitch the f****** thing up,' while making to drive an imaginary ball with his left arm.

The last ball was quite full and cut back, but I blocked it well enough before engaging in a bit of light-hearted banter with McGrath. I was pumped up, and as he stood at the end of his follow-through glaring at me, I said: 'Just remember, you can't say anything.'

That was a reference to the fact he has a suspended punishment hanging over him after his verbal volley at Al during the Melbourne Test in December, so if he stepped over the line again he could be in trouble.

He thought about this for a while then cupped his hand to his ear as if to make out he didn't hear me. I responded by doing the same, and nothing more was said in my hearing before he headed off to the fence.

All good clean fun, no swearing, and as far as I'm concerned, full of the passion you'd expect to find in a final.

I was feeling great, but that feeling didn't last. In the next over I clipped Dale straight off the middle of the bat, but straight to Mark Waugh at mid-wicket. He threw the ball up and claimed the catch, nodded at me to say he thought he'd caught it, but I wasn't convinced and stood my ground.

As far as I could see, I thought he'd got his hands around the ball rather than under it, so the ball hit his hands and the ground at the same time. He wouldn't necessarily have known that, so I stayed where I was and waited for a decision.

I expected it to go to the third umpire, but Hair looked across at Daryl Harper at square leg, got the nod, then gave me out without any referral. I wasn't pleased, but when you're given out you have to go, so off I went.

I got back to the dressing room just in time to see some replays on the television, and none of them showed what had happened clearly. It didn't make me feel any better.

Neither did our loss at the end of it all. Murgers said later that straight after the match he'd never seen me look so angry, but although I was furious inside I knew I still had to do my post-match duties, the Channel Nine presentation ceremony and the other television and radio interviews required.

I can't say I was in the best of moods for them, but I think I just about managed to keep my cool in the face of questions like: 'You'd expect to win that game from 198–4 wouldn't you Alec?'

By the time I got back to the dressing room the lads had left so Murgers, Malc and myself just sat and reflected for a while before driving back to the hotel. I was calmer now, but still felt empty. Not much time for reflection though, as I had to pack for our trip to Melbourne the next morning. The sooner the next game comes around the better.

Friday 12 February and Saturday 13 February

2nd one-day Final, Australia v England, Melbourne. Australia 272–5 (50 overs, Lehmann 71, Martyn 57, Gilchrist 52) beat England 110 (31.5 overs, Warne 3–16) by 162 runs.

I reckon everyone's mind wanders from time to time, and I couldn't help it when mine did just that as we stood on the MCG for the presentations at the end of the Carlton and United Series, the end of our Australian tour.

As the stage was being prepared on the outfield, I immediately thought of the last time I'd been on this ground for a ceremony like this. It was in March 1992, and it was after we'd lost the World Cup Final to Pakistan.

This was the type of deja vu I could have done without, but here I was, seven years on, and a loser again. For all that though, the feeling was inescapable, as I found out when I mentioned it to Hicky and Harvey, the two other survivors of that side still around here. They said they were thinking exactly the same thing.

But unlike seven years ago, this time we had been hammered, a frustrating and disappointing end to a one-day series that promised much, but in the end delivered little.

That little was at least the consolation that Hicky was named joint player of the series with McGrath after his three centuries, plus one or two other telling contributions. But if a player makes three hundreds and we win just one of those matches, I suppose it also shows how much the rest of the batting failed.

And it certainly failed today. Needing to win to stay in the best-of-three contest and set a testing but not impossible 273, we just folded like a pack of cards. It started with Knighty's run-out after a mix-up with me, was followed by three successive ducks, and from 13–4 we were only realistically saving face.

The Aussies played the type of confident cricket you'd expect from a side that's won its last six or seven matches, and for us it looked like the end of a long, hard tour.

Not that I think you can blame tiredness for the way we played. Six of our side had only been in Australia for six weeks, and while it has been a long tour for a few of us, I felt fine going into the game and not jaded at all. I know that when I get home I'll just flop into a chair or bed and do as little as possible for a couple of weeks. But while I'm on tour I never struggle on the tiredness front.

In any case, we had an extra day's break before the match because of the weather. When we left Sydney on Thursday morning it was raining again and we just thanked our lucky stars we'd got the game in rather than having to hang about. If it hadn't been played on Wednesday, it would have gone ahead the next day, and we would have had to fly to Melbourne on Friday morning for an afternoon game.

Once we were on the plane to Melbourne we thought that was it for weather problems as the reports were that it was fine there. But we arrived in cloudy conditions and by the evening it was drizzling.

It cleared up for long enough on Friday for us to practice on the outfield and even have the toss and the national anthems, but during the singing it began to rain quite hard and never let up for the rest of the day.

As for the Anthem, after the problems on Wednesday in Sydney, this time the bloke doing the singing didn't seem to know the tune so got his timing for each line hopelessly wrong. In the end, as Frank Sinatra would say, he just did it his way.

We weren't to know we wouldn't play on Friday when Warney and I tossed up and it was a tricky decision to know what to do when I won it with my usual call of heads. It was humid, overcast and we expected the new ball to move around. But with rain around and the outfield damp, gripping the ball wouldn't be easy and under the current rain rules batting first would give you an advantage. So I decided to bat and Knighty and I were all set to go, just like Athers and I during the Test here, when the rain really set in.

And that was it for 24 hours. It was fairly steady rain for the rest of the day, and the lads had to amuse themselves. Harvey, Creepy, Hicky and Headley formed the card school, Knighty, Nass and I had a short indoor net, and most of the rest of the lads had some lunch and dozed or chatted to the Aussies.

Meanwhile, Channel Nine showed highlights of our game against Sri Lanka in Adelaide. It was the first time most of us had seen the coverage, and it was a real eye-opener. The stump microphones picked up Ranatunga telling Emerson he was in charge of the game, while the commentators seemed to think the umpire should stand where he was told by Ranatunga and Murali, even though the Laws say he can stand wherever he wants to get a good view of the action. All very interesting.

Play was eventually called off at around 5 o'clock even though we could start as late as 7.20 to get a 25 overs-per-side game in, as there was no chance of a let-up in the rain. In fact, it continued for most of the evening as well, but the groundstaff did a great job, as they had in Sydney on Wednesday, and we were able to get away on Saturday with only a fifteen minute delay.

There was a new toss though. That's because the playing conditions here are different to back home. In England, if two days are set aside for a match, you take as much time as you like during those two days to get the overs in. But in Australia, if you don't finish a game in one day, or at least 25 overs of the second innings, you have to start a whole new game on the reserve day. Each to his own.

This time it was Warney who had the problem of what to do when the coin came down tails, and he reached the same conclusion as me. With the weather still threatening he batted first.

First up we went well. Goughie and Al bowled well and Goughie even managed to get rid of Mark Waugh. Before the game Murgers told me an amazing fact given the number of times they must have faced each other this winter, that Goughie hadn't got rid of him all tour. That surprised me, but when I thought about it I reckoned he must have had him dropped a few times!

This time Hicky clung on to a fast edge at second slip, but although the new ball moved a little, the pitch played pretty well considering it had been under cover for the past 24 hours. Gilchrist and Ponting hit through the line cleanly and also chanced their arms if any of the bowlers dropped short, Ponting pulling Vinny for six.

They were looking ominously set when we struck twice in quick succession. First, I threw the ball to Smokey and Ponting clipped his first ball low to short mid-wicket where Harvey took a good, sharp catch. Then Gilchrist hit a sweep right in the middle of the bat off Crofty only for Knighty to make ground to his right at deep square-leg and take a top-class, tumbling catch.

So, all of a sudden we had two new batsmen to attack, but credit to Lehmann and Martyn, they played well. Crofty and Smokey kept it tight and they never got away from us, but they kept the board ticking over at four runs per over and could afford to see those bowlers off after the fast start they'd got. Then, when Goughie, Al, Ealy and Vinny each came back, they immediately started to attack, refusing to let them settle.

Lehmann seemed to go in the back during the innings but that actually counted against us. He knew he'd struggle to bat through, so he opened out a bit earlier than usual and got 29 from his last 20 balls before he fell with almost eight overs left.

Ealy managed to stem the flow briefly through a combination of some reverse swing and me coming up to the stumps, but Shane Lee came in at the death to play a great little short innings. In the last over Al was searching for a full length, but over-pitched twice and Lee clubbed low full-tosses over mid-wicket for six. Good hitting, and he finished with 20 in just nine balls.

By then Lee had been dropped by Hicky, running in at deep mid-wicket. It wasn't an easy catch as he was moving quite quickly and he juggled it before it went down, but it was one Hicky would normally expect to swallow. And after all the missed chances he's suffered on the trip, I suppose it was quite appropriate that Goughie was the bowler to suffer.

Australia had got 79 from their last ten overs, and with the pitch looking good I reckoned we had a great chance of winning, although I knew chasing a score as large as 273 isn't all that easy under lights. But very quickly, it all went pear-shaped.

I suppose I was partly to blame for the start of our decline. In the second over Knighty dropped the ball short on the off-side and called me for one. I started off but then saw Ponting screaming in from cover and sent Knighty back. But by that stage he was far too far down, and he was yards short when Gilchrist, who'd got up to the stumps pretty quickly, whipped of the bails.

McGrath got in on the act in the next over when he had Hicky caught at third man cutting, and next ball Nass was given out caught behind as he pushed forward to leave us in tatters. Then when Harvey edged an ambitious stroke at Dale, it felt like the Test in Adelaide all over again as I leaned on my bat at the non-striker's end.

I wasn't going to go down without a fight and managed to slam McGrath over mid-wicket twice for old-time's sake, but the game was up when BJ came on. Second ball he gave me some width with a full ball, and I tried to hammer it through extra cover. Maybe I tried to hit it too hard, maybe it wasn't really there, but I miscued it straight up in the air to Lee at extra cover, and was on my way even before it came down.

From 43–5 the game was over and the only question as the clouds got lower around the ground was whether we'd be bowled out before the rain came back. When Warney pitched his flipper just right to get rid of Al, the answer was an emphatic yes.

We had been hammered, no getting away from that, and Bumble took it especially badly. He is a real heart-on-the-sleeve, passionate man, and although we were all upset at the way we'd lost, he was especially cut up.

After the presentation but before I saw the press, I spoke to Bumble and Grav and discussed what had happened. It may not be the best time for clear assessments, but I thought it was useful, and I think they did too. The bottom line was that our batting failed to click for the umpteenth time, and that has cost us the one-day series. If we can get that right I still believe England can be a match for anyone.

The press conference wasn't as much of an inquisition as I'd expected – maybe some of the journalists are tired at the end of a long tour – and there was a nice touch at the end. Kenny Casellas, the cricket writer of the *West Australian* newspaper whom I've known for years through my time in WA, called for silence and said a quick word of thanks to me for my co-operation during the trip. Once he'd done that, all the press boys gave me a round of applause.

That was nice, and I must say I've enjoyed my jousts with the likes of Aussie reporters Malcolm Conn and Robert Craddock. They have been good sports through the tour and the only sad part about the quick finish is that it's stopped me having a drink with them.

I did have a drink with the Aussie boys though, and as you'd expect they were in good form with music blaring out from their dressing room and players exchanging shirts. Interestingly though, I reckon some of them are going to be pretty tired by the start of the World Cup in May as the likes of Mark Waugh and Shane Warne are off to the West Indies for almost three months next Wednesday. At least we've only got three weeks in Lahore and Sharjah between now and meeting in Kent on 2 May.

The travelling, pressure and hotels aren't fun all the time, but it's still not a bad way to earn a living.

The World Cup and 1999/2000 South Africa Tour

A Summer of Frustration

During a six-month period after returning from Australia in February 1999, I experienced the sort of ups and downs that test you out psychologically. I came through it all eventually, and got my mind attuned to the fresh challenge of fighting for my England place, so that I was ready for a gruelling tour of South Africa – but at times it was a hard slog. At the end of September, when the whites were put away for a few precious weeks, I was done in, physically and mentally. Only then could I reflect properly on the roller-coaster that I'd been on since late March.

In chronological order, I'd been dragged into an unhappy dispute over our financial terms for the forthcoming World Cup, at a time when we should have been concentrating on getting it right on the field. We had spent a fortnight in Sharjah, losing a one-day triangular series that was basically an irrelevance in terms of playing World Cup cricket in England a month later. Then came the hammer blow – being eliminated from the World Cup in our own country, before we even got to the closing stages. After that, I was kept in suspense for a few weeks, before I was sacked as England captain. I stayed in the Test side, but had to come to terms with my place being on the line as we lost the series to New Zealand, with all the England players copping some deserved flak. Then I tried to eliminate from my mind the worrying speculation that I wouldn't be picked for the South Africa tour. I made it, but not for the subsequent one-day series, which surprised and disappointed me. All in all, there was enough on my plate to test my strength of mind, and I was grateful that I could rely on my experience, accumulated over a decade of international cricket. There was one cheering event, though, towards the end of the season. Surrey won the county championship for the first time since 1971, when the team was captained by my father. That at least ensured a difficult summer ended on a high note.

Sharjah first. I don't think we should have been there at that stage of our World Cup build-up – and that has nothing to do with our three defeats out of four against India and Pakistan. The die had been cast about this trip long before I had been made captain, so I had to grin and bear it, but it wasn't a relevant exercise. The players should have been resting from match conditions so soon after we ran out of steam in Australia in mid-February. Over the previous twelve months, we had been in the Caribbean, then a full summer in England, followed by four-and-a-half months in Australia. Then, after three weeks' rest, we were in Lahore for ten days' training before Sharjah. In my opinion, we would have been better off going to Lanzarote for fitness training rather than being in Lahore and Sharjah, where the conditions – dusty, temperatures close to forty degrees – were totally dissimilar to what we would expect in England, in the middle of May, at the start of the vital World Cup games. I believe we should have gathered earlier in England in April, to re-acquaint ourselves with the conditions, thereby utilising our home advantage. Instead we were in Sharjah, unable to put our World Cup strategy into action. Because of the dry pitches out there, you can use a pinch-hitter at the start of an innings, and the ball will also reverse-swing. Yet I knew that in England a month later, the ball would move around off the seam, the pitches would be conducive to those types of bowlers, and that you wouldn't see much spectacular pinch-hitting on English pitches early in our season. We'd gone to Sharjah with guys like Gus Fraser, Ian Austin, Vince Wells and Mark Ealham, who were in the squad for the World Cup in England, but not in the expectation that they'd be heroes in totally different conditions out in the desert. So we were never at the races in that tournament. You want to win every game for your country, though, and that Sharjah experience wasn't a happy omen.

The England players were also getting distracted by a simmering dispute over money. Negotiations for our World Cup contracts had started the previous November, in Brisbane, when the international tours' director at the ECB, Simon Pack, had a short meeting with me. It wasn't exactly an ideal time – the afternoon before the first Test of an Ashes series – and all I said was that we ought to be given more for winning the trophy, and for getting through to each stage. Simon said there was only so much money in the pot, so it looked as if the ECB wasn't going to budge. That was it until we got out to Lahore, when we had a players' meeting to discuss the money situation. Then we asked if Simon Pack could come out to see us in Sharjah, but he didn't. Instead, we met up with Tim Lamb, the ECB's chief executive and David Acfield, the overseas tours' committee chairman – both former county players, and both sympathetic. We all piled in with our opinions and although both Tim and David could see our points of view, it became essentially a 'them and us' situation. It was stressed by all of us that the pride in playing for our country was paramount, that there was no intention at all of holding the ECB to ransom. We just asked for a fairer distribution of any available money. Negotiations didn't break down – they never really started. We didn't get any extra money. I was dragged into the discussions as captain, along with Gus Fraser and Neil Fairbrother, and although it was right for the skipper to represent unhappy players, I'm sure I was categorised as the 'shop steward' in the dispute. I wonder how much all that told against me when I lost the captaincy? I'll never know.

We were based at Canterbury for our warm-up matches at the start of May. We'd have preferred to be at Leicester, where they have the best net facilities in the country, but India had the good fortune to be based there. That frustrated both myself and our coach, David Lloyd. We felt that we should have been the beneficiaries of any advantages that stemmed from being the home country. Certainly in the two previous World Cups I'd played in, the host countries – Australia, New Zealand, India and Pakistan –- were less inconvenienced by long journeys and inadequate practice facilities than the visiting countries. Why couldn't we do the same? We always aim to do the right thing on behalf of our opponents in England, rather than using home advantage.

So I wasn't at my best with the press for various reasons on the day before our first World Cup game, at Lord's, against the holders, Sri Lanka. I felt there had been a lot of negative comment about our supposed greed over our contracts, and over our performances in the warm-up games. After our acrimonious match at Adelaide a few months earlier, I knew this one would be billed as Stewart versus Ranatunga, but I was determined not to carry that onto the field. I was also concerned about my opening partner. Nick Knight hadn't been at his best in Australia, and had started the English season with some low scores, but he had done well for us over the past three years. Yet Nasser Hussain had batted well against us for Essex in a recent friendly. In the end, Nass stayed in the team for the duration, and played well, but Knighty was unlucky to miss out. He's still got plenty of time to prove he's an international cricketer.

I was pleased at our eight-wicket win in that first game, and my 88 didn't do my morale any harm either. Our next match, against Kenya, was another routine victory – by nine wickets – but in retrospect, we took too long, 39 overs in fact, to get the 203 needed. At the time, two easy wins seemed more important as we sought to build up a momentum, but run rates were eventually to become a consideration, especially in view of the scale of our defeat in the next game – at the Oval against South Africa. We were all out for 103 in just 41 overs, to lose by 122 runs, and that's a heavy margin in a one-day game. It would prove to be a damaging blow to us. I made an error in sticking South Africa in after winning the toss. Knowing the Oval as well as I do, I should have batted first, but after consulting a few of our senior players, we felt that South Africa would be happier to chase, rather than setting us a total. In hindsight, I should have definitely gone with my gut feeling. We were blown away by Allan Donald, who came on as the fourth bowler because he can't control the white ball early on. To complete a bad day, I was out first ball. I was concerned about the manner and margin of our defeat, but still felt confident that we would go through to the next stage. South Africa were the favourites in my book, so there was no disgrace in having a bad day against them. As long as we beat Zimbabwe and India in the next two games, we'd be certain of qualifying – assuming that South Africa, as expected, would roll over Zimbabwe. That game turned out to be a nasty shock to us.

In our match against Zimbabwe, we saw off the opposition comfortably enough, by eight wickets. We should have knocked off the 168 needed in thirty or so fewer balls to improve our run rate, but we wanted to make sure of a comfortable win to boost our morale after the Oval setback. A win is a win at this level, and we felt our fate was still in our own hands. Beat India at Edgbaston and we're through. But that weekend in Birmingham turned out to be one of the worst experiences of my career. At the end of it, I was driving south, with my team out of the World Cup and my head soon to be served up on the sacrificial platter.

The bare facts are that we lost to India by 63 runs on the second day, after a thunderstorm had cut short our reply to their 232 for eight on the Saturday. I was later criticised for bowling first, with storms forecast, but you don't play a cricket match on the basis of a weather forecast, and to this day, I believe that with luck, we'd have bowled them out cheaply. Time and again, we beat the outside of the bat, as the ball swung in humid conditions, but we didn't get a nick. By the time the storm came, we were three down for not many, and I was one of the batsmen dismissed. But I still believed we could win next day. We had enough specialist batters left. As the rain hammered down at Edgbaston on that Saturday evening, we sat in the dressing-room and watched Zimbabwe pull off a fantastic win over South Africa at Chelmsford. Very little was said. We all knew it was in our hands now, and it was a fairly subdued night at the team hotel. At that stage, Zimbabwe had under-performed in the tournament, while South Africa had looked awesome. The result at Chelmsford was a huge blow to us, but we knew what we had to do now. Defeat the next day and we were out of the World Cup – in the first round. It didn't bear thinking about.

But the unthinkable happened. After the rains, the wicket sweated up overnight, and gave help to India's high-class seamers, Prasad and Srinath, while their leg-spinner, Kumble, had too much know-how and class for our middle order. We needed a special innings from Neil Fairbrother or Graham Thorpe, but we never recovered from the hammer blow of losing Thorpey to a decision by the umpire, Javed Akhtar, that still baffles me. Srinath was bowling around the wicket to the left-hander and won an lbw decision, when many felt the ball wouldn't have hit a sixth stump. Now I know that was just one dismissal in a poor batting display, but Thorpey is a match-winner in such situations, and it knocked the stuffing out of us.

There were tears in the dressing-room afterwards, as we sat with our private thoughts. I was aware that, realistically, this was my last chance of winning the World Cup, and as captain, I felt it deeply. Nothing can compare to losing the Final, as we did in Melbourne in 1992, but this came pretty close. I had to face the press soon afterwards, and I just sleepwalked through it all, giving a good impression of Alan Shearer as I offered platitudes rather than anything original. When I got back to our dressing-room, I was dismayed that a few of our boys had been phoned up by their counties, who had assumed their players would now be available for one-day matches over the next few days. The Lancashire boys and Nass all turned out for their counties, whereas the Surrey lads were treated more sensitively, and given some time off to lick our wounds. That episode summed up the amateur side of English cricket. No one should have been made to go through with a county appearance so soon after this shattering weekend. Can you imagine David Beckham having to play a Worthington Cup match for Manchester United, the day after England had gone out of the World Cup? The sooner our national cricket team gets priority over county considerations, the sooner we'll start to do ourselves justice.

As I drove home from Edgbaston, I had a blank feeling, as I tried to rationalise where I, and the team, had gone wrong. Could we have done things differently? We should have scored more quickly against Zimbabwe and Kenya, it's true, but the real crunch was Zimbabwe's shock win over South Africa and our defeat by India, in the space of a day. Our heavy defeat by the South Africans was also relevant. Whatever the reasons, we were out and I prepared for the inevitable inquests and the atmosphere of doom and gloom that was bound to hang around for some time. I was aware that a sacrifice might be necessary and that I'd be at the head of that particular queue. At the Edbgaston press conference, I'd parried the inevitable question about my future with the hope that I'd carry on if requested, but it was now up to David Graveney, as chairman of selectors. On that bleak Sunday, I wasn't thinking too far ahead. A fortnight later, when I still hadn't been re-appointed, the writing was firmly on the wall.

I was finally put out of my misery on 24 June, more than three weeks after our Edgbaston exit. I was at Edinburgh Airport, travelling back after a Benson & Hedges match for Surrey against Scotland. Grav had already been to see me a few days earlier, and I'd appreciated him taking the trouble to drive from Bristol to Surrey to discuss things. We talked around the subject for an hour, and he left with me still unsure whether I would keep the job. When he rang me at the airport, Grav couldn't get through on my mobile phone because the batteries had run down, so he contacted Surrey's coach, Keith Medlycott, to ask me to ring him. We were checking in our bags, so I walked away to find a quiet place. After getting the initial pleasantries out of the way, Grav broke the news of my sacking and told me that Nass was going to be announced as the new England captain later that morning. It was a fairly short conversation. Grav probably found it harder than I did, because that phone call was always going to come – it was just a matter of Grav telling me that I'd be playing in the first Test, although he didn't say whether or not I'd be keeping wicket. We ended the conversation in a civilised fashion – I thanked Grav for letting me know in advance of the official announcement – and then I rang Lynn and dad to break the news. I left a message of congratulations on Nasser Hussain's mobile phone and he rang back later, pledging his full support. I told him to captain the side his way – the same advice that Athers gave me when I took over from him the previous year – because it's vital that you have no regrets about how you've done the job when it's over. It's too important a job not to be true to yourself. I had no personal problems at all with Nass about the decision – players never fall out about such matters, because it's out of their control. I felt a little annoyed that my fate couldn't have been decided earlier, that the whole issue had dragged on far too long. I wonder how many soundings had been taken? Had the decision to sack me been taken purely on cricketing grounds, by a small group of relevant people, or were other issues involved? I'll never know. What did bother me was that I'd lost the Test captaincy on the back of defeat in a one-day competition. Yet as a Test captain, I'd helped secure that series win against South Africa the previous summer, and we had done creditably in Australia. I remain convinced that if Michael Slater had been given run out in the Sydney Test when everyone knew he was out, then we'd have squared that series at 2–2, rather than losing it 3–1. In previous World Cups, we had lost under Mike Gatting, Graham Gooch and Mike Atherton, yet they had all kept the England captaincy on their return. Was I being treated differently?

I soon got the disappointment out of my system, though. Playing for England remained my major priority and I was prepared for the inevitable media curiosity about my state of mind when I got to

Edgbaston for my first Test back in the ranks. I was asked if I felt I'd been made a scapegoat, and diplomatically, I said it was up to the press if they wanted to use that word. It was business as usual with the rest of the lads, though. No one was walking around me on eggshells, worried about my reaction to losing the job. When we had a team meeting on Tuesday lunchtime, Nass made a point of thanking me for my previous work as skipper, and for my support over the past week. He was now in charge, and would do the job his way. Very sensible, I thought. Mind you, old habits die hard. When the usual round of bat signing had started, I signed at the top of the first one, subconsciously thinking I was still captain! Athers had made the same mistake when I took over from him at Edgbaston in 1998, and we all had a good laugh about it. I was over my disappointment, delighted to be opening the batting again – always my preferred position – and committed to giving all my support to our new wicket-keeper, Chris Read. My morale was fine, it remained a great honour to play again for England, and I was really up for the match. But it just so happened that I had the worst Test match of my career. I got one and nought, and dropped two catches at second slip which I normally would have taken. I had no idea why I shelled out two regulation catches. There were no problems of concentration, and I didn't go along with the idea in some newspaper quarters that my eyes had gone at the age of thirty-six. I simply had a bad game personally, but at least we'd won the Test. Before I left Edgbaston, Nass had told me that I was in the side for the Lord's Test, and I appreciated his support. But I knew I was under pressure now.

When I pitched up at Lord's, I thought that I was playing for my Test career. To me, that was unfair – after all I'd scored a hundred only a few months earlier in the Melbourne Test, and only two more Tests had been played by us since – but I wondered if the media would be influencing the selectors against me. I knew I had to perform, and I went out there not feeling as confident as someone should be who has played more than eighty Tests. I made fifty in the first innings, and although it wasn't a fluent innings, I hung around. I played well for my 35 in the second innings, but then my shot selection let me down, when I tried to hit the spinner, Daniel Vettori over mid-wicket. That's one of my nominated shots when the left-armer operates over the wicket, but this time I got it wrong. Out for 35, and that sparked off another collapse. We lost by nine wickets and I got some stick for that shot. Fair enough – but it's got me a lot of runs over the years, and a fair amount of applause from spectators who like my aggressive style. The execution of that stroke has to be spot-on, and that's the hallmark of a Test batsman. I was at fault on this occasion, but that happens sometimes when a positive player is trying to dictate to the bowlers.

So we came to Old Trafford, with the New Zealanders on a high and England struggling. We hadn't underestimated the opposition for one moment, we knew they had some very good players. But we also knew that if we played to our potential, we should win the series. That was the problem. We could have picked a better-balanced eleven for Old Trafford. Our stand-in captain, Mark Butcher – replacing Nass, who had broken a finger – wanted me to keep wicket, but he lost out to the other selectors. Athers was back, to open with Butch, so I dropped down to number three after opening in the first two Tests. We managed to get away with a draw, and I was pleased with my 83 not out on the last day. I wasn't at all fazed at Butch standing in for Nass as captain, despite my credentials. When Nass broke his finger in the field at Lord's, Thorpey took over, while I went down to fine leg. That was fine by me – my time had gone – and it was more important for England to improve, no matter who was in charge.

Nass was back for the Oval Test, and I had the wicket-keeper's gloves on again. But we lost badly, getting ourselves out in both innings – as distinct from being got out. Top international sides are full of batters who don't give it away. We were still short of that consistency. So we were now at the bottom of the table of Test-playing countries, according to a cricket magazine that had dreamed up the notion – and although the press made much of that, it was impossible to take seriously. We were down, but not out, and nobody would convince me we were the worst Test side in the world. But we had to take the criticism on the chin. We had played poorly, lacking in confidence, and I felt sorry for Nass when he was booed by some of the Oval crowd as he stood on the main balcony, going through the necessary media responsibilities. Until you actually experience something like that, you cannot appreciate the hurt. Athers and I knew all about it. When you've been around as long as we had, you can almost write the comments yourself. This time, the stick was even more intensive after our early World Cup exit, then a disappointing defeat to New Zealand. We just had to swallow our pride and hurt, and vow to turn it round in South Africa.

Exactly a week after we'd lost at the Oval, I had a call on my mobile from a cricket writer to say 'Bad luck, you're not going on the tour'. He'd been at Lord's for the Nat-West Final, and all the gossip in the media centre was that I hadn't made it – nor Ramps or Phil Tufnell. My mind was in turmoil for the rest of that Sunday evening. Nobody phoned me, though. Next day, Grav rang to say that reports of my demise as a Test cricketer were premature. I was going, but not for the one-day triangular series to follow. He said they were now building for the next World Cup, which struck me as rather a long way off, but never mind. I was disappointed at missing out on the one-dayers, because I always want to play every game for my country, but I would have been very upset if that media mole had got it right. Next day, I saw on teletext that the final place had rested between me and Ramps, but I was unaware that Ramps opened the batting, with a Test average of around forty, and kept wicket. Strange reasoning. Where did that line come from?

At least there was some personal and professional satisfaction for me before the summer was over, when I joined the boys in celebrating our championship victory. I could only play nine of the games, but it was great just to be a part of it. When the season finally ended, it dawned on me how tired I was. It never hits you when you're playing, but when it was all done, I just slumped in front of the television for a few days. But a week's holiday with my family recharged my batteries and by the time we left for South Africa three weeks later, I was again raring to go. I set myself new targets – a hundred Tests and further progress up the run aggregates' table for England. Never believe that international cricketers take no notice of facts and figures! At this stage in my career, they can be an important motivation. The main point for me was that I wanted to keep playing for England, as long as possible, and to help make us a better team. A disappointing series of setbacks over the previous few months hadn't blunted my ambitions.

Another Losing Tour

The 1999/2000 tour to South Africa followed a depressingly familiar pattern in my England career. We promised so much at times, we had good days, excellent sessions – but then threw the advantage away by not nailing down the coffin. Not for the first time, I found myself wondering how the Australians would have dealt with certain key situations where we fell short. That remains the yardstick we need to be judged by. Yet it was frustrating to lose to South Africa by 2–1. I believe we weren't flattered by that margin, especially as a few experts had us down as 5–0 losers at the start of the series – even more so after losing the first Test by an innings. When it came down to it, we lost the series after playing our one bad game of the tour, at Cape Town, when we really needed to put it together. No excuses for losing that Test, and with it the series. It was the ninth time we had lost a Test series away from home during my time with England, and I'm desperately hoping that soon we develop the consistency to turn these tours around.

The build-up to the first Test couldn't have gone better. The practice facilities – particularly at Centurion Park – were excellent, and nothing was left to chance by a first-rate management team. Nass clicked straight away with our new coach, Duncan Fletcher, which was important. They were both on a steep learning curve at the start of a new experience in their respective careers, and it was important that the chemistry was right. Duncan proved to be a first-rate successor to David Lloyd. He came to see me for a chat before the tour and I was immediately impressed. On the tour, he proved to be excellent at man-management, staying on the same level emotionally, whether or not things were going well. A straight talker, he'd praise at the right times, then have a quiet but firm word when we had failed individually or as a unit. He never slagged off the players in public and kept the hard words in-house.

Throughout the South Africa tour, Duncan knew instinctively when I was happy with my wicket-keeping. During an interval he'd just say 'Well done' in passing. Only a sentence, I know, but even to an experienced player like me, that meant a lot. With my batting, he looked closely at my game and asked my opinion about the way I played. I go back and across and play quite deep in my crease and Duncan asked why I did that. As with all the other players, he'd get you talking about your own game, coming up with the answers eventually, and he would never impose his views. His fielding drills were excellent. If he spotted one of our players wasn't up to par in catching practice, they'd have five extra skied catches to take before getting off the hook. I rate Duncan Fletcher very highly after touring with him. He's definitely England's gain and South Africa's loss. I could see why he had been so successful with Glamorgan, Western Province and South Africa's 'A' side.

Duncan told me he wanted me to keep wicket and to bat at five. He wanted to split up our three experienced batsmen in the order – that was Athers, Nass and myself – and I could see the sense in that. In the lead-up games to the Test series, I was frustrated at failing to get enough runs, even though I was playing well enough, but I was happy with the standard of my wicket-keeping. The more I've done it, the better I've got at it and I was mentally locked into the job of an all-rounder again. Fletch kept on stressing that we were there to compete against South Africa, rather than look for a specific target. He was right; you can achieve anything if you hang on in there, and it was up to us to show mental resolution against such strong opposition.

So we came to Johannesburg and the first Test in good heart. Yet when we saw the wicket on the first morning, it was clear the match was going to be a lottery, dependent on the toss. It was overcast and for some reason, the pitch was rather wet. Win the toss and bowl in conditions ideal for the faster bowlers. We lost it and were all out for 122. Yet we must give credit to their opening bowlers, Shaun Pollock and Allan Donald. You still have to utilise the conditions properly and when they had us 4 for two, I think you could say that they were doing just that! Our three most experienced players were all out for nought, including yours truly, first ball to an inswinging yorker. Michael Vaughan, on his Test debut, saw two wickets fall, before he faced a delivery. Donald wasn't at his best, yet still took six for 53, including the key wicket of Athers, bringing one back into him on a full length to bowl him. Clever work – he knew that Athers looks to leave a lot early on, and he surprised him with the inswinger. That was typical of South Africa's thoroughness and attention to detail.

We could offer some justification for being dismissed so cheaply, but we should have bowled better when they batted after tea on that first day. Pollock had bowled the ideal length to make our batsmen play on a pitch that was offering a lot of sideways movement, but we allowed their batters to leave too many deliveries. We bowled fractionally short throughout their innings, and they got away with 403 when 250 was par. So we were really up against it after two days, especially now that the wicket had dried out, leaving indentations that had hardened, which meant variable bounce. Before our second innings, we talked about the need for resolution, to hit the stray deliveries for four, to expect the odd rogue delivery, and hope to earn any luck that came our way. But we got off to the worst possible start, when Athers was caught behind off a beauty from Pollock. How ironic – coming into this Test, Athers had been batting as well as I'd seen him for several years, and now he walks off with a 'pair'. Athers admitted later that those two balls would have got him out at any stage of his career.

I came in to join Butch on 41 for three, in deep trouble, and we added 104 in contrasting styles. I played positively, while Butch dug in solidly until he was given out, unluckily lbw. I think it's fair to say that most people watching the game thought the ball pitched outside leg-stump and Venkat, one of the best umpires in the world, had got it wrong. These things happen, but you could do without them when you're staring down the barrel. Soon we had lost three wickets quickly. Chris Adams was caught behind, trying to impose himself on Donald, then I didn't get over an off-drive and Jonty Rhodes caught me at cover for 86. Either side of him, and it's four, with me in sight of a hundred, but I got out, playing positively on an untrustworthy pitch. I felt it was worth the risk.

I thought we did well to take the game into the fourth day, with the pitch so much in favour of the quicker bowlers. Pollock and Donald took nineteen of our twenty wickets in the match, which tells you all you need to know about their quality and the favourable conditions for them. The day after our defeat, we had a very constructive team meeting after nets. We agreed we couldn't hide behind the bad luck with the toss, or some borderline umpiring decisions going against us.

241

It was necessary to look at areas where we could improve – where we must bowl in future, and how we should bat. All of us agreed that the performance had to be upped. If we needed any incentive, it was in the way we had been written off completely by the South African press, including some one-eyed comments from Kepler Wessels, their former captain, who really ought to have known better than dismiss us as just a village green team. We'd keep those newspaper headlines in mind as we tried to get back into the series.

We played well at times in the next Test, at Port Elizabeth, but again it was in patches and we ended up relying on an heroic innings from Nass to get us a draw. I felt we deserved at least that, but it was frustrating to see us waste good positions. On the first day, after we at last won the toss, we had them 91 for four, but Jonty Rhodes and Lance Klusener pulled it round and Klusener's 174 brought them to 450. We all knew about Jonty's worth in a crisis, but Klusener was hugely impressive. He took the attack to us, playing properly, and although we fed his favourite scoring area by giving him too much width, this was a genuine Test innings, not that of a one-day slogger. When he was joined by the best number nine in world cricket – Mark Boucher – Klusener just went up another gear, and they put on another hundred. It was frustrating for us, but another indication of what's needed when you bowl at the highest level.

We showed commendable bottle when we batted. Nass and Athers added 155 in a top-class stand, and although the captain missed out on a deserved hundred, his aggression and readiness to play the hook shot was just what we needed to see. Athers' century was fluent, masterful and a vindication for taking him on tour. He still looked an opener from the top drawer, and I know the South Africans thought that as well. When they batted again on the fourth day, I thought they were over-cautious in building up a big lead. It seemed to me that they were looking for ways to stop us winning by occupation of the crease, whereas the Australians would be looking to see how they could win, by scoring at speed. The South Africans should have tried getting after us, even though we bowled really well in that second innings. If they'd got us in on the fourth evening, we would not only have faced a tricky forty minutes or so but they would then have been able to take a second new ball late on the fifth afternoon. As it was, they only bowled 77 overs at us, with Nass leading the rearguard action. I think Hansie Cronje is a good captain, he never seems to lose control out in the middle. Like the West Indies of old, the South Africans are good at coming in for the kill when they sense it, or they'll set back the field, and wait for another chance. Hansie can rely on Donald and Pollock for the key wickets, then keep it quiet while they are resting. They are very disciplined in the field, and their approach is attritional and successful up to a point, because they are the second best side in the world, in my opinion. But I question whether they'll ever match Australia consistently with that approach. Australia dare to win by risking defeat and a feature of the captaincy of both Mark Taylor and Steve Waugh has been their imaginative, challenging declarations. They believe in tempting the opposition, because they back themselves in tight corners.

The standard of umpiring in the Port Elizabeth Test received general condemnation, but before I talk in detail about it, I must say that both Steve Bucknor and Rudi Koertzen are fine umpires. Umpiring at Test level is also the hardest job of all. But I think both umpires were below par in this Test and that most of the decisions went against us. Now I know that the South Africans feel that crucial decisions went against them in the Leeds Test of 1998 that we won narrowly to take the series – but Athers and Freddie Flintoff both got a couple of dodgy ones at Leeds, and we were unlucky at times earlier in the series. But that's now history. So is Port Elizabeth and I have to stress that the contentious decisions by the umpires were never seen by us as bias, nor did the fervent atmosphere out in the middle harm our personal relationships with the opposition players. You only had to see the way we mixed over a few beers at the end of this Test series to appreciate that. The controversial decisions were not cut and dried errors and that's what bothered me. Television ought to have been made available in its entirety to reach the correct decision.

When Chris Adams caught Jacques Kallis at silly point in their second innings, there was no doubt in my mind that it was a genuine catch. I was two yards from the incident. I don't blame Kallis for not walking, though. I never have a go at a batsman for standing his ground, although Grizzly was upset that neither umpire Koertzen or Kallis would take his word that it was a clean catch. The problem was that the host broadcaster could only offer inconclusive television evidence, so the umpire had to side with the batsman, giving him the benefit of the doubt. But Sky showed a different angle a few minutes later which proved beyond doubt that Kallis was out. Surely, if you're going to use modern technology, you ought to make sure that it's in full working order? Remember Michael Slater's reprieve when run out in the Sydney Test earlier in the year? If you're not going to use every available camera angle, then forget the third umpire and give it back to the umpires out in the middle, relying on the naked eye and their own experienced judgement. It seemed daft that Sky's extra camera angles couldn't be amalgamated with the other ones, so that the television umpire could make the decision swiftly. It was too late to hear from Dr Ali Bacher afterwards that plans to do just that were under way.

On the final day, a few questionable decisions went against some of our batsmen, and they might have been vital if it hadn't been for Nass' brilliant innings that secured us a draw. I thought that we handled the situation exceptionally well, kept our thoughts to ourselves and didn't publicly complain about not getting the rub of the green. The players don't make the umpires' job any easier by refusing to walk and by appealing too much, I agree – but what annoys me in particular is that the giant electronic screen at the ground shows a decision time and again, in slow motion. The cameras now magnify the area between ball, bat, pad and stumps, so that any mistake is glaringly obvious. So the crowd gets on the umpire's back, he gets extra pressure from aggrieved players and he becomes unsure of himself, so his judgement can be affected. I believe the way round this is to show the incident once at normal speed, once in slow motion, and leave it at that. The guy in the white coat is doing his best out in the middle and he doesn't deserve all the hassle. Every batsman who is dismissed watches the big screen as he walks back. I do it to know what shot I played, and if I was at fault – not to show dissent at the decision. Usually, the action replay has gone by the time you get back to the dressing-room, so I see no harm in looking at it on the way back. But it's time replays were curtailed in the interests of the umpires. By all means, show the replays on televisions away from the ground, but they inflame situations at the ground.

We took a lot of satisfaction from emerging with a draw from Port Elizabeth and we genuinely felt we were still in the series as we came to Durban. Christmas was just around the corner as we were joined by our partners and families, and it was great to see our closest ones. But we were there to work, and we discussed this just before we arrived in Durban, a few days before Christmas. The hardest part of touring for me is to be away from Lynn and the two children, but Lynn met me just before I broke into the England side and knew the score right from the off. I've had four Christmases at home since I became a professional cricketer in 1980, but it's great to have the family with you on Christmas morning, to see the kids open their presents. But then it was back to work, and nets later that morning. In fact, during the fortnight that Lynn was with me, I took her out four times at night. The rest of the time it was room service and pizza for the kids. Glamorous life, touring!

That Durban Test was played in draining humidity. Apart from Colombo in 1993, it was the worst Test I'd ever played in for discomfort. I was grateful that the fitness programme had been instituted in recent years by Dean Riddle, then Nigel Stockhill, because we certainly needed a lot in the tank during the Durban Test, swiftly followed by another in Cape Town. With Durban finishing on 30 December, and Cape Town starting on 2 January, we faced a gruelling period. Afterwards, I worked out that by keeping wicket for a total of seven days in those two Tests, I had put in the equivalent of 2,600 squats. No wonder I felt tired after Cape Town! I was glad that fitness work has always been important to me in my career.

Considering that the outfield on Christmas Eve was a bog due to heavy rain, the groundstaff in Durban did remarkably well to get the Test started on time. When we pitched up on that first morning, we were amazed to hear that Jonty Rhodes had been dropped from the side, on his home pitch. They wanted to play Nantie Hayward, their impressive young fast bowler and have the left-arm spin of Paul Adams for added variety, but we never thought that Rhodes would be sacrificed. Some of our guys – particularly Athers – find his bubbly attitude irritating, but I don't mind him, and I respect his temperament. Four years earlier in the Johannesburg Test, he'd given me some verbals and I shouted back 'Make sure you enjoy your last Test!', and that upset him. Since then, full credit to the bloke. He's Australia's Steve Waugh in pressure situations, who'll take the attack to the bowlers. Jonty is my type of player and South Africa were weaker without him.

For a time, we were in with a good shout of winning that Durban Test until the flat wicket and fatigue got to our bowlers. Two players stood out: Nasser Hussain and Andy Caddick. On the first day, I admit I thought we were a little too cautious. At 135 for two off 85 overs, I felt we were fifty runs light, but Nass wanted to make sure we didn't throw away the advantage of winning the toss. I was in for the second over next morning, and Nass and I then took them on. I came out to play my usual forcing game, and it worked. I felt very comfortable at the crease and soon I was motoring. By lunch, I was on 72 and Nass told me just to keep on playing. Nass is as good an attacking player as England can pick, but this time he reined himself in and let me take them on. I was there with him when he got to his hundred and what a responsible, mature innings it was. I kept reminding him during our partnership that Graham Gooch once told me 'You've never got enough' and I hope that spurred him on during his marathon innings, spread over more than ten hours. Unfortunately, I wasn't there with him at the end. I was plumb lbw to Hayward for 95, a faster delivery that would have taken out middle stump. But it was one of my best innings for England, and I was pleased that I'd helped Nass to a respectable total.

The next day belonged to Andy Caddick. We bowled them out for 156, making them follow on and Caddy's figures of seven for 46 would have been even better if Shaun Pollock hadn't chanced his arm late on, slogging a few boundaries. Caddy's line and length were perfect for that pitch, he made them all play. He used to be yard too short, but bowling on such a good wicket at Taunton has made him tighten up onto a disciplined length. To be a top fast bowler at Test level, you need pace, bounce and movement and he had all three that day in Durban. It made me ponder the wisdom of Caddy not going to Australia under my captaincy the previous year, and I have to say he was very unlucky not to make it. Contrary to some rumours, there has never been any personal problems at all between me and Caddy. In the Caribbean, early in 1998, he had bowled indifferently at times. With Darren Gough back and fit after missing out on that tour, he would obviously be in contention for the home series against South Africa. I'm a big fan of Dominic Cork and Angus Fraser and when I became captain, I wanted them in my side. We did win the Test series with those three playing important roles and when we considered the tour party to Australia, I wanted the variation of Alan Mullally, plus Alex Tudor as the promising young fast bowler. So Caddy was very unlucky not to make it, and in hindsight, we got it wrong. I spoke to him at the end of the 1998 season, explaining that there just wasn't room for him and he went away to prove me wrong. Good luck to him. I honestly believe that being out of the England side for a year made him a better bowler.

The last couple of days took a lot out of Caddy and our other bowlers as we battled hard to bowl them out a second time on a wicket that got flatter and flatter. We had a genuine glimmer on the fourth evening, when they were just 41 ahead with six wickets left, but Mark Boucher, coming in as nightwatchman, scored a classy hundred and Gary Kirsten made 275, after looking out of touch until then. Gary admitted afterwards he expected to be dropped if he failed again, and it was a tremendously gutsy effort to hang in there and save the game for his side. We had a dilemma about enforcing the follow-on, because we wanted to rest our bowlers. Nass talked it over with me and Athers, and we felt that with the sessions expected to be shorter because of the uncertain weather, we could keep them fresh. But the expected rain never materialised and after Boucher stayed with Kirsten, we were never in the hunt. Boucher is a very fine all-round cricketer, and will be a top player for years to come in international cricket. On the field, he's very vocal, and we hammered him in England in 1998, when he was very immature with some of his comments. Off the field, though, he's a nice chap and I enjoyed talking cricket with him over a drink. Like me, he started off as a batsman and only started keeping wicket in first-class cricket when Steve Palfryman was away on World Cup duty in '96. He's come on in leaps and bounds since then. Gary Kirsten's monumental innings was hugely impressive and it was no hardship to congratulate warmly a nice guy, who gets on with the game, and never makes a fuss. When Butch bowled him round his legs with an off-break that was fairly full, it spoiled Gary's day, because he was one run away from beating the all-time individual innings in Tests for South Africa. Butch looked rarther sheepish, but at least that ended the Test and we could get off. Gary batted for fourteen-and-a-half hours – some batsmen don't manage that in an entire Test career! The most I've ever batted in an innings was for seven hours when I scored 164 at Old Trafford against South Africa in 1998, so the mind boggles at such a feat of endurance. Athers was rightly celebrated for his monumental 185 not out at Johannesburg in 1995, but Gary batted for two sessions longer than that! You do get into a zone when it's going well for you, but that's some achievement.

It had been a very long time out in the middle at Durban and there were some tired bodies on the plane as we flew out that night. We had stuck at the task well, fielding splendidly and we still felt that we could win in Cape Town. Admittedly they'd feel good about escaping at Durban, but we had shown that their batting was vulnerable, something we maintained all series. The England players spent the next couple of days in the shade, feet up, lying low to conserve energy. You can safely say that not a great deal of alcohol was consumed by the players over the New Year festivities. Getting back into the series was far too important.

We threw away the Cape Town Test. On the first day, after winning the toss and batting on a good pitch, most of us got out when well set. Butch was caught at third man, and Athers and I fell to deep backward square leg, on the hook. It was the old story about shot selection, but the pull or the hook has brought us both many runs at Test level. Mine was definitely an ill-judged stroke to a ball that was quicker and higher than the one I'd swatted to the boundary in the previous over. If I had my time over again, I wouldn't have played that shot, because it cost us dearly. Allan Donald, enjoying the verbal jousts with me, then picked up his pace and swept through us. From 213 for three, we were all out for 258, when we needed a minimum of 400 on that pitch. When they batted, our bowlers stuck at it well after a disappointing initial burst. Chris Silverwood put his hand up and fully deserved his five wickets. He's such a great trier. Yet they still lead by 159 at the start of the fourth day, and with Andrew Flintoff breaking down with a fractured bone in his foot, we were deep in trouble. We didn't escape.

We were all out on the stroke of tea, to lose by an innings. The only hard luck story was the lbw decision that went against Nass. B C Cooray gave it in favour of the bowler, yet that was the first time I've seen someone edge a ball to the boundary and be given out lbw! After that, a few decisions went our way, with Chris Adams being reprieved twice in an over and Athers also getting away with a catch to silly point, but it was a big blow to lose our captain and leading batsman at 40 for one in such a bizarre fashion. Then we crumbled again, just like we did four years ago in Cape Town. All out in just sixty overs on a good wicket – what a time to put in our first poor performance of the tour! Until then, we had been competitive but in front of thousands of our supporters, we had let ourselves and them down. For me it was a familiar feeling to lose a Test abroad like this, but such familiarity made it no easier to bear.

Nass and Fletch waited until we had flown to Port Elizabeth before we had our post-mortem. Nass did most of the talking, then opened up the discussion. We agreed we had been ill-disciplined in our batting in Cape Town, and quite rightly, Athers and I were singled out in that meeting for criticism. Nass said that two batters with more than 6000 Test runs each shouldn't have got out to ill-executed shots when set. We were all frustrated at ourselves, having played poorly at a crucial time in the series, and it was no consolation that we had disappointed so much for the first time on tour. We all sat there with our heads down taking the hard words in the right professional manner.

The priority now was to go home 2–1 losers, rather than 3–0. We would be trying like hell to win at Centurion Park in the final Test. Pride in performance and patriotism were the motivating ingredients, plus a genuine conviction that we weren't that inferior to South Africa.

That Test was basically a tale of two days. On the first, shortened to 45 overs due to rain , they made 155 for six, which I thought was thirty too many. I thought that our bowlers sprayed it around too much, giving them too many 'four balls' on a wicket that was doing a bit. On reflection I was a bit hard on our bowlers, because the damp run-ups did hinder their rhythm. Not that this was likely to matter because it rained for the next three days and we didn't get on the field.

On the final morning, it was bright and sunny and all the talk was about a meaningless few hours of play and the inevitable draw. As I bumped into Hansie Cronje while both sets of players were practising, he shouted '270 in seventy overs – how does that sound?' and I answered 'Too many – 250 sounds better'. I told him to speak to Nass, but nothing came of it and we went out to field. After around forty minutes, we'd seen enough of the pitch to realise that it was playing better than we expected after all the rain. The ball wasn't jagging around, so Nass threw the gauntlet back at Hansie. After a double forfeiture, the target was 249 in 76 overs – not all that generous, because in a Test match you can always slow down the scoring rate with two bouncers an over and spearing it down legside, just inside the call of 'wide'. But it was a fair declaration and with so many England supporters there, we owed it to them and to the game of cricket to go for it.

Now I know that some believed that the final day demeaned the image of cricket, but I disagree. When South Africa batted, they weren't given any lob bowling to speed up the rate, and then we really had to compete against their bowlers, who tried their hardest. They were unlucky to lose Paul Adams with a dislocated and fractured finger, picked up in the field, before he'd bowled one ball. He would have kept it tight, as well as troubling us. Adams was a bowler who had improved a great deal since we had last seen him in a Test series.

At 102 for four, there was plenty of time for us to win, but also for them still to bowl us out. So Michael Vaughan and I played normal Test match cricket, looking to put away the bad ball, but attempting nothing suicidal. After Hansie had bowled a couple of tight overs, I got after him and the race was on. I got out for 73, pulling at Hayward to be caught behind, and after a clatter of wickets, we got home in the final over when Darren Gouch pulled one for four, using one of my bats. After using it for throw-downs, Goughy was delighted with it, so I lent it to him. I doubt if I'll ever get it back now!

To those who doubt the authenticity of our win, you should have witnessed the scenes of jubilation in our dressing-room when Goughy smacked that four. The South Africans tried so hard to bowl us out, with Hayward impressing me particularly at the death. If they had won, they'd have been crowing about a 3–0 series win. It was a full-on game out in the middle, they were totally committed. It was a nice atmosphere when we had a beer with them afterwards and we swapped shirts and enjoyed a gossip. That's how cricket should be played, in my opinion – hard on the field, but no legacy of that afterwards. We're at fault here. We're rather too keen on getting back to the hotel to shower, rather than hanging around for a natter. The South Africans and the Aussies do that, and they're at each other hammer and tongs out in the middle. You can form friendships for life and learn about cricket by talking to the opposition after the game's over for the day, and that doesn't mean you are less committed once play starts the following day.

That night, as we celebrated at Centurion Park, Nass came over to me, shook my hand and said 'Thanks for all your help on tour, you've been brilliant'. I appreciated that. Playing for England has always been the vital thing for me and every captain has my fullest support. I mention that conversation with Nass only to scotch a daft rumour that surfaced when I returned to England. A South African journalist somehow decided that Nass and I had had a row in the dressing-room on that final day. I couldn't believe it and when the denial from Nass appeared in the *London Evening Standard* a few days later, I rang through to our operations manager, Phil Neale to tell him I knew nothing about this. I recall a jocular remark from Nass when he told me he was putting me up the order to supervise the run chase. He quipped, 'Go on Stewie, prove me wrong about not picking you for the one-dayers', and we had a laugh about that. When I got out, having played well, I sat down beside Nass and said, tongue in cheek, 'That good enough for you captain?' and again we shared the joke. I was fully committed to the run chase, and that daft story infuriated me.

Some sections of the press tried some mischief-making about my omission from the one-day series, but I wasn't uptight about it. I think you can build too early for a tournament that's three years away, but that's the prerogative of the selectors. Having picked Chris Read as the wicket-keeper/batsman for the one-dayers in South Africa, it was right to stick with him, even though Andrew Flintoff's departure through created a space for another all-rounder. So they drafted in Craig White instead of me, and that wasn't a problem to me. Of course, I would have preferred to stay on, but I know the captain has to make tough decisions and I respect that.

Our morale and team spirit was very good out in South Africa, and Nass and Fletch deserve credit for that. They worked well together, with Nass the main spokesman in team meetings, not afraid to tell players to their face where they've failed. Fletch is the quieter individual, but when he speaks you listen. At Cape Town, he waited for a few days after my first innings dismissal before he had a quiet word with me. He told me I'd played very well for my forty-odd but I said, 'Forties mean nothing if you throw it all away.' He said, 'Yes, but you're a very good hooker and puller. That one was on to you too quickly. Just make sure the execution is right.' We both knew that I'd cocked up, but Duncan chose the right time to talk it through constructively.

As for Nass, he has learned a lot about captaincy under Keith Fletcher and Graham Gooch and he had time to absorb things at England level before the job came to him. He has the necessary ruthlessness, and by necessity he's had to learn to be a little more remote from the rest of the team. But I believe the Fletcher/Hussain partnership will be good for English cricket, if they are given time to blossom and they maintain consistency of selection.

There were several plus points from the Test series, despite the result. Michael Vaughan impressed as a calm, composed batsman. Scoring 69 to get the Man of the Match Award at Centurion Park will have done him the world of good, because he needed a major innings after looking comfortable at the crease but then getting out for middling scores. I see him in the middle order for the time being. He needs to get used to Test cricket before being exposed at the top of the order. He's a great lad and already he's getting the mickey taken out of him for being an FEC (Future England Captain), but he's too sensible to take notice of that. Just get on with your game, and everything else will happen.

I think Freddie Flintoff will turn into a vital part of England's future. He should be a genuine all-rounder in a year or so. Only Klusener hits the ball as hard as Freddie in world cricket, he's a great catcher and his bowling is coming on in leaps and bounds. Duncan Fletcher was very impressed with him in South Africa, and if he carries on learning quickly, he could be a star. He's now seen at close quarters what's needed to be successful in Test cricket, and I'm convinced he has the hunger. The more he plays, the faster he'll make progress. Freddie needs consistent support, because he has that extra ingredient.

Chris Silverwood impressed with his heart and willingness to learn, while Andy Caddick was the pick of the bowlers, even though his efforts in Durban took a lot out of him. Goughy didn't bowl as well as he would have wished, but he still took just two wickets less than Caddy. People forget how that long lay-off affected him. In 1996, I was out for several months with a badly broken finger and I know how much you lose in confidence during such a long period away from the middle. There's a lot left in Goughy. All he needs is time in the middle and to recapture his rhythm. His ability to bowl the magic delivery is his strength and I rate him very highly. I believe that Caddick and Gough will work well as a unit for a few more years.

England must show more faith in their players. Unless you're a genius, it takes at least ten Tests to get used to the special pressures, as the likes of Jacques Kallis and Steve Waugh discovered. If they'd been English, they might have disappeared from the Test arena for good after unimpressive starts. Chris Adams found the transition from county to Test cricket very difficult and he was honest enough to admit it. He has an excellent record in recent years in county cricket, and on figures alone, deserved to be picked for South Africa. But Chris struggled and he admitted that until you step up to the highest level, you have no idea just what a gulf there is between that and the domestic cricket you play at home. The sooner that gap is reduced, the better. It will come with better match wickets and practice facilities, so that bowlers have to earn their wickets, and we need to show faith in our chosen players. I'm sure Nass and Fletch will try for that.

After the Test series, Athers had some strong words to say about the relevance of county cricket in an interview on BBC Radio 5 Live. Athers said that county cricket was no preparation for playing at Test level and he got a lot of flak for allegedly denigrating our domestic game. But Athers shouldn't be shouted down – a cricketer of his vast experience should be listened to. We all want to make our domestic game stronger and try to reduce the gap, as they've done in Austrailia and, to a lesser extent, South Africa. Athers prefers regionalisation to two divisions but I believe we should give promotion and relegation a go for three or four years. If not, look at it another way and that might mean regionalisation. One way to help narrow that gulf is to beef up the sides who play the tourists. How about six matches of four days' duration each against them? The tourists could play a full England 'A' side, the current county champions and then four regional teams. Those four regional sides should include the best players available, even if that means pulling out guys from a county team that's currently playing.

For me, our main error on the tour to South Africa was to come without another experienced batsman. I'm all for taking along younger players to learn the ropes, but against a side of South Africa's stature, we needed a Hick or a Ramprakash to supplement Athers, Nass and myself. Thorpey would have been ideal, but he asked to be excused for personal reasons, and that's fair enough. Judged at the highest level, our other batsmen didn't put their hands up, apart from Vaughany at Centurion Park, and that cost us. We needed more back-up. It'll be interesting to see who's in the shake-up for this summer's Test series against the West Indies. Thorpey would always be in my best eleven. Then there's Hicky and Ramps, Nick Knight as well. I like the look of Vikram Solanki. Two years ago, I picked him out as the young batsman most likely to succeed and he looked good when he joined us in South Africa. Some good batsmen are going to miss out, that's for sure.

I hope and expect still to be in the frame. I still feel fit enough and I'm enjoying my cricket just as much. The buzz involved in playing for England is still just as strong, and I feel I kept wicket well in South Africa, with just a couple of errors. I improved my Test batting average, and believe I justified the selectors' faith in me last September when some saw me as past it. There are still many targets ahead of me – a hundred Test appearances, further progress up the England runs table and the prospect of winning back the Ashes against the Aussies in 2001. I'm now eighth in the all-time England runs list and I was very pleased to end the nineties as the highest scorer of Test runs in that decade, ahead of some great players from other countries. Not bad for someone whose batting is supposed to be affected by keeping wicket! It sounds boring, but I just want to go on and on as long as possible, without my performances dipping. Consistency in sport isn't to be scoffed at.

Cast of Characters

Players

Alec Stewart – Stewy, PP (Peter Perfect), Squeaky (as in squeaky clean). Captain, wicketkeeper, top-order batsman.

Nasser Hussain – Nass, Beaky, Conehead. Vice-captain, middle-order batsman and 1999 beneficiary at Essex.

Michael Atherton – Ath, Dreed. Opening batsman and former captain.

Mark Butcher – Butch, Booch. Opening batsman and occasional (very) medium-pacer.

Dominic Cork – Corky, Dom. All-rounder.

John Crawley – JC, Dogger, Creepy, Creeps. Middle-order batsman, occasional wicketkeeper, regular short-leg.

Robert Croft – Crofty, Blobby. Off-spinner and professional Welshman.

Angus Fraser – Gus, Gussy. Seam bowler.

Darren Gough – Goughie, Dazzler. Fast bowler.

Dean Headley – Headless, Deano. Fast bowler.

Warren Hegg – Chuck, Chucky, Heggy. Wicket-keeper.

Ben Hollioake – Pelican, Pelly. All-rounder.

Alan Mullally – Big Al, Al Mullal. Seam and swing bowler.

Mark Ramprakash – Ramps, Rampo, Bloodaxe. Middle-order batsman.

Peter Such – Suchy, Rocky. Off-spinner.

Graham Thorpe – Thorpey, Chalky, Chalks. Middle-order batsman.

Alex Tudor – Tudes. Fast bowler.

Graeme Hick – Hicky, Arnie. Middle-order batsman, occasional off-spinner and reinforcement to the original 1998/99 Ashes tour party.

Management and Back-up Staff

Graham Gooch – Zap, Goochie. Tour Manager.
David Lloyd – Bumble, Dave. Coach. Retired after 1999 World Cup.
Bob Cottam – PB. Assistant Coach.
Wayne Morton – Fizz. Physiotherapist.
Dean Riddle – Riddler. Fitness Consultant.
Malcolm Ashton – Malc, Ashtray. Scorer/Administrator.
Brian Murgatroyd – Murgers, Flipper-foot. Media Relations Officer.
Steve Bull – Bully. Sports Psychologist.
Peter Philpott – Flipper. Leg-Spin Coach.

Carlton & United Series – Additional personnel

Mark Alleyne – Boo-boo. All-rounder, occasional wicketkeeper.
Mark Ealham – Ealy. All-rounder
Neil Fairbrother – Harvey, The General. Middle-order batsman.
Ashley Giles – Splash, Ash. Left-arm spinner.
Adam Hollioake – Smokey. All-rounder.
Nick Knight – Knighty, Stitch. Opening batsman.
Vince Wells – Vinny. All-rounder
David Graveney – Grav. Tour Manager.
Dean Conway – Deano. Physiotherapist.

1999/2000 Tour to South Africa – Additional personnel

Chris Adams – Grizzly. Batsman, occasional medium-pace bowler.
Andrew Caddick – Caddy. Fast bowler.
Duncan Fletcher – Fletch. Coach.
Andrew Flintoff – Freddy (as in Flintstone). All-rounder.
Chris Silverwood – Spoons, Spooner. Opening bowler.
Michael Vaughan – Virge (as in Virgil from Thunderbirds). Batsman.